Arnold Svenberg
March 11, 2006

Yuma

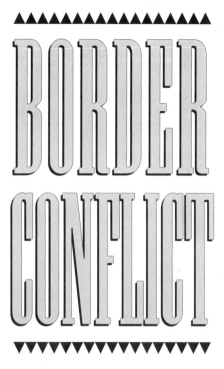

BORDER CONFLICT

VILLISTAS, CARRANCISTAS
AND THE PUNITIVE EXPEDITION
1915–1920

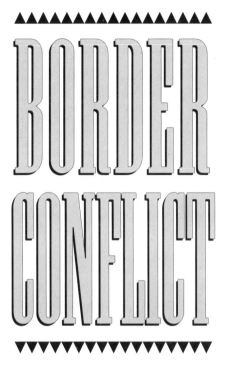

BORDER CONFLICT

VILLISTAS, CARRANCISTAS AND THE PUNITIVE EXPEDITION 1915–1920

by Joseph A. Stout, Jr.

TEXAS CHRISTIAN UNIVERSITY PRESS

Library of Congress Cataloging-in-Publication Data

Stout, Joseph Allen
    Border conflict : Villistas, Carrancistas and the Punitive
      Expedition, 1915-1920 / by Joseph A. Stout, Jr.
        p. cm.
    Includes bibliographical references and index.
    ISBN 0-87565-200-X (alk. paper)
    1. United States. Army—History—Punitive Expedition in
Mexico, 1916. 2. Mexico. Ejército Constitucionalista—History.
3. Carranza, Venustiano, 1859-1920. 4. Villa, Pancho, 1878-1923. 5.
Wilson, Woodrow, 1856-1924. 6. Mexico—Foreign relations—United
States. 7. United States—Foreign relations—Mexico. 8. Mexico—
Foreign relations—1910-1946. 9. United States—Foreign relations—
1913-1921. I. Title. II. Title: Villistas, Carrancistas and the Punitive
Expedition, 1915-1920. F1234.S86 1999
973.91'3—dc21
98-46676
CIP

Cover and text design by Bill Maize; Duo Design Group

▲▲▲▲▲▲

For my Father,

Joseph A. Stout,

who lived in Mexico City

long enough to drive

like a *Chilango*

▼▼▼▼▼▼

CONTENTS

▼▼▼▼▼

PREFACE

▼▼▼▼▼▼

Border Conflict is a study of Venustiano Carranza's Constitutionalist army and its activities in 1916 and 1917 when the United States Punitive Expedition, under command of General John J. "Black Jack" Pershing, searched Chihuahua, Mexico, for Francisco "Pancho" Villa. Although the focus is on the Carrancista army, the work includes a look at the activities of the Punitive Expedition that President Woodrow Wilson sent into Mexico to capture or neutralize Villa, who had led almost 500 men across the international border and attacked Columbus, New Mexico, on March 9, 1916.[1] *Border Conflict* also examines diplomatic efforts to resolve differences through a joint diplomatic commission held in the United States during the summer of 1916. I have used Mexican foreign relations documents, Carranza's correspondence and other materials in Mexico City to explain the conference as Carranza viewed it.

Based largely on Mexican primary and secondary sources—*Border Conflict* also illustrates Carranza's military problems on the northern frontier of Mexico, the internal dynamics of the Constitutionalist army and Carranza's effort to resolve these difficulties. I wish to show what part the Constitutionalist army played in chasing Villa in Chihuahua during 1916 and to detail military activities during that year. At the same time, I seek to place the campaign in the context of the Punitive Expedition in Mexico and how it affected U.S.-Mexican relations.

Constitutionalist troop commanders probably reported more success than they enjoyed against Villa, and their exaggerated body counts are unreliable. I believe, nevertheless, that accounts of major confrontations in Chihuahua are mostly accurate. I have included general military aspects of the Mexican Revolution to establish a background for the events on the frontier in 1916 and 1917.

In my examination of the armies of the United States and Mexico, I attempt to explain qualitative differences: leadership, tactics, logistics, past combat experience, command structure, military education and preparation for the campaigns of 1916. Tactical differences explain in part why neither army was able to find Villa and why Villa was so resilient.

I take the position that Carranza and the Constitutionalist army were dedicated to Villa's destruction—despite contrary beliefs of members of Wilson's government and of many high-ranking U.S. army leaders. Carranza, in my opinion, worried more about Villa's successes and his threat to the Constitutionalists than about the presence of United States troops in Mexico. To understand the nature of the problem that Constitutionalist and United States armies faced in capturing Villa, I offer background about Villa and his relationship to the United States, to the Constitutionalist government, to the Constitutionalist army and to the Mexican Revolution.

Based on my interpretation of military correspondence between commanders and Carranza, the "First Chief" saw the presence of the United States expedition on Mexican soil as a political threat—and perhaps long-term military threat to his regime—but between 1915 and 1919 he considered Villa, Emiliano Zapata and Félix Díaz as the most immediate and dangerous military problems. In his rhetoric—publicly and in diplomatic correspondence with the United States—Carranza spoke out vigorously against the United States and its involvement in Chihuahua. Carranza knew that the United States occupation of Veracruz in 1914 had threatened the strategically important seaport and oil-producing region. The arrival of the Pershing expedition in Chihuahua posed no threat to Veracruz. Sparsely populated and a long way from Mexico City, U.S. forces in Chihuahua, a center for numerous ranching and mining enterprises, were not a serious preoccupation.

By 1916 Carranza, aware of heightened public opinion in the United States and apprised of the war in Europe, realized that he had little to fear from across the border. After Pershing's troops had been in Mexico for some time, however, Carranza realized that Villa was using the gringo presence to his advantage. Villa loudly and publicly blamed Carranza for tolerating American violation of Mexican sovereignty. Carranza ultimately ordered his army to oppose United States troops if they attempted to move south into central Chihuahua. Carranza's stand contributed to a deadly confrontation at Carrizal in June, 1916. But Carranza had no intention of provoking war with the United States. Nevertheless, some high-ranking officers of the Constitutionalist army, including Manuel M. Diéguez, indicated, perhaps partially as polemic, that they were more than eager to make war with the Americans. In the U.S., General Hugh Scott, chief of staff of the army, felt that war with Mexico was inevitable.

Carranza and Wilson understood the problems and recognized each other's position in domestic politics. During 1916 especially, the heads of state sought to avoid any military escalation. The confrontation of 1916 occurred, however, for several reasons: first came Villa's attack on Columbus, New Mexico; Carranza took a hard-line nationalist stand; and Woodrow Wilson (backed by American industrialists) tried to protect United States interests in Mexico. Collision was unavoidable. Carranza knew that all-out war was possible, but he did not want a conflict. He had to tread carefully between promoting nationalism as a unifying ideology of the Revolution—which dictated that he could not let Wilson set the parameters of the conflict—and not becoming involved in open war. Carranza's stance strengthened his position with many of his country-men. Despite his aim not to provoke war, Carranza took steps to prepare for hostilities. He intensified espionage in the United States and may have been involved in the Plan of San Diego.[2]

How close did the two countries come to war in 1916? Some historians assume that war was imminent. I argue that the nations were not on the brink of war in 1916, but that Wilson and Carranza were spar-ring for diplomatic and political advantage in their respective countries. Neither nation could afford the strife. Carranza, however, wanted to control revolutionary Mexico and to forestall criticism that he willingly tolerated the Punitive Expedition. For Wilson 1916 was an election year in which Wilson suffered Republican criticism for his handling of the

Mexican situation. Both leaders engaged in considerable rhetoric for personal, political and nationalistic reasons.[3]

Wilson's desire to bring stability to Mexico centered on assurances that United States citizens and their properties would be protected. Diplomatic historian Mark T. Gilderhus writes that Wilson believed in "legal procedures," and that he wanted to promote "the orderly processes of just government based upon law, not upon arbitrary or irregular force."[4] Wilson felt that the elimination of Victoriano Huerta would open the door. He also hoped that he could influence the course of the revolution by playing hostile factions against each other. In 1916, according to Gilderhus, Wilson wanted "neither a declaration of war nor an intervention." The American president did not see the Punitive Expedition as a military solution to United States-Mexican problems, but he believed its deployment would help protect the United States border and maintain U.S. prestige in Europe. Ultimately, Wilson hoped to influence the revolution according to his principles of liberal capitalism.[5]

I have used information from Carrancista military and diplomatic communications to demonstrate what the Constitutionalist army was doing while Pershing's troops were in Mexico. I have done so also to illustrate that—at least in military correspondence—Carranza showed no fear of the Punitive Expedition, nor did General Jacinto B. Treviño, Carranza's northeastern frontier commander. In fact, all military telegrams between Carranza and Obregón and other frontier commanders about the battles between Constitutionalists and Villistas demonstrate the effort Carranza made to eliminate Villa. They show that his main concern was Villa, and they clarify his attitude toward the United States.

My research in Mexico occurred over several years. I spent many hours over two summers at the Archivo Histórico de la Secretaría de la Defensa Nacional unsuccessfully trying to get access to the service files of Alvaro Obregón, Francisco Murguía, Jacinto B. Treviño and others. I was able to obtain most of the same material in other places, however. According to the most recently published guide to documents in Defensa, there are few items there that are not in various other archives.[6] Copies of all telegrams between Jacinto B. Treviño and Venustiano Carranza are accessible in the Archivo Histórico del General Jacinto B. Treviño at the Universidad Naciónal Autónoma de México. Copies of many thousands of Constitutionalist military documents—the originals of which are probably in Defensa Nacional—are also in el Archivo Histórico del General Juan Barragán at UNAM. Several hundred of Obregón's military telegrams are in the Fideicomiso Archivo Plutarco Elías Calles y Fernando Torreblanca in Mexico City. Carranza's telegrams are available at the Archivo Histórico de Estudios de Historia de México Fundación Cultural de Condumex. Much information can also be found in the Archivo Histórico Genaro Estrada, Secretaría de Relaciones Exteriores (both in Mexico City). Newspapers containing information about battle activities can be found at the Hermeroteca Nacional at UNAM, at the Biblioteca del Archivo General de la Nación, and at the Biblioteca Miguel Lerdo de Tejada, all in Mexico City. Battle reports and newspapers accounts must, of course, be used carefully, but they often underscore what is in military correspondence. Secondary sources are numerous and range from some that are fairly good to many of little value. The best Mexican source on the Constitutionalist army is the three-volume *Historia del ejército y de la Revolución constitucionalista* by Juan Barragán Rodríguez. The volumes do not include all the confrontations between the Constitutionalist army and the Villistas, especially during 1916. Barragán's work is based on research in the Archivo de la Defensa Nacional, but is biased in favor of the Constitutionalist army. Federico Cervantes' *Francisco Villa y la Revolución* is a respectable source that also provides information about Villa in the 1916 campaign.[7]

I owe a debt of gratitude to many professionals in Mexico who helped me with the research: Lic. Josefina Moguel Flores at Condumex; Lic. Roberto Marín Maldonado at the Archivo Histórico de la Secretaría de Relaciones Exteriores; Lic. Norma Mireles de Ogarrio, Directora General of the Fideicomiso Archivo Plutarco Elías Calles y Fernando Torreblanca; Lic. Patricia Galeana, Directora del Archivo General la Nación; Dra. Angela Moyano Pahissa, formerly of UNAM and later at the Instituto Polytécnico de Monterrey en Querétaro; Lic. Armando Ruíz, formerly at the Instituto Nacional de Antropología y Historia (INAH) and now at the Biblioteca Miguel Lerdo de Tejada; and Marta Ochoa Esquivel, Técnico Academico del Archivo, UNAM. Prof. y Lic. Hector Jaime Treviño Villareal, Subdirector del Archivo Histórico de Nuevo León, provided documents.

Lic. Alfonso Vásquez Sotelo, Director del Instituto Estatal de Documentación de Coahuila, also assisted with materials, as did Lic. Beatriz Carrillo González at the Secretaría de Relaciones Exteriores and Rodolfo Beristáin of the Archivo General de la Nación early in the study. Susana Morales Feregrino, María Esther González Hernández and others retrieved and copied documents for me at the various archives in Mexico City.

In the United States, Douglas Richmond of the University of Texas at Arlington read the manuscript critically and suggested numerous changes. Without his help, this book could not have been completed. Sam Brunk of the University of Texas at El Paso suggested materials to examine. Friedrich Katz asked me difficult questions leading me to reexamine my treatment of recruiting soldiers for the Villista and Constitutionalist armies. My colleague Professor Michael M. Smith, who has examined many of the documents of Carranza's regime, read the original draft and suggested it needed to be placed in wider context. He also read the completed draft and offered valuable suggestions for final revision. Suzanne Pasztor sent me a copy of her Ph.D. dissertation on Coahuila during the revolution. Professors William Beezely, Don Coerver, Linda Hall, Pedro Santoni, and Juergen Buchenau encouraged me to complete the effort. A. T. Row, editor at TCU Press, helped make this a better book. Although I had considerable help with this study, any interpretations or errors are mine.

Finally, I wish to express my appreciation to Dean Smith L. Holt of the College of Arts and Sciences at Oklahoma State University and to his able director of research, Associate Dean Jack Bantle as well as his staff, particularly Toni S. Shaklee, for their help on this project. The history department also provided research support. Early in the study, Dr. Anita May and the Oklahoma Foundation for the Humanities provided financial support.

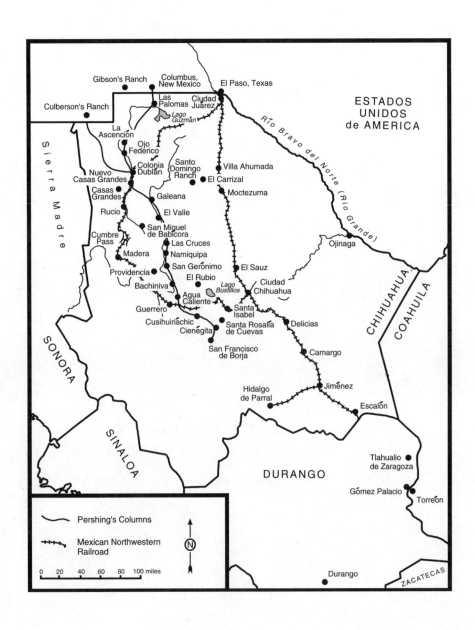

Gibson's Ranch

Columbus,
New Mexico

El Paso, Texas

ESTADOS
UNIDOS
de AMERICA

Culberson's Ranch

Las
Palomas

Ciudad
Juárez

*Lago
Guzmán*

Río Bravo del Norte (Río Grande)

La
Ascención

Ojo
Federico

Santo
Domingo
Ranch

Villa Ahumada

S i e r r a   M a d r e

Colonia
Dublán

El Carrizal

Nuevo
Casas Grandes

Galeana

Moctezuma

Casas
Grandes

El Valle

Rucio

San Miguel
de Babícora

Ojinaga

Cumbre
Pass

Las Cruces

CHIHUAHUA

COAHUILA

Madera

Namiquipa

El Sauz

Providencia

San Gerónimo

El Rubio

Bachiniva

*Lago
Bustillos*

Ciudad
Chihuahua

Agua
Caliente

Guerrero

Santa
Isabel

Cusihuiriáchic

Santa Rosalía
de Cuevas

Delicias

Cienégita

San Francisco
de Borja

Camargo

SONORA

Jiménez

Hidalgo
de Parral

Escalón

S I N A L O A

Tlahualio
de Zaragoza

DURANGO

Gómez Palacio

Torreón

Pershing's Columns

Mexican Northwestern
Railroad

N

0   20   40   60   80   100 miles

Durango

ZACATECAS

CHAPTER 1

VENUSTIANO CARRANZA, PANCHO VILLA AND THE UNITED STATES

▼▼▼▼▼▼

Early on June 21, 1916, United States Army troopers under command of Captain Charles T. Boyd of the Tenth United States Cavalry crossed open ground approaching the village of Carrizal, Chihuahua, Mexico. Almost immediately, they came under heavy machine gun fire from Mexican Constitutionalist soldiers who held the town. The Mexicans had a clear line of fire from barricades they had erected and from buildings facing the troopers' approach. The odds were hopelessly in favor of the Mexicans, and the fire devasted the American ranks. Boyd and twenty-two others were killed or wounded. When the firing ceased, the Mexicans held twenty-four Americans captive.

At 4 A.M. Boyd had led his command of African–American troopers to the outskirts of Carrizal in search of the elusive Francisco "Pancho" Villa, who on March 9, 1916, had led almost 500 followers across the international border and attacked the tiny village of Columbus, New Mexico. The United States responded by sending General John J. "Black Jack" Pershing and approximately 5,000 men into Chihuahua to capture and punish Villa. Pershing failed, and his expedition served little more than to escalate diplomatic and military tensions between the two countries.

Internal instability in Mexico and international difficulties with its northern neighbor began soon after Mexico acquired independence from Spain in 1821. Independence brought dilemmas. The country suffered as successive individuals or factions gained and lost power quickly and violently. Such turmoil strengthened regional *caudillismo* and was not conducive to stability and progress. Mexico's weaknesses cost dearly. First, Mexico lost Texas in 1836. As a result of the war with the United States that ended in 1848 with the Treaty of Guadalupe Hidalgo, much of what is the present-day American Southwest, including New Mexico, Arizona and California, fell to the U.S. The country remained in political and military chaos until 1876 when Porfirio Díaz, a general officer in the Mexican army, garnered the support of business, army, political and church elites to reach the presidency. He ruled from 1877 to 1911. The Porfiriato was marked by peace and prosperity—as well as foreign investments. Díaz, however, was also notorious for his dictatorial methods.

Díaz took control by making the defiant *caudillos,* or *cabecillas,* subject to the central government. Then he proceeded to destroy provincial militarism and to professionalize the national army. He retired twenty-five percent of the active-duty generals, all of whom were civilians who had obtained their positions either during the 1860s in the War of the Reform or later against French invaders. To bring a degree of professionalism to the officer corps, Díaz established the Military Academy (Colegio Militar) at Chapultepec, which trained and graduated 4,500 of the approximately 9,000 officers in the army by 1900. Still, at the turn of the century most generals were not professionals but corrupt opportunists. Díaz tried to create a volunteer Federal force, but—with the exception of officers—it was comprised mostly of conscripts and uneducated Indians. In short, the army was weak and ineffective.[1]

In Díaz's push toward modernization, his government made a concerted effort to bring stability and development to the country, including the northern frontier. Díaz also encouraged foreign investment, and the country slowly prospered. Although economic development moved forward, not all Mexicans shared in the increasing wealth. The poor remained at a subsistence level, while elites of the church, the army and the land-owning class became wealthier with each passing year.

By 1900, however, Díaz faced opposition from middle-class leaders in the north who became alienated from the regime. In 1910 Díaz announced that he would not seek reelection, but quickly reneged and declared his candidacy. Because elections had historically been fraudulent, opponents saw no hope of ending the Porfiriato other than by armed rebellion.

One of the more articulate of Díaz's opponents was Francisco I. Madero, son of a well-to-do Coahuilan hacendado. Madero had attended the University of California at Berkeley and was well informed about democracy. He suggested the rallying cry for the rebellion when he called for "Effective Suffrage—No Reelection." In 1910, Madero announced that he would be a candidate for the presidency. Díaz, demonstrating his power, had Madero arrested. Madero's family obtained his release, however, and Madero fled to the United States. There he proclaimed his Plan de San Luis Potosí, calling publicly for the overthrow of Díaz by any means.

By November 1910, the rebellion against Díaz had begun. Regional *cabecillas* such as Pascual Orozco, Jr., Francisco "Pancho" Villa and Emiliano Zapata were involved almost from the beginning, while others like Alvaro Obregón and Plutarco Elías Calles waited to see what would follow. Zapata, a budding entrepreneur, raised the standard in Morelos, calling for the redistribution of lands to the peasants. Hundreds joined Zapata, and even more flocked to serve Madero in the north. Motivation ranged from true revolutionary sentiment to a desire for personal profit or adventure. Some middle-class Mexicans hoped ultimately to break the hold of foreign investors who controlled much of Mexico's natural resources and transportation infrastructure. Others only wanted a better life for their families, while a few sought to combine revolutionary activities with banditry.[2]

Pancho Villa might be considered a revolutionary, a reformer, an opportunist, a nationalist, a rebel or a bandit. Few would disagree, however, that he was a legend in his lifetime—a man whose reputation became even larger in the years after his death in 1923. To many Mexicans, Villa remains a symbol of the Revolution. Today's Americans have a quite different view of Villa. Some conjure up a romantic Hollywood image. In the community of informed scholars north of the

border, Villa remains controversial. Some see him as a Mexican Clyde
Barrow, while others view him as simply a revolutionary leader. Villa's
brutality against his enemies, his destruction of property and his activities
along the border ultimately prompted many Americans of Villa's era to
condemn him as a cutthroat and sadistic killer.

Villa remains elusive. He embodied a little of all the characteristics
people of his time and of later eras have attributed to him. He occasionally took from the rich and gave to the poor. He supported the rebellion
against Díaz, fought against the usurper Victoriano Huerta, and eventually
opposed both the leaders and the direction of the Mexican Revolution.
E. Alexander Powell, a United States author who met the famous revolutionary in 1911, helped readers visualize Villa. He was:

> . . . stockily built and of medium height—not over five feet ten,
> I should guess—with the chest and shoulders of a prize fighter
> and the most perfect bullet-shaped head I have ever seen.
> Receding from the back of the neck and jaw, it tapers upward
> in the most extraordinary fashion. His head is covered with
> black hair as crisp and curly as a negro's: his skin is the color
> of a well-smoked meerschaun [sic]; a small black mustache
> serves to mask a mouth which is cruel even when it is smiling.
> The most attractive feature of the face is the eyes which are
> large and brilliant and extraordinarily piercing. Indeed, they are
> really not eyes at all, but gimlets which seem to bore into your
> very soul. I can describe him as a man that I would not care to
> meet in a lonely neighborhood on a dark night.[3]

Accounts of Villa's origins are cloudy and may be fact or fiction. He
is said to have been born Doroteo Arango in about 1878 near or in Río
Grande, Durango, the son of peasants who worked for and lived on Don
Arturo López Negrete's huge hacienda. Like similar thousands, Villa's
parents, Augustín Arango (who was not Villa's biological father) and
Micaela Arambula, barely survived. It is almost impossible to ascertain why
Villa first turned to banditry. He probably related the story that he became
an outlaw as a consequence of the actions of Don Arturo's son. Villa
said that Leonardo López Negrete lusted after his sister and raped her. In
retaliation Villa killed the son and fled. Villa also told another tale in which

Plutarco Elías Calles (Archivo Fotográfico, Centro de Estudios de Historia de Mexico, Condumex).

General Francisco "Pancho" Villa (AHUNAM, Archivo Octavio Magaña Cerda).

he left the hacienda without permission to work on a nearby ranch that offered higher pay. Don Arturo sent men to retrieve the errant boy. They brought him back in shackles and flogged him brutally. Once recovered, Villa left the hacienda again. He spent his days and nights hiding from the authorities but was soon captured. He later claimed that while he was incarcerated he heard stories of bandits who robbed from the rich and gave to the poor, prompting him to consider the outlaw life. He asserted that he saw the injustices inflicted on the poor and dedicated himself to effect change.

As a bandit, Villa said he did whatever he could to fight a system that abused peons. When he heard of Francisco Madero's rebellion against Díaz, for example, he led his men into the movement. Madero welcomed his support and in 1911 named Villa a colonel. In the same year Villa married Luz Corral, a young woman he had met earlier, and established a home in Ciudad Chihuahua.[4]

Others opposed the regime of Porfirio Díaz and joined Madero. Ricardo, Enrique and Jesús Flores Magón campaigned against Díaz through the use of propaganda. When propaganda failed, they turned to more aggressive means. They then fled to the United States for safety. Neither the Flores Magón brothers, Zapata nor Madero had enough followers to topple Díaz, but Madero ultimately united the disparate groups long enough to overthrow the aged dictator.

Fighting against Díaz broke out in different regions of Mexico. On the northern frontier Abraham González, Pascual Orozco, Jr., and Pancho Villa fought Federal troops. By early 1911, Mexicans throughout the country joined the Madero-led Revolution. Ciudad Juárez fell to the Díaz opposition; then Torreón and other cities across the nation capitulated. On May 21, 1911, Don Porfirio resigned and went into exile. Madero nominally rose to power, but Mexico remained so factionalized with local *cabecillas* struggling for control that the country continued in turmoil. Emiliano Zapata in Morelos, Pancho Villa, Pascual Orozco, Jr., and Abraham González in Chihuahua and Venustiano Carranza in Coahuila did not support parts of Madero's programs. Moreover, the Flores Magón brothers, who had organized against Díaz from their base in the United States and had orchestrated an invasion of Baja California, also were unhappy with Madero's leadership. In the eyes of some, Madero had not moved rapidly enough in bringing social reform. Finally, Madero alienated church leaders and lost their political support. Madero hoped that the national army would back his efforts, but again he erred. Madero's attempt to retire many of the revolutionary generals prompted rebellion within the army. Generals Bernardo Reyes, Victoriano Huerta, and Félix Díaz (the latter Don Porfirio's nephew), ultimately conspired to overthrow Madero. Huerta was a capable military commander, a graduate of the Colegio Militar, and the original organizer of the División del Norte. He had led the forces that suppressed a Pascual Orozco-led rebellion in Chihuahua. Some elements of Huerta's Division of the North were later incorporated into Villa's División del Norte. (Many of the Huertista officers were graduates of the military college. Others were trained engineers, but the elites chose not to join Villa.)

It was most likely while Villa was a member of Huerta's division that he learned basic elements of strategy, particularly the use of artillery, which came from his association with Felipe Angeles, one of the most famous artillerymen of his day. He also learned the need for sanitation, as well as the value of a competent medical service. Villa added his new talents to his knowledge of the terrain and his natural audacity and intuition.[5]

When Madero learned of the opposition, he promptly jailed Generals Reyes and Díaz, but the conspiracy continued. On February 9, 1913, guards released the two men. Shortly thereafter Reyes was shot to death while trying to capture Madero. Bloody fighting between Madero loyalists and opposition army units lasted ten days. In the end, Félix Díaz formed an alliance with General Victoriano Huerta. On February 18, they met with United States Ambassador Henry Lane Wilson, who evidently encouraged the ouster of Madero by promising U.S. recognition of the counter-revolutionary regime. (The Taft administration had recognized the Madero government previously.) On February 18, 1913, late in the day, the conspirators had Madero and his vice president, José María Pino Suárez, arrested. On the night of February 21 as they were transferred from the national palace to the federal penitentiary, Madero and Pino Suárez were killed "while trying to escape." They were, in fact, assassinated. Who ordered the executions remains a mystery. Huerta, however, had sufficient support from the army to gain and temporarily hold the position of president.

Huerta believed he had sufficient support to maintain the office and hoped to restore the Díaz system of control. His regime was primarily a military one, however, and events quickly proved him wrong. He soon realized that he faced a resurgent popular movement and that he did not have the military resources to ward off the opposition. His critical weakness was the poor quality of the Federal troops. The recruits—frequently peon and Indian conscripts—had no reason to fight and little stomach for battle. Adding to the problem, regional *cabecillas* opposing Huerta determined to carry out their version of the revolution. Northerners under the leadership of Venustiano Carranza, governor of Coahuila, insisted that Huerta had violated the Mexican Constitution of 1857 when he assumed power. Carranza formed what he called the Constitutionalist movement— designed to restore the tenets of the Constitution of 1857—and enlisted the support of other regional leaders. Along Mexico's northern frontier, Alvaro Obregón of Sonora, Pancho Villa of Chihuahua and others joined the effort by signing the Plan de Guadalupe and calling for Huerta's ouster. Although never a Constitutionalist or a Carrancista, Emiliano Zapata in the south helped Carranza by fighting Federal troops in his region. The coalition agreed upon little other than the overthrow of Huerta.

Woodrow Wilson, who had been inaugurated president in March 1913, immediately recalled Henry Lane Wilson and refused to recognize Huerta's government. Wilson established an arms embargo against Mexico, hoping to bring down the regime. At home, the president was increasingly pressured to intervene. Ironically, the U.S. had a history of meddling in Mexico's internal affairs when it suited American interests. An incident at Tampico, where a number of U.S. sailors were briefly detained by Mexican authorities, that led to the spring 1914 American occupation of Veracruz (a major shipping port), is a good example. With the arms blockade and with American troops in southern Mexico, Wilson effectively choked off Huerta's supply route, crippled his ability to ship petroleum and stiffled the collection of critical import taxes. Additionally, revolutionary armies were marching against Huerta in the south and the north. Simply put, the regime was doomed, and Wilson got his wish: Huerta resigned in July 1914 and fled into exile. In the final analysis, however, it was Huerta's attempt to militarize the country and reinstate the programs of the Porfiriato that caused his demise, not the United States.

Wilson ordered his troops out of Mexico on November 23, 1914. Carranza had gained the upper hand. Before Wilson withdrew troops, however, he demanded that Carranza guarantee protection of American citizens in Mexico and exoneration of Mexicans who had worked for United States authorities in Veracruz.[6] The opening of the port supplied Carranza with tax funds to import supplies to pursue his goal of eliminating his enemies.

On March 26, 1913, approximately 100 revolutionary *cabecillas* met with Carranza, withdrew recognition of the Huerta regime and created the Ejército Constitucionalista. Carranza became "Primer Jefe," or First

Chief of the Constitutionalist army, a civilian rank he chose for himself. Nonetheless, the newly created Constitutionalist alliance proved almost uncontrollable because of discord among commands. Carranza had to break down clan loyalties in the revolutionary groups to establish a functional, unified army. On April 18, 1913, Villa in Chihuahua and Obregón

Above: left to right, General Cándido Aquilar, Henry Fletcher, Venustiano Carranza, Roque Estrada, and General Benjamín Hill (AHUNAM, Archivo Octavio Magaña Cerda).

Left: United States Ambassador Henry Lane Wilson (Archivo Fotográfico, Centro de Estudios de Historia de Mexico, Condumex).

in Sonora agreed officially to fight under Carranza's leadership. Villa and Obregón opposed Federal forces that were numerically—but not qualitatively—superior.[7]

Originally a guerrilla force, the Constitutionalist army did not have the strength to fight the Federals in head-to-head battle. The rebels (as those who opposed the Federals may be called) weakened enemy strength with harrassing tactics, isolating and destroying detachments and attacking supply and transportation systems. The Federals ultimately abandoned the countryside, retreating to city garrisons. Obregón proved a capable commander as he retreated deeper into his northern territory, pulling the Federals into positions far from logistics and reinforcements. When Obregón attacked, it was on his terms. Villa also demonstrated his military prowess against Federal troops. Drawing on his bandit past, he paid scant attention to formal strategy, yet Villa wreaked havoc with hit-and-run tactics. By the time the Federal army surrendered in late 1914, there were about 150,000 armed rebels in the country, and Villa's 40,000 fighters, the largest concentration of Constitutionalists, resembled a professional army in organization and operation.

The alliance, however, among the disparate revolutionary forces remained uncertain. The factions agreed, therefore, to a joint conference at Aguascalientes. Carrancista officers were in attendance at first, but because of the proximity of Villa's army, Villa's influence over the proceedings and Carranza's unwillingness to cooperate with Villa or Zapata, the Carrancistas withdrew. Convention delegates eventually declared Carranza in rebellion and refused to support him. The representatives elected General Eulalio Gutiérrez provisional president of Mexico.[8] Gutiérrez served until early 1915.

Carranza refused to accept the convention proceedings, hoping to maintain his government in Mexico City. Without sufficient military strength to defend the capital against Villa (who may have had command of 70,000 men by this time) and Zapata, however, Carranza left Mexico City and established his administration in Veracruz. Villa and Zapata finally met at Xochimilco, just outside of Mexico City on December 4, 1914, to discuss cooperation between their armies. They had some goals in common. Both hated Carranza, and they agreed on the course of the revolution in general. But both wanted to dominate the coalition.[9] The result: a rift between the two factions. Their inability to cooperate created considerable disorganization among their forces.[10] Carranza would not have to face a concentrated Villista-Zapatista force. The First Chief wanted to eliminate Villa, Zapata and, ultimately, Félix Díaz; at the same time, he hoped to end United States influence in Mexico, heading off any incursions like the 1914 occupation of Veracruz. Carranza viewed all of his adversaries as threatening, not only to himself but to the type of constitutionalism he wanted to establish.[11] Carranza's most significant military problem was that he did not command a field army personally and had to rely on cooperation from his generals.

Venustiano Carranza's stubborn opposition to the financial and diplomatic meddling by the United States had more to do with revolutionary nationalism than any innate hatred of *los yanquis*.[12] Carranza supported nationalism as the basis of his ideology of social justice. His determination to lessen American influence in Mexico led to a confrontation with Woodrow Wilson.

The Mexicans believed that both the Drago and Calvo Doctrines should be observed by the United States and Mexico. Argentine Foreign Minister Luis Drago had written earlier that nations could not employ force to collect foreign debts owed to its citizens. Carlos Calvo, also an Argentine, suggested that in addition to the principle of non-intervention expatriates should be subject to the same laws as citizens of the host country. Calvo argued that foreigners could not appeal to their mother country for help and that the mother country could not intervene in the affairs of another nation on behalf of its citizens. When Wilson stepped in to defend United States citizens and business interests in Mexico, Carranza would not hear of it. As Robert Freeman Smith writes, "Revolutionary Nationalism and U.S. hemispheric hegemony now had completely locked horns."[13]

Carranza's appeal to Mexican citizens' nationalism and his opposition to United States intervention provided a unifying ideology to rally support against other factions that he considered in rebellion. Carranza promised a more equitable tax system, and agrarian laws that would give the common man more opportunities and a better standard of living. He proposed accomplishing these goals by gaining the backing of various sectors of Mexican society and by closely controlling the exploitation of natural resources.

This nationalistic zeal infected students, who strongly supported Carranza. It also influenced hacendados, peasants and elements of the various armies to stand with Carranza against the First Chief's foes. Carranza effectively used rhetoric to recruit for his army and to win support for his view of the Revolution. His actions were not as radical as he often made them sound. Although his generals occasionally confiscated haciendas, Carranza ordered most of the properties returned. In January 1915 he promised restoration of peasant lands that hacendados had taken. Though the program failed, it did increase his image among the lower classes temporarily. Wealthy land owners and businessmen also supported Carranza financially and provided a stronger economic base for the First Chief's military activities than either Villa or Zapata could sustain.[14] Carranza's reforms, although sometimes only temporary and often only rhetoric, helped expand his power base and gain support from most sectors of Mexican society.

Carranza appealed for help on a national scale. For example, he pressured local governors and military commanders to act against merchants who charged unfair prices or hoarded commodities that were in short supply. In Chihuahua, he ordered goods seized from merchants who did not cooperate and forced the sale of the merchandise at fair prices.[15] Where poor rural populations were scant, as in Chihuahua, he courted the middle and upper classes.[16] Across the country, Carranza created a new bourgeoisie who shared power with existing political and economic elites.

But the military took precedence over all else. Carranza tailored his military policies to match local sentiment. If the local population called for radical reforms, he sent radical generals to the region. In spite of his efforts, however, between 1915 and 1917 Carranza's army—still dominated by regional *cabecillas*—never resembled a national force. Carranza armed civilians, organizing *defensas sociales* (which he refused to subordinate to regional chieftans) to act as counterpoint to his often unruly army.

Villa's forces during the same period may have been more unified and professional than the Constitutionalists. After Villa's bloody defeat at Celaya in April 1915, however, his army disintegrated and became largely a guerrilla force. Villa became more radical after 1915, confiscating hacienda land and cattle and appealing to the poor. Such moves provoked the middle classes; after 1915, Villa had more difficulty financing his struggle against Carranza. The presence of the Punitive Expedition in 1916 also changed the relationship between Villa and Carranza. Both sides used United States intervention in Chihuahua to encourage local citizens to join their armies.

Additionally, Félix Díaz threatened Carranza when he returned to the country early in 1916 with the support of conservative United States businessmen. Díaz tried to capture the city of Oaxaca. Later he moved on to Veracruz, where—by 1917—he established control over part of the state.

To defeat Villistas, Zapatistas, Felicistas, as well as other opposing groups, and to discourage the United States from further intervention, Carranza relied on diplomatic efforts and on Alvaro Obregón. Carranza did not trust Obregón but needed his military skills. The Constitutionalist army wanted to confine Zapata to Morelos, eventually defeat him, and isolate Villa in the northern frontier.[17]

Obregón proved to be the most effective military leader of the period. Born in the Alamos District of Sonora, Obregón was the youngest of eighteen children. He grew up with Mayo Indians and spoke their language. The Mayos strongly supported him and later many joined his army. Obregón's education consisted of tutoring by his older sisters and a short stint in a school at Huatabampo. He worked in a machine shop, later sold shoes and eventually taught school. His greatest strengths were his understanding of machinery and a photographic memory. He supported Madero and fought with Carranza until 1917. In all his battles, he was cool under fire, using techniques of surprise and bluff and demonstrating his outstanding memory for details and terrain. Obregón would study his opponent's habits, bypass objectives of little significance and concentrate entirely on destroying his enemy.

On January 5, 1915, Obregón captured Puebla, forcing the Zapatistas to flee toward Morelos. Obregón did not pursue. He recognized that his most dangerous foe was Villa, and on January 28, 1915, he reoccupied Mexico City, forcing the Villistas to withdraw without a fight. While in Mexico City, Obregón recruited for his army and enlisted many recruits from the growing labor organization Casa del Obrero Mundial. On March 10, 1915, he moved north.

Also in early 1915, Carrancista General Jacinto B. Treviño, commanding Constitutionalist forces at the oil fields near Tampico, withstood a seventy-two-day seige by Villista Generals Manuel Chao and Tomás Urbina at nearby El Ebano. While Treviño's defense was important, more significant were Obregón's victories against Villa.

In late March 1915, Villa and Obregón marched toward a violent confrontation at Celaya, Guanajuato. On March 31, 1915, the Constitutionalist army reached Querétaro, occupying Celaya on April 3. Villa, aware of the movement, feared that Obregón might deploy men between units of Villa's army if he did not advance far enough south. Villa stopped first at Aguascalientes, then moved south toward Celaya. By April 4, Villa had concentrated at Irapuato, thirty-five miles west of Obregón. On this occasion Villa would not have the services of General Felipe Angeles, whom Villa had ordered to remain at Torreón. Angeles, who enjoyed the respect of many on all sides of the fighting, was a distinguished-looking officer. His thin face and neatly trimmed mustache gave the appearance of a natural bearing of command.[18] Many military officers considered him a "military genius" and the best artilleryman in Mexico.[19] Angeles had studied military tactics in France and had graduated from the Colegio Militar, where he later taught mathematics and eventually became superintendent.[20] Angeles suggested to Villa that their forces were far too widely spread out to engage Obregón so far from the Division of the North's supply base. Angeles told Villa to retreat slowly north to draw Obregón away from his supplies and reinforcements. Angeles' goal was total destruction of Obregón's army, while Villa wanted to protect territory. Villa was determined to attack Obregón and would not listen to wise counsel. Villa was under the mistaken notion that if he could destroy Obregón's army in one great battle, he could easily defeat elements of the Constitutionalist forces in Jalisco and other places as well.

Villa's well-organized army was equipped with Mauser and Remington rifles. Villa, however, often was impulsive and was not formally schooled in the military arts. Without the help of Angeles, Villa's battle strategy was less than sound. In the ensuing conflicts, Villa seemed to have forgotten the lessons he had learned from his earlier experience fighting the Porfirian Federals. Nevertheless, he did many things correctly out of intuition. He frequently attacked late at night or in the early morning, using darkness to shield his troops. Generally, he began his assaults with an artillery barrage that forced the enemy to return fire and reveal their positions. Villa provided water trains and medical services for his men. He paid attention to the small details that made an army successful.[21] And, despite occasional mistakes, his leadership and personal bravery often carried the day.[22]

In preparation for the fight at Celaya, Villa asked Zapata to attack Constitutionalist forces with the objective of severing supply lines to Obregón and to Mexico City. Zapata agreed, but only made a half-hearted effort. Villa was on his own.

Celaya, a town of about 25,000, was criss-crossed and surrounded by canals and drainage ditches. The waterways offered Obregón strong defensive positions. He skillfully posted his troops, concentrating them in trenches behind barbed wire.[23] The struggle would consist of two deadly battles; Obregón successfully held his position each time. Villa sent his men forward on April 6 but did not accompany the initial attack; instead, he trusted his generals to lead. They did so, but not in coordinated movements. The Villistas entered battle dispersed against a Constitutionalist army that was solidly concentrated and positioned. Villistas attacked in a mass, uncoordinated cavalry and infantry frontal assault, hoping to overrun the enemy. The initial attack proved costly. Villistas paid a high price in men and ammunition. They also failed to dislodge any of the Constitutionalist forces, partly because of Obregón's troop deployment and tactics and the recklessness of Villa.[24] Obregón had ordered General Fortunato Maycotte to lead his cavalry toward the Villistas until contact was made, then fall back into the defenses of Celaya. Action began at about 10 A.M. on April 6 and lasted until the morning of April 7. At one point Villistas reached the center of the city, but were driven off. Obregón used the moment to launch a cavalry attack against Villa's flank. Villa's only chance for victory had passed. He had squandered his ammunition and again lost many of his followers. Following the fight, the Constitutionalists dug in, and the Villistas regrouped at Irapuato.

On April 11, Villa sent Obregón an ultimatum, challenging him to come out and fight or Villa would fire artillery at Celaya, possibly killing many civilians. Obregón did not consider leaving his defenses because he knew that a force caught out in the open field would be cut to pieces by the Villistas. He knew, too, that he had a tactical advantage and was determined to maintain it. At 6 A.M. on April 13, Villa again attacked, opening the second battle of Celaya. The fight lasted more than twenty-four hours as Villa's thirty 75 mm and 80 mm guns shelled the Constitutionalists. Villa attempted many frontal assaults on the trenches on the western edge of the city but could not penetrate. Once Villa attacked, the Constitutionalists fought patiently until the Villistas expended their offensive energy. Then Obregón sent his cavalry to strike the Villista left flank, which sent the enemy from the field in panic. Villa withdrew to Aguascalientes, leaving behind almost half of his artillery and 6,000 to 8,000 men killed, wounded or captured. His reckless frontal assaults destroyed any remaining offensive capability of the División del Norte.

Nevertheless, Villa maintained a sizeable army, and on June 1, 1915, he engaged Obregón again at Trinidad near León de las Aldamas. Felipe Angeles, who was present as the battle took shape, recommended that Villa take up a defensive position in León. Villa again refused to follow the advice and struck quickly. The battle began on April 29 and lasted more than a month. During the fight, Obregón was wounded in the right arm and had to have the limb amputated. At times delirious, he was unavailable for several days. But General Francisco Murguía went on the offensive, striking the center of Villa's lines. The attack shattered the Villista front and sent Villa's men fleeing from the field. Again, Villa had expended his offensive energy and the Constitutionalist counterattack held León. Villa withdrew to Aguascalientes.

Early in July 1915, Villa fought his final large-scale battle of the campaign against the Constitutionalists. The two armies collided at Aguascalientes, and, as in the previous engagements, Villa made serious tactical errors. Again, he refused to listen to Angeles, who, just before leaving to represent Villa in the United States, had advised against the confrontation. Angeles predicted to others that Villa would lose the fight. He was correct. By summer's end Villa was forced to withdraw north to Torreón. Although he had lost battles and his army was largely destroyed, Villa was back in familiar territory where he enjoyed considerable local backing. One of Villa's strengths was his ability to bounce back from losses. One soldier later wrote that Villa never let such things discourage him for long.[25] Villa and his remaining confederates returned to the guerrilla tactics that had been successful against the Federal army in 1913.

Meanwhile, the Constitutionalist army savored success against the Zapatistas in Mexico City. Constitutionalist leaders marched their troops to Cerro Gordo and by July 10 were poised to capture the capital. The next day General Pablo González led his troops into the city, forcing the Zapatistas to withdraw southward. Constitutionalist occupation of Mexico City, however, was temporary. Carranza ordered his troops withdrawn in a few days. On August 2, 1915, the First Chief again ordered his forces to occupy Mexico City. He took control of the capital and the surrounding area. He felt confident enough—even before the occupation—to announce that "at last, after five years of warfare ... the revolution is about to end ... the Constitutionalist Government has control over seven-eighths of the national territory."[26]

▼▼▼▼▼▼

President Woodrow Wilson and then Secretary of State William Jennings Bryan (Robert Lansing replaced Bryan in 1915) had been watching the Mexican situation carefully since 1914. Wilson was chagrined at the conditions south of the Río Grande and suggested that Mexico "has been swept by civil war as if by fire."[27]

Villa, likely aware of Wilson's attitude, saw an opportunity to provoke the United States president. Villa was also unconcerned about what action the United States might take toward Mexico. He remarked in June 1915 that he did not particularly care if the United States intervened south of the border.[28] Villa responded to Wilson's comments by insisting that Carranza had violated the principles of the constitution and was the cause of the suffering in Mexico.[29] In any event, Wilson remained hopeful that during 1915 he could bring Carranza and Villa together for peaceful discussions. Wilson demonstrated his lack of understanding of the severity of the conflict in Mexico, just as he had underestimated the war in Europe. Despite the bloodshed, Wilson believed that all parties were willing to sit down and negotiate. Wilson was wrong. Villa made it clear that he was not interested in peaceful talks with Carranza; similarly, the First Chief offered "that under no circumstances would he treat with Villa."[30]

Public opinion in the United States endorsed Villa to some extent, and the sentiment increased as Carranza's intractibility became obvious; the First Chief came under open criticism in the United States. A June 11 *New York Times* editorial reflected the American attitude when the editor wrote that Carranza "lacks the extraordinary personal force of Villa, who seems, however, to be quite immune to civilizing processes."[31]

Conversely, U.S. officials, including some high-ranking military officers, favored Villa as the man most likely to protect United States interests in Mexico. After all, Villa had remained patient with the United States and had not criticized the invasion of Veracruz. On October 19, 1915, however, Wilson and some members of the State Department, in an effort to protect American interests, backed Carranza and officially recognized the Constitutionalist government. Villa, of course, was furious and soon retaliated.

During late summer and fall of 1915, Villa withdrew to Chihuahua and Coahuila, establishing his headquarters first in Torreón, Coahuila, and

President Woodrow Wilson and his cabinet. Clockwise: the President, W.G. McAdoo, J.C. McReynolds, J. Daniels, D.F. Houston, W.B. Wilson, W.C. Redfield, F.K. Lane, A.S. Burleson, L.M. Garrison, W.J. Bryan (Woodrow Wilson House, Washington, D.C.).

then at Ciudad Chihuahua. Once he reached Torreón, Villa was not allowed any respite. Constitutionalist forces from Sonora and points south relentlessly pressured the Villista army, trying to confine it to a limited area. As Constitutionalist strength grew, Villa was driven from Torreón and turned to raiding Constitutionalist posts and villages to isolate small garrisons from reinforcements and destroy them.

As the guerrillas got closer to the border, Wilson worried that the fighting would spill over into the U.S. On August 10, 1915, Villa journeyed to El Paso to meet with General Hugh Scott, who was sent by Wilson to analyze the situation and to talk with Villa. The revolutionary leader suggested to Scott that he and Carranza should agree to a three-month's cease-fire, during which talks could begin. Villa knew well that Carranza, who now held the stronger hand militarily, would not agree.

By mid-September it was obvious to American officials that Constitutionalist strength in the northern states was growing and Villa's strength was declining. Most of the time Villistas remained dispersed, joining forces only to attack cities or other strategically important sites. In Coahuila, Constitutionalist troops captured the capital of Saltillo and drove the Villistas into eastern Chihuahua.

The success of the Constitutionalists did not go unnoticed in the United States. In September 1915, George C. Carothers, an American consular agent in Torreón, advised his superiors that Villa's fortunes were waning and that Villa might attack some point in the United States to spark intervention. A clear indication that Carranza was winning the war is evidenced by changes in editorial content of the *Periódico Oficial,* the government newspaper of Chihuahua. Villa's last remarks were published in October 1915; by January 1916, Carranza's decrees were printed regularly.[32]

Villa's once-proud Division of the North had slowly dwindled as it moved northward to avoid confrontation with Constitutionalist forces. Losses were discouragingly heavy, and Carranza's army seemed only to gain strength. Some disheartened Villista generals fled to Texas or headed for safety in the Sierra Madre of Chihuahua and Durango. Adding to his troubles, Villa knew that the United States' de facto recognition of Carranza's government meant that the Villistas would have trouble securing money and ammunition to continue the struggle.

Villa was bitter at the United States for abandoning him in favor of Carranza and predicted "Revolution after Revolution." Villa remained primarily concerned with Carranza's army, but even the wily northern leader recognized that his military fortunes were in decline. Villa probably realized that an action provoking the United States intervention in Mexico would be his only chance to defeat Carranza. Villa also knew that if he could force the United States to violate Mexican sovereignty by sending large numbers of troops across the international border, Carranza would look weak or appear to be cooperating with the gringos. Villa probably speculated that United States intervention would make recruiting troops—ostensibly to fight the Americans—easier. Various revolutionary and governmental factions had employed similar methods several times. Seeking support in the United States for his position, Villa constantly offered proclamations that found publication north of the Río Grande. On one occasion he insisted that,

> Mexico is my country. I shall not run away from it. Here I have lived and here I have fought. Here I shall fight and here I shall live. Here, also, I shall die, and that probably soon, but I am content.[33]

Later Villa exclaimed:

> Save your ammunition and rifles, for it soon would be the American invader against whom you will fire them, and not against your brothers. Intervention is coming sooner than you know, and when it does, fight for your country and you will find General Francisco Villa beside you.[34]

By late fall 1915, Villa's pronouncements took on a desperate tone. He recognized that he would probably not be able to challenge the Constitutionalists on a wide-based military scale in the future.

The Constitutionalists kept the pressure on. In Sonora, General Plutarco Elías Calles, operating from Agua Prieta, threatened Villa's sanctuary in Chihuahua.[35] In November, Villa led his troops to Sonora, where they engaged and lost to Calles but refused to leave the state. Angered that U.S. officials had allowed Constitutionalist reinforcements to reach Agua Prieta by using railroads north of the international border, Villa raided in Sonora for several days, then fled back to Chihuahua with what was left of his army.

In late 1915 and early 1916, Carranza decreed publicly that Villa had to be eliminated. The First Chief ordered his troops in the northeastern frontier, nominally under command of General Jacinto B. Treviño, to intensify their search for Villa throughout the state. The task of finding and eliminating Villa in the terrain of northern Mexico was formidable. Chihuahua is 94,000 square miles of arid, rocky, desert and mountain landscapes, with little vegetation and even less water. Hundreds of caves and canyons provided hiding places for the Villistas. During the winter, it can be bitterly cold, and in summer temperatures can reach more than 100 degrees. Rainfall is rare. When it does rain, the deep arroyos cut by rushing waters are dangerous to man and beast. Inhabited sparsely except for the major towns, most of Chihuahua was and is a harsh and unfriendly place. Furthermore, many of the inhabitants either supported Villa or feared him enough to make them unwilling to help Constitutionalist troops. Finally, the Chihuahua citizenry made capable soldiers. For more than a century they had fought raiding Apaches, scalp hunters and bandits. The tradition of self-defense helps explain the effectiveness of Villa's army before 1915 and even to some extent in later campaigns against the Constitutionalists.

Into this landscape Carranza ordered the struggle against Villa to continue until he was killed or defeated. Carranza, however, soon found himself in a position similar to that of Huerta a few years before. Carranza controlled Mexico City, but he had not subdued his opposition, especially in isolated areas of the country. Zapata still presented a problem in Morelos and the south, but that threat was localized. Villa posed the greatest danger to the Carrancistas, particularly as he turned to guerrilla warfare, banditry, looting and extortion. Although Villa's power had declined, the Carrancista army was not yet capable of subduing him. The ongoing plague of bickering generals and logistical problems precluded success. Since the organization of the Constitutionalist government, regional *cabecillas* had cooperated with Carranza only as long as it was profitable. By 1916, the Constitutionalist army (at least on paper) numbered about 200,000, including about 50,000 officers, 500 of whom were generals. Many officers and enlisted men, however, were loyal only to local chieftans. They shared no real concept of nationalism, particularly those from the far northern frontier. Before Carranza could beat Villa and his other enemies, he had to take control of this force and build a smaller, more efficient and obedient army.

CHAPTER 2

FIND VILLA!

▼▼▼▼▼▼

By early 1916, Carranza was determined to take control of Chihuahua. He ordered General of Brigade Jacinto B. Treviño, Constitutionalist commander of the northeastern frontier, to do everything in his power to eliminate Villa and to protect larger villages and railroad centers. He told Treviño to deploy enough troops to search every mile of mountain and desert. The First Chief's mandate: get Villa and his surviving forces. Because Treviño did not have enough troops to garrison the entire state, Carranza ordered Alvaro Obregón to send additional units to Chihuahua and Durango to keep the pressure on the enemy.

Carranza never ceased in his efforts to capture or kill Villa before or after the arrival of the Punitive Expedition. Once American troops entered Chihuahua, General John J. Pershing, President Woodrow Wilson and others in the United States government insisted that Carrancistas were of no help in pursuing the revolutionaries and, in fact, actually obstructed the process. This is inaccurate. Carranza placed the northeastern frontier under the command of Treviño, who had fought competently for the Constitutionalists since Carranza had organized the movement. Treviño assured the First Chief late in 1915 that the northeastern frontier was secure and that only small bands of Villistas were roaming about Chihuahua causing minor trouble. Treviño's optimistic appraisal was not an accurate analysis of the military situation for 1915 or for what 1916 would bring to the Constitutionalists.

Treviño was well qualified to lead troops against Villa. He was born in 1883 at Villa Guerrero, Coahuila, and educated in his home state until

winning an appointment to the Colegio Militar in 1900. In 1908 he graduated and was commissioned an artillery officer. In 1913, as a captain in
the Mexican army, he supported Francisco Madero, who sent him that
year to Saltillo to organize irregular troops in the state. When General
Huerta overthrew Madero, Treviño opted to support Carranza, also from
Coahuila, in his effort to remove Huerta. Treviño helped Carrancistas win
the battle of Anhelo on March 7, 1913. Carranza subsequently appointed
him lieutenant colonel and jefe del estado mayor (chief of staff) for the
Constitutionalist army. In 1914 Treviño led the Constitutionalist defense
of El Ebano, Tamaulipas, against Villistas. For seventy-two days his men
held out, finally forcing the Villistas to retreat. On April 15, 1915, Carranza
rewarded Treviño by appointing him general of brigade and naming him
commander of the Army of the Northeast. Treviño fought Villistas until
Carranza sent him to Europe in 1919 to study the French, German and
Spanish armies. In May 1920 he rebelled against Carranza, ultimately
supporting Obregón. He retired from the army in 1927 but received
a presidential appointment to general of division in 1941. He held
numerous other army and civilian posts until his retirement in 1966.[1]

In late 1915 and early 1916, Villa recruited and reorganized.
Carranza, probably more pessimistic about Villa's demise than Treviño,
ordered General Francisco Murguía to take up positions in Durango so
his troops would be in place to assist Treviño. Murguía had been with
Obregón in the major battles against Villa in 1915 and had proven more
aggressive than other commanders. Carranza had considerable faith in
Murguía; it would be justified in 1916. Murguía, although not trained
as a soldier, exhibited traits desired in a professional military leader.[2] He
was bold and aggressive but not careless. In a 1916 conversation with
then Colonel Juan Gualberto Amaya about a conflict with the United
States, Murguía showed his understanding of Mexico's predicament
when he suggested that "our military situation before our powerful
neighbor is ridiculous." He believed, however, that with great sacrifices of
men and an aggressive stance, Mexico might have a chance to make
the invading American troops pay a high price in lives lost. He suggested
"that only audacity would offer probabilities of success" and that the

Mexicans "would have to use surprise and night attacks," among other non-traditional tactics.[3]

Murguía, with his disposition for attacking and his understanding of the overall situation, appointed General Arnulfo González military governor of Durango.[4] With the changes that Murguía made, Carranza now hoped that the Constitutionalist garrisons were ready to deal with a resurgence of Villismo. In fact, he claimed that Villa would not be able to find sanctuary anywhere because Constitutionalist forces were searching every corner of Chihuahua for him.[5] By the end of 1915, however, Carrancista military leaders realized that Villa was far from defeated; the guerrilla leader aggressively attacked towns and rail centers throughout Chihuahua, forcing Carrancista troops on the defensive. Villa chose the time and place of confrontation. Villistas later remarked that Villa almost always knew the location of government soldiers. Villista veterans also alleged that government troops raped, pillaged and otherwise abused local villagers, precluding any local support.[6]

Examples of government units confronting Villistas at various locations abound, and they demonstrate Carranza's commitment to defeating Villa. One unit under Major Gáspar de la Garza fought Villistas in a bitter battle at Payasos, Tamaulipas, late in December 1915. Other Constitutionalist field commanders had almost daily contact with the Villistas. On January 6, 1916, Treviño sent General José Cavazos, a native of Nuevo León, and his column to establish bases at San Antonio and Cusihuiriáchic. Four days later, Villistas under command of generals Rafael Castro, a Coahuila native, and Pablo López, born in Chihuahua and a close confidant of Villa's, attacked railroad train No. 41 near Santa Isabel. The train was traveling between Chihuahua and Cusihuiriáchic. The Villistas robbed the passengers, herded eighteen American citizens off the train and brutally executed them as they tried to escape.[7] Only one American, who had scrambled into the brush, survived. Although Villa was not present at the time, he was probably nearby and may have ordered the assault.[8]

Treviño advised Carranza of the fatal attack and said that he had sent a regiment under Colonel José Villanueva Garza toward Santa Isabel

Pancho Villa (center) and some of his troops in typical Villista attire, 1915 (Archivo General de la Nación).

with orders to pursue. Garza was to coordinate his efforts with those of General José Cavazos, commander of the Sixth Military Zone. But by the time government troops converged on the point of attack, the Villistas had dispersed and fled into the mountains of Durango.[9] The Constitutionalist forces pursued and caught up with one group that included Villista Generals José Rodríguez and Carlos Almeida and a Lieutenant Colonel Nevárez. Rodríguez—a favorite of Villa's—fell captive to the Constitutionalists in a skirmish at Las Varas and was executed on January 14, 1916. His body was displayed publicly in Ciudad Chihuahua as a warning to those who helped the guerrillas.[10]

Carranza was notedly pleased with the turn of events.[11] On January 16, 1916, Constitutionalists captured a few more Villistas, including Colonel Manuel Baca Valles; they placed this unfortunate officer before a firing squad, shot him and put his body on public display in Ciudad Juárez.[12] Carranza took additional measures to focus Constitutionalist efforts on Villa when he pronounced Villa a bandit outside the law and called for his capture and execution. Mostly for propaganda purposes, Carranza insisted that Villa was on the run, that all railroads were protected by government soldiers and that the state of Chihuahua "was completely pacified."[13]

American officials were greatly concerned about the killing of U.S. citizens in Mexico. Charles A. Douglas, legal counsel for the Constitutionalist government, advised Carranza that the episode was being politically exploited by Carranza's enemies in the United States. Republican newspapers, for example, suggested that the murders were further evidence of Carranza's inability to control his countrymen. Douglas advised that Carranza demonstrate good faith in pursuing Villa by offering a reward of at least $50,000 for the bandit's capture.[14] Mexican Ambassador to the United States Eliseo Arredondo counseled his government that American journalists were accusing Carranza of having no control over Mexico and that some U.S. politicians and writers were urging the United States to intervene.[15]

Carranza was clearly aware that propaganda aimed at Americans was a powerful tool. In fact, he had devoted considerable time and money to convince U.S. citizens that he was capable of handling the situation. His backers and agents in the United States tried to improve his personal image and offset negative publicity.[16] Nevertheless, his main concern remained Villa, not public opinion in the United States. Treviño was still far more confident than Carranza that Villa was under control. He advised Carranza in mid-January that troops under the command of General José Cavazos had occupied and were campaigning from Ciudad Guerrero. They had captured 87,000 Mauser cartridges, seventy-four Mausers, four prisoners, 600 boxes of dynamite, forty horses and a machine gun.

General Francisco Murguía arrived in Durango and assumed command on January 15, 1916.[17] Seeing that Murguía had the advantage, Villa left Durango for Lagunera, Chihuahua. Few Constitutionalist troops were in the region, and Villa knew that he would have more freedom to operate there. Villa hoped to concentrate his troops with those of Generals Luis Hilario Castro, Severiano Ceniceros and Bernabé González—all near Casas Grandes, Chihuahua. Together the concentrated force would move on to the Laguna region near Torreón. These Villistas already had enjoyed some success against the Carrancistas, having fought and routed Constitutionalists at Hidalgo de Parral on January 15, but they, too, had suffered losses, including four men killed and three captured. On January 19, Colonel Cruz Maltos' (sometimes spelled "Maultos") Constitutionalist Zuazua Brigade engaged Villistas under General Manuel Tarango at Hacienda La Joya. In the confrontation, government troops claimed to have killed ten enemy and pursued the survivors to Rancho El Alamo, where another brief skirmish took place.

While this news seemed positive for the Constitutionalists, the problems within Carranza's army were evident. Lack of unity and cooperation among commanders still plagued the force. On January 1, General Arnulfo González had reflected on the problems when he complained to Carranza that the frontier was in a "ridiculous" military condition: various area commanders issued contradictory orders and many senior officers developed their operations independently as if no chain of command existed.[18] The problem reflected the very nature of revolutionary armies and the lack of professionally trained leaders.

Logistical woes also continued. Two days after González wrote Carranza of his opinions, General Juan Marero advised the First Chief that his troops had been in a vicious fight with Villistas, but "we had to abandon our position, for we ran completely out of ammunition." Marero had asked Treviño for reinforcements and ammunition but had received none.[19] On January 6, General González and his forces fought for seven hours against Villistas near Yerbañez, Durango. González complained that he retreated only after running out of ammunition.[20] Difficulties and shortages notwithstanding, Constitutionalist commanders claimed successes. On January 10, General Luis Gutiérrez led government troops in pursuit of Villistas in the Pedricena area. Gutiérrez reported that in a running shootout he had dispersed several hundred enemy troops, but in the process had lost eighteen killed and about that number wounded. Apparently, he had no enemy body count to report.[21]

Another problem along the frontier was that Carranza—directing from Querétaro—tried to take personal control of his forces. On many occasions he ordered Treviño to move troops. He communicated directly with field commanders who were supposed to be under Treviño's orders.

In short, the only unity of command was the active role that Carranza took. His failure to work through Treviño, however, contributed to chaotic military operations. He should not have corresponded with field commands without passing the communications through Treviño's headquarters, nor should he have received messages directly from the field commanders, especially when the communications were complaints about Treviño or another sector commander.[22] Alvaro Obregón was painfully aware of the organizational problems. Obregón suggested that "such disasters [battle losses] were the result of the lack of unity of command in the region" and lack of leadership.[23] Lastly, Constitutionalist troop strength at all locations varied, and, in most instances, neither Treviño nor General Alvaro Obregón (soon to be named secretary of war) knew for certain the number or fighting trim of the troops at any particular location or time.

Other difficulties existed. The mere survival of the Constitutionalist troops and their families depended on Carranza's ability to pay them. When they were paid, they got only one and three-quarter pesos per day, not enough to feed themselves or their families. According to General Mariano Arrieta, pay was at the heart of several problems.[24] Troops sometimes received their wages in gold or silver, but more often in paper money that declined in value daily. Most merchants would not accept the scrip. In purchasing power, twenty-five silver pesos was equal to twelve in gold, while fifty pesos in paper money was worth only two pesos in silver. As a consequence, soldiers were loyal to whoever paid them and changed sides to follow the money.

By the end of January 1916, Treviño—then en route to Torreón— devised a plan to block Villa's access to the Mexico-U.S. border by dispersing troops across the frontier. He circulated the plan to frontier commanders and to town officials.[25] In Cuidad Chihuahua, General Luis Herrera led the Brigada Benito Juárez.[26] In the center of the state were the Zuazua and Benjamín Garza Brigades, while General Cavazos and his troops were in the Sierra del Noroeste. General Francisco A. Espinosa was in the district of Santa Rosalía de Camargo with his brigade, while on a line from Parral to Jiménez were General Petronilo Hernández and

Colonel Emiliano Triano's forces. In the Plaza of Ciudad Juárez and on a line from the northwest were the troops of General Gabriel Gavira. Finally, Lieutenant Colonel José Riojas operated from Ojinaga west along the border.

All told, Treviño had forty-four generals, 1,347 field-grade officers, 3,699 other commissioned officers and 11,118 enlisted men. Treviño admitted that not all of the command, especially local men who might have once fought for Villa, could be trusted to stand against their former comrades. Despite this, Treviño insisted that as of January 1916 "the zone under my command is pacified, and there exist only some parties of bandits who are pursued tenaciously by our forces."[27] On January 22, Treviño assumed personal command at Torreón.[28] General Ignacio C. Enríquez agreed in part with Treviño's assessment of conditions. According to Enríquez, many soldiers would fight the Villistas, but there were insufficient arms and ammunition.[29]

At the end of January, Treviño reorganized the frontier defenses, establishing four sectors. General Luis Gutiérrez was at Parras, General Matías Ramos in San Pedro de las Colonias, General Ignacio Ramos at Gómez Palacios and General Fortunato Maycotte at Ciudad Lerdo. Under Maycotte were Generals Gonzalo Novoa, Francisco Manero and José V. Elizondo. Each sector was to send out patrols to search for and, the leaders hoped, destroy the enemy.[30] Despite Treviño's efforts, Villa continued his attacks. On January 31, sixty Villistas under Villa himself sacked a government train near Las Lagunas, Chihuahua, robbing the passengers, killing one American citizen and capturing and executing former Villista and now Constitutionalist General Tomás Ornelas.[31] Carranza recognized that publicizing such Villista successes would not help the Constitutionalist cause. Early in February 1916, the First Chief demanded that newspapers not run articles on Constitutionalist losses.[32]

Between February 7 and 12, 1916, government troops again confronted Villistas. Enemy troops attacked Hacienda de Guadalupe in General Matías Ramos' sector.[33] Two hacienda employees were killed and several others wounded. Constitutionalists pursued the Villistas. One unit under Colonel Evaristo Pérez caught and dispersed them near Hacienda

Buen Arigo. Others of Ramos' command fought Villistas at San Pedro del Gallo and San Luis del Cordero; they captured five Villistas, several horses and some weapons. Also during early February, General Gabriel Gavira, a reliable and competent officer then commanding at Cuidad Juárez, sent 150 cavalrymen in two columns toward Bosque Bonito and Moctezuma.[34]

On February 15, 1916, commander of the Third Military Sector in the Laguna Region, General Ignacio Ramos, fought Villistas under the command of Generals Canuto Reyes, Hilario Rodríquez and Margarito Salinas near Lomas de Derrame. After a brief fight during which the Villistas suffered a few wounded, they broke up only to concentrate later at Rancho del Derrame. These small and apparently marginal successes did little to curtail Villista activity,[35] but the incidents demonstrate that Carranza still focused much of his attention upon Villa and the northern frontier. He sent General Luis Gutiérrez a message telling him not to try to occupy or protect all of the towns, but "dedicate your forces to pursuing parties of bandits with the goal of quickly exterminating them."[36]

Despite reports from various sectors indicating progress, the dispatches were not an accurate appraisal of the situation. On February 21, General Ignacio C. Enríquez said that he was "desperate" and needed more troops at once.[37] Villistas were also causing trouble for General Francisco Murguía in Durango. On February 24, approximately 1,500 Villistas waged a heavy firefight with Murguía's troops that lasted from 2 P.M. until dark. When the Villistas withdrew, they left fifty dead on the field. Murguía did not pursue for two reasons—the impending nightfall and fear that the enemy would charge his position again at dawn.[38] Villistas did not attack the next day. Rather, they broke up into smaller groups and attempted to cut the railroad between Durango and Torreón.[39]

On March 3, 1916, Treviño placed General Luis Gutiérrez in command at Ciudad Chihuahua. On that day Gutiérrez began to move his men from Torreón to that city. At the same time, Murguía worked to secure the area near Ciudad Durango. He sent troops to protect the rail line to Torreón and others to suspected Villista hideouts. In the process of defending the region, Murguía lost two officers, three noncommissioned officers and four soldiers.[40]

On March 6, 1916, General Gutiérrez advised Carranza that Villa was north of Ciudad Chihuahua, possibly preparing to attack Ciudad Juárez. Gutiérrez added that the Constitutionalist forces were moving into position to block Villa. Little did the Constitutionalist leaders suspect what would follow in the next few days.[41]

CHAPTER 3

THE RAID ON COLUMBUS

▼▼▼▼▼▼

Columbus, New Mexico, was not much of a town in 1916: a hotel, one bank and a few other enterprises constituted the main business district. There was no electricity, often a water shortage and indoor plumbing was a luxury few enjoyed. Most of the buildings were constructed of adobe; some had glass windows and screens, but most windows were simply open to the elements. The El Paso & Southwestern Railroad tracks bisected town east and west; a dusty road called Main Street ran thirty-two miles north to Deming and a couple of miles south to Mexico. Streets were unpaved and rain—when it came—made them impassable quagmires. Most often dust blew and the heat in the summer was intense. Monotonous terrain surrounded Columbus: cactus, tumbleweed, sand, and, in the distance to the north, the peaks of the Tres Hermanas Mountains.

About 300 people called Columbus home. Across the international border, the Mexican Revolution had been raging for almost six years; before that, nomadic Native Americans and bandits had plagued this part of the frontier. Because of the hazards, a United States army detachment was stationed at Columbus in an encampment called Camp Furlong. The troops occupied the southeast quadrant of the town.[1]

The men of the Thirteenth United States Cavalry were not particularly pleased with their assignment. The commanding officer, Colonel Herbert J. Slocum, a wealthy Ohioan and a competent officer, had done everything he could to protect his command and the surrounding area.[2] Slocum was aware of the political and military problems south of the border. During the first week of March 1916, he had heard that Villa was just south of Columbus. On March 7, 1916, he received a dispatch from Headquarters, Southern Department, Fort Sam Houston, Texas, in which General Frederick Funston, commanding the department, advised him that Villa might cross the line. No one knew whether to believe the rumors. Funston thought that Villa might be seeking sanctuary, but he did not think Villa would attack to the north.

Evidence continued to mount during the first week of March, however, that Villa was up to something. On March 7, Slocum interviewed two Mexican nationals who claimed that they had blundered into Villa's camp about fifteen miles south of Columbus. Juan Favela and Antonio Muñoz, employees of the Palomas Land and Cattle Company of Chihuahua, said that they and an American, William K. Corbett, had been working cattle along the Casas Grandes River when a band of Villistas surrounded them. Corbett surrendered. The two Mexicans escaped. Although this report placed Villa near Columbus, the army could not legally send patrols into Mexico to find out what Villa had in mind.

Determined to learn what he could of Villa's intentions, Slocum offered Muñoz $20 to return to the Villista camp and report back. Muñoz accepted the cash and headed west to Gibson's ranch, arriving on March 8. There Muñoz talked with Major Elmer Lindsley and a detachment of the Thirteenth Cavalry. Lindsley furnished Muñoz with field glasses and a rifle and drove him to the border. That same day Muñoz arrived at Boca Grande and discovered that Villa had just left. Muñoz told Slocum later that he thought the entire Villista band numbered approximately 120 men. He believed they had headed south. Slocum, unfortunately, trusted the report.

Slocum had more pressing problems than he could easily resolve. The War Department had told him to protect Columbus, as well as to patrol a sixty-five-mile-long stretch of the border from Noria in the east to Hermanas in the west. Slocum's twenty-one officers and 532 troopers faced an impossible task. The camp commander had not been derelict in his duties. He had driven across the region after receiving Funston's warnings. At one Mexican port of entry, Slocum had talked with

Carrancista troops about Villa. He learned nothing. In fact, Slocum reported, the Mexicans were hostile.

Returning to Camp Furlong the next day, Slocum warned his men to be ready for anything. He sent reinforcements to Lindsley—seven officers and 151 men—and dispatched two officers and sixty-five men to stand guard at the border gate. He retained seven officers and 341 men, including seventy-nine noncombatants, to protect Columbus. He also dispatched day and night patrols along the border. On March 8, Slocum nervously checked his preparations and contemplated additional precautions. Darkness arrived early that time of year and, as the sun set, Slocum must have realized how dark the village would be. The only sources of light on the streets were an occasional kerosene lamp and the moon.

The Villistas were closer than anyone realized, and they had been for several days. On March 7, when Muñoz and Favela made their escape, they were unaware that others were already captives of the band. Corbett surrendered and was taken to the Villista camp and added to other hostages. The foreman of the ranch for whom Corbett worked, the outfit's cook, James O'Neil, and an African American named Edwin R. "Buck" Spencer all shared the same fate. Spencer survived, probably because he was black and the Villistas saw him as a victim of the whites. He later told authorities that when a Villista colonel sent word to Villa asking what to do with the captives, Villa said to shoot them or hang them and that he intended to arrive in time for the show.

By midnight on March 8, Columbus was dark, and there was little sign of life. A little before 1 A.M. on Thursday March 9, 1916, part of the darkly clad Villistas slipped across the border about three miles west of Palomas. At the Palomas crossing, U.S. troops were completely unaware of the presence of the Villistas. Villa and the rest of his men crossed later. When the raiders arrived within a mile of Columbus, they split again into two columns, each containing approximately 250 men. Villa dispatched one group to attack Camp Furlong and the other to strike the Columbus business district. Despite Slocum's warnings, the American troopers were unprepared for an assault.

Lieutenant John P. Lucas' adobe hut was almost in the middle of the two Villista columns as they began the assault.[3] Lucas awoke at the sound of hoofbeats and was the first person to hear the approaching raiders. He could see little except Mexicans wearing traditional sombreros when he peered out the window of his hut. Lucas was alone and quickly retrieved the .45-caliber pistol that he had left loaded and hanging on the wall. He positioned himself in the middle of the hut determined to kill as many Mexicans has he could when they entered. The second soldier to realize the presence of the Villistas was Private Fred Griffin of K Troop. Griffin saw the Mexicans and shouted at them to halt. They fired, wounding him in the stomach. He killed three of them before he died. Meanwhile, Lucas, thrashing about in the darkness of his hut, had finally found his trousers, but not his boots. He raced barefoot out the door toward the barracks where his men were trying to get dressed and organized.

From another part of town, Lieutenant James P. Castleman had heard the gunfire and as he ran from his hut collided with a dismounted Villista.[4] The startled Castleman fired at the fleeing invader, then ran to join F Troop. Sergeant Michael Fody already had rallied the unit. Castleman quickly assumed command and led his men toward the center of town. Dropping to the ground, they returned the shots. Castleman prodded his men on. Private Jesse P. Taylor was wounded when he was hit in the leg. At a barbed-wire fence near the edge of the business district, the men again came under heavy Mexican fire during which Private Thomas Butler was hit twice. Butler continued on, but by the time the men reached their objective, he was hit several more times. Butler died.

Lucas, even with his feet painfully exposed to the rocks and cactus, had been active too. After the fight, he said that he felt nothing at the time; only later did he realize the severity of the wounds to his feet. Once Lucas reached his men, he led them to the supply shack to get French-made Benet-Mercie machine guns and ammunition. Lucas did not wait for the others. He grabbed a weapon and headed toward the railroad tracks with two men. He opened fire only to have the gun jam.[5] He returned to the ammunition shack and got a similar weapon and, with a Corporal Barmazel, raced back and began firing at the raiders. By this time riflemen had joined Lucas and the group exchanged fire with the Mexicans for ninety minutes.

While Lucas and others fought to defend the business district, the men at Camp Furlong were also under seige. The Villistas first attacked the stables. Even army cooks—already preparing the morning meal—got into the action. They opened fire at the Villistas with shotguns normally used for hunting game. As the Mexicans broke through the door of the cook shack, soldiers hurled boiling water on them and hacked away at the raiders with axes, leaving a bloody scene in the shack.

After two hours, the Villistas broke off the fight and headed south toward the border. During the shooting, Colonel Slocum had taken position on a nearby hill from which he watched the retreat. Major Frank Tompkins asked Slocum for permission to chase the Villistas, and Slocum agreed.[6] With the help of Captain Rudolph E. Smyser, Tompkins organized H Troop for the pursuit.[7] Within twenty minutes thirty-two men were riding for the border. Lieutenant Castleman mounted up twenty-seven men of F Troop and joined the chase. The Villistas knew that Americans would follow, so they left a detachment to slow down the pursuit. The U.S. troopers killed thirty-two of the rear guard. Tompkins later wrote that on catching up with the Villistas, he and his men "deployed at wide intervals and advanced toward the enemy at a fast trot, the enemy firing all the time but their shots going wild."[8] The raiders were killed in Mexico, and Tompkins realized that he had violated international law and Mexican sovereignty. Tompkins sent a messenger to ask Slocum what to do. Approximately an hour later he received instructions to do as he thought best. Tompkins decided to press his chase further into Mexico. He followed the retreating Villistas about fifteen miles into Mexico until his men ran out of food and water.[9] His command suffered no casualties, but, according to one report, "Major Tompkins was shot through the hat, his horse was shot under him, and two of his troopers lost their mounts."[10]

On the return trip to Columbus, the troopers counted almost 100 dead Villistas, as well as dead horses and lost equipment. Except for the men Tompkin's command had killed, the rest probably died of wounds received at Columbus. Tompkins and his column returned to Columbus at a little past 1 P.M., having marched seven-and-a-half hours and covered twenty-five miles of rough territory.

The returning cavalrymen found a sobering scene. Smoke rose over the city; fires had recently burned out and the stench of burning human flesh filled the air. Soldiers and civilians had dragged the bodies of sixty-seven Villistas to the outskirts of town, poured kerosene on them and set them afire.

The rest of the United States knew of the attack on Columbus shortly after it began.[11] Mrs. E. G. Parks, a night telephone operator on duty in Columbus when the attack commenced, had been hit by flying glass as the bandits sprayed bullets in her direction. She remained at the switchboard until she had raised the Deming operator and told her to sound the alarm. News spread immediately in other ways. Associated Press chief George Seese of El Paso had sent a telegraph agent to Columbus to see if rumors about Villa attacking along the frontier had any credibility. On March 3, Seese boarded a train for Columbus to join the telegrapher. He reported the raid immediately after it ended.

Although news was spotty at first, it soon became known that nine civilians and eight soldiers had died and many others were wounded. No accurate count of dead Villistas was made, though it was clear many had been killed. Eight bandits fell captive to United States forces. One newspaper report claimed that the Villistas who got away "dropped considerable material and loot which they had gotten in town."[12] Captured Villistas confirmed that Villa had led the attack. Further proof of Villa's presence came from correspondence found on the battlefield, including copies of letters to Emiliano Zapata asking him "to march north and join in the attack on the U.S."[13]

Additional evidence of Villa's presence came from Maud Hawkes Wright, who had been taken hostage by the Villistas a few days before the raid. She was held for ten days. Wright later told authorities that she and her husband had ranched near Colonia Hernández, approximately 120 miles south of the border. On March 1, 1916, she was at the ranch house with her small daughter when twelve members of Villa's band appeared. Colonel Nicolás Hernández advised her that she was a prisoner of the

Villistas. Her husband and another American returned during the confrontation and were also captured. The daughter was left with a Mexican woman at the ranch, and the prisoners were forced to ride with the group. Evidently, Villa condemned the two men. Mrs. Wright never saw her husband again.

For the next three days and nights Mrs. Wright was forced to ride with the bandits. When she asked Villa to free her, he responded that he might after the attack; he turned her loose as he fled Columbus. Wright later retrieved her daughter and described her ordeal. Villa, she offered, had been dressed in civilian clothes until the day of the attack. Then, she said, he "appeared clad in trim military uniform and rode one of the three handsome sorrel chargers which had not been ridden during the long march."[14] Wright also recounted that Villa had earlier ridden "among the men, cursing and threatening to shoot any man who ran away."[15]

News of the assault on Columbus reached President Woodrow Wilson late on the morning of March 9, and he immediately considered retaliation. It was an election year, and Wilson recognized that the Republican press, which was intensifying its attacks on him, would criticize him. Republicans would profit politically if he did not act. On March 10, Wilson called his cabinet together to discuss the possibility of sending army units across the international border. Opinions varied about the course of action, with Wilson favoring some military response.

General Funston in San Antonio, Texas, already had decided that the army should be dispatched. On March 10, he recommended such an action in a telegram to the War Department. On that same day Wilson sent a telegram to Carranza advising him that the United States considered the attack a very serious matter and that it was the responsibility of the Mexican government to punish Villa. Specifically, Wilson asked Carranza if the Constitutionalist government had any advance notice of Villa's intentions. Two U.S. special agents then in Mexico communicated the notice—John R. Silliman and John W. Belt passed the message to Mexican Foreign Relations Secretary Jesús Acuña.

On March 9, Carranza also learned of the Villista attack. The word came from Consul Andrés G. García in El Paso and from General

Plutarco Elías Calles in Sonora, both of whom telegraphed the First Chief. Both indicated that the United States was in an uproar over the incident. Fearing a major confrontation, Calles told Carranza that he had concentrated troops at El Tigre, Bacerac and Bavispe to confront Villistas should they head west from Chihuahua or to fight United States troops who might cross into Sonora. Calles awaited orders.[16] Carranza advised all Constitutionalist commanders to be cautious while diplomatic efforts proceeded. In his reply to Wilson, Carranza reminded the American president that, in the nineteenth century, reservation Indians from north of the international boundary had crossed almost weekly to attack villages in Mexico. Carranza doubted that any additional Villista attacks would occur on United States soil, but if that occurred, then Mexico and the United States should discuss terms of "hot pursuit." The Mexicans would consider any other reaction—sending a military expedition, for example—"an invasion of National Territory."[17] Carranza made the statement knowing of the political pressures Wilson faced. Carranza advised General Agustín Millán at Veracruz to resist any United States landing at that port. Carranza also told United States officials that the Mexican people should not be held responsible for the attack by a few bandits and that any invasion of Mexico would be viewed as a declaration of war.

Diplomatic exchanges and threats meant nothing, however; within twenty-four hours of the attack, Wilson had decided to pursue Villa.[18] Public outcry forced action. The United States would not be patient with Carranza or Villa. Newton D. Baker, newly appointed secretary of war, and General Hugh L. Scott, army chief of staff, ordered the expedition into Mexico and told General Funston to draw up specific plans. Capturing or eliminating Villa would not be easy. One correspondent for the New York Times opined that Villa would disappear into the mountains, and his "capture would tax American ingenuity."[19]

By March 12, Washington was ripe with talk of war. Diplomatic notes were exchanged daily between Carranza and Wilson, the First Chief holding fast to the demand that no United States troops be sent to Mexico. On March 14, American troops stationed at Palomas thought

Villista prisoners at Columbus, New Mexico (Arizona Historical Society, Tucson, photo #28358).

United States cavalrymen salute fallen comrades after the raid on Columbus (Arizona Historical Society, Tucson, photo #53925).

that the Carrancista commander across the line had received orders to oppose any force crossing into Mexico. They knew that Carranza was using the press in Mexico to incite Mexicans against a potential intervention.[20]

Once Carranza realized that the United States would send troops to capture Villa, he backed away from a military confrontation, saying there was no need for war. Carranza offered no explanation to the United States for Villa's attack, but Manuel Calero, former ambassador to the United States during the Madero administration, suggested that Villa wanted to strike "the government that until a few months ago he considered his friend." Calero offered that Villa's action was "the rage of a desperado, a madman if you wish. You must remember that until about six months ago Villa considered himself the pet of the U.S.A."[21] In fact, he had good reason to believe he was the favorite. General Scott admired Villa and once remarked that even with all his faults, he was "a far better character than Carranza."[22] Scott had met Alvaro Obregón and Villa and had formed strong opinions about the two men. Scott had observed the fighting in Mexico for a number of years and ultimately disliked Carranza so much that he recommended to Wilson that the United States not recognize the Carrancista government. Scott was also certain that Wilson did not want "to provoke the Mexicans by a show of force on the border."[23] Scott did not understand the Mexican Revolution or Carranza's aims. While Villa's motives for attacking the United States might not have been clear, Wilson's determination to send troops into Mexico in search of the revolutionary leader was evident.

Wilson reacted to public pressure that called for retaliation against Mexico, not only for the raid but also because of the nationalist direction that the Mexican Revolution seemed to be taking. International intrigue, possibly involving the Germans in Mexico, may have influenced Wilson. He might have believed initially that the Germans were behind the raid on Columbus. The Germans were undoubtedly pleased that the United States was getting involved in Mexico militarily. Of significance, too, was that the Germans provided arms and ammunition to the various revolutionary factions in Mexico.[24]

▼▼▼▼▼▼

To fifty-five-year-old John J. "Black Jack" Pershing fell the task of organizing and leading the expedition. Pershing was born at Laclede, Missouri, on September 13, 1860. In 1882 he entered the United States Military Academy. He graduated thirtieth in a class of seventy-one and was assigned to Fort Bayard, New Mexico, where he participated in the last of the major campaigns against hostile Apaches. He later served in the northern plains against the Sioux. In 1891 the army assigned him to teach ROTC cadets at the University of Nebraska. He served in the Spanish-American War in 1897 as a first lieutenant in the Tenth Cavalry, an all-black unit. In 1899 the army assigned him to the Philippines to help pacify the islands.[25] After his tour in the Pacific, he was ordered to Washington, D.C., where he became popular among members of Congress. In 1906 President Theodore Roosevelt promoted Pershing to brigadier general. In the fall of 1913, Pershing received a new assignment as commander of the Eighth Infantry Brigade at the Presidio of San Francisco. The next year, as the Mexican Revolution spilled over into the United States, Pershing was transferred to Fort Bliss, where he commanded the Sixth and Sixteenth Infantry of the Eighth Brigade. Pershing believed his assignment only temporary, but as conditions between Mexico and the United States deteriorated, he realized he would be in El Paso for some time.

Pershing accepted his assignment to find Villa, fully aware of the complexity of the task. He knew that in the state of Chihuahua alone there were 94,000 square miles of mountains and deserts—too many places for Villa to hide. There were few roads, and only a single rail line ran north from Ciudad Chihuahua to Ciudad Juárez. Because Carranza refused to let American troops use Mexican trains, Pershing had to rely on trucks and animals to move men and supplies. One newspaper reporter wrote that the campaign occasioned "the first autotruck companies to be organized for the United States Army." Shortly after the pursuit began, the government accepted bids for fifty-four trucks, fifteen motorcycles and two "wrecking trucks" for Pershing's campaign.[26]

When the Punitive Expedition—as Pershing's columns would be called—entered Mexico, the American army had a total troop strength in the continental United States of 24,602. Pershing had units of the Seventh, Tenth, Eleventh and Thirteenth Cavalry and two batteries of the Sixth Field Artillery to lead into Mexico. Perched on the border, the general's command included 4,800 men and 4,175 animals.

Wilson, through Secretary of War Baker, specifically ordered Pershing to capture Villa if possible. If not, he must sufficiently disperse the Villistas so they could no longer threaten the United States.[27]

CHAPTER 4

THE PUNITIVE EXPEDITION

▼▼▼▼▼▼

The United States army that entered Mexico on March 15, 1916, was a more highly polished force than the Constitutionalist army of Mexico. In 1916 the total strength of the American army stood at 108,399, the bulk of whom were stationed in the Philippines, Hawaii and the Panama Canal Zone. There were also 132,194 national guardsmen in varying degrees of readiness. Late in the nineteenth century the army progressively became more professional. In 1903, Elihu Root persuaded Congress to create a "general staff system" that along with the Army War College (created in 1900) began systematic studies of war, including ultimately Plan Green—largely a defensive scheme—in case of war with Mexico. The general staff finalized the system in the 1920s, continuing the defensive posture.

The Punitive Expedition was similar to operations against Native Americans. It was the first campaign, however, to employ motorized devices like trucks, motorcyles, tanks and airplanes—equipment that was already being used extensively in Europe—and it helped to prepare the army for future engagements overseas. One of the units in the campaign that had long experience in the Indian wars was the Tenth Cavalry, comprised of African-American troopers.[1] The Tenth was stationed at Fort Huachuca, Arizona, when it received orders to join Pershing.

The arrival of Pershing's troops in Mexico did not mark the first time that American soldiers had crossed into Mexico, nor would it be the last. Between the annexation of Texas to the United States in 1845 and the death of Venustiano Carranza in 1920, American soldiers crossed the border on numerous occasions. Each time the Mexican and American governments hurled challenges, charges and threats at each other.

Throughout the nineteenth century, the international border remained the focus of difficulties that plagued both countries. Diplomats had tried to resolve the problems. In the Treaty of Guadalupe Hidalgo (1848), the United States agreed in "Article XI" to make an effort to stop Native American raids launched from the U.S. In the Gadsden Purchase Treaty of 1853, Article XI was abrogated and the two countries agreed to guidelines that established a joint boundary survey (going west from El Paso to the Pacific coast) that would clarify the international line. Yet outlawry and raids by hostile Indians continued to curse the frontier until the end of the century. During this period, native warriors, most of whom lived on United States government-established reservations, frequently left to raid into Mexico. Indigenous tribesmen living in northeastern Mexico crossed into the United States to raid. After the attacks, the perpetrators returned to their camps on either side of the line. Mexican and United States army troops usually pursued them, often into the neighboring national territory. As a result, the countries signed a formal border-crossing agreement in 1882 that allowed hot pursuit of hostile Indians for a short distance across the border and for a limited time. With the surrender of Geronimo in 1886, the United States finally confined the native tribes to reservations, and much of the violence ceased. Diplomatic relations improved between 1880 and 1910, although the frontier remained a troublesome, disputed area.

It would remain highly charged and violent from March 1916 until January 1917 as U.S. cavalry units faced hostile Villistas and Constitutionalists.

▼▼▼▼▼▼

General John J. Pershing divided his forces into two converging columns, a tactic often used in the Indian wars, in an effort to trap Villa before he could move too far south. The columns entered Mexico twelve hours and fifty miles apart. Major Frank Tompkins of the Thirteenth Cavalry headed out of Palomas, while the other column, with Pershing in command, entered south of Hachita, New Mexico. Neither column

U.S. troops of the Punitive Expedition in Mexico take a rest from the campaign, 1916 (El Paso Public Library).

encountered any resistance crossing the international line. Pershing pressed ahead toward Nuevo Casas Grandes, approximately seventy miles away, where he would meet scouts from the other column and exchange information. The units quickly realized that they would learn nothing about Villa from local citizens. In passing through Palomas, Tompkins remarked that the village was almost deserted, except for an elderly couple. Tompkins described the village as unimpressive, for it "consisted of about thirty adobe houses scattered about a spring."[2]

On the march, men of the Punitive Expedition suffered. It had not rained in that section of northern Mexico for nine months, and it was through difficult terrain that the troopers filed. Sergeant J. L. Thompson wrote that "we went in singing, and we thought we were having a lot of fun. Then we hit deep sand and heat. It was awful and we had to conserve our water, for we each had but one small aluminum bottle filled with brackish water from the shallow wells at Columbus for the first day's supply."[3] Sergeant W. P. Harrison recorded that in his group everybody was serious, for there was not a bit of breeze "and dust hung over the road like a curtain. The alkali got in our eyes and down our throats, it sifted into our shoes and through our clothing. The sun beat down upon us."[4] Conditions were so severe that the pack-mule train fell behind and did not arrive at the assigned destination until almost twenty-four hours after the main body of men. Infantry, along to protect camps and supply lines, suffered greatly. One officer wrote that the region was all "canebrake cactus, Yaqui Indians and rattlesnakes."[5] Each trooper carried food, water, ammunition and a nine-pound Springfield 30.06 rifle.

On the second day's twelve-hour march, Pershing covered fifty-five miles and reached Colonia Dublán, just north of Nuevo Casas Grandes, at sundown. There Pershing waited for Tompkin's force, which had a greater distance to travel. Once Tompkins arrived, Pershing learned that the column had encountered no resistance from the Carrancista forces or from Villistas. On March 18, Pershing quickly sent about 600 men of the Seventh Cavalry to scout the area toward and near San Miguel de Babícora, but he sent the Tenth to Madera, another thirty-five miles to the south. Despite Carranza's objections, Pershing pressed the Mexican railroad into use. The train that arrived at Colonia Dublán on March 19 was in poor shape. Major Tompkins wrote later that "the box cars had to be ventilated by cutting holes in the sides, and many repairs had to be made on all cars."[6] Another officer remarked later that it appeared to him that the freight cars had been used by Mexican troops, for "fireplaces of clay and stones were still in them. In some places, the fires had burned through the floors."[7]

When Colonel William C. Brown's Tenth Cavalry reached Babícora on March 22, they learned that Villa had not been in the vicinity for days.[8] Carrancista Colonel Maximiliano Márquez told Major Ellwood W. Evans of the Tenth Cavalry that Villa and his band definitely were not in the nearby high country but might be about forty miles away on the other side of the mountains.[9] The information provided to Evans and Brown proved false, and the Americans believed that they were purposely misled.

Pershing continued to push his men and sent patrols sweeping through valleys and across deserts looking for Villa. Part of the Villista party that attacked Columbus passed through Palomas ahead of the

United States units and quickly moved south. Villa himself had passed through El Valle, recruited for his force, then journeyed on to Namiquipa. He arrived on March 18, the day after Pershing marched to Nuevo Casas Grandes. Namiquipa, a village of about 3,000 people who were accustomed to defending themselves from Indian attacks, was armed and had a reputation for supporting the Revolution. Shortly afterward, Villa attacked a nearby Constitutionalist force and captured two machine guns and approximately a hundred horses. On March 20, Villa led his men away from Namiquipa. Four days later American soldiers under Colonel Brown arrived at the village. Villa evidently headed across steep rocky trails through the wooded sierra toward El Rubio about thirty-five miles south of Namiquipa. There, on March 24 and 25, he prepared to fight Constitutionalist troops stationed at Guerrero.[10]

Meanwhile, the Tenth Cavalry continued to have problems with rail transportation. On March 19 at 5:30 P.M., after patching the cars and loading horses and men, the column headed south. With only two days' rations, the troopers were soon forced to forage for food. For thirty-two days government supplies failed to catch up with the columns. By 8:15 A.M. on March 20, the dilapidated train arrived near El Rucio (just south of Colonia Dublán), where officials advised Colonel Brown that some of the load must be taken off before the train could continue. Brown ordered his cavalry off the train and headed overland to Babícora. There he learned that Villa had passed through only two days earlier. Brown's men fed and watered their horses and then began a treacherous trip along a rocky trail.[11] They traveled twenty-seven miles to Chávez and on to El Toro, where on March 23 they waited for Major Ellwood W. Evans and his men.

Brown sent a civilian guide scout toward Babícora, where Constitutionalist troops were located, and to the area between there and Namiquipa. One Carrancista soldier told the guide that Villa had recently been at Namiquipa and Santa Clara. When Brown learned this, he immediately went to talk with the Carrancista commander. The Mexicans told him that Villa was probably east of Namiquipa, near or in Cañon de Oso. Brown notified Colonel George A. Dodd, who was near Namiquipa with units of the Seventh Cavalry.[12] Then at 7 A.M. on March 25, Brown led his troopers toward Namiquipa. On arrival, he conferred again with local Carrancista commanders and learned that Villa was last seen seven miles east of town. The Americans rode east for nine miles but found no Villistas. They established camp in Cañon de Oso. The local Carrancista commander told Brown he would scout the area and report back if he found Villa.

Two days passed and Brown concluded that the Constitutionalist commander had not sent out scouting parties, nor was he going to forward any information. Brown ordered his men to the trail once again and headed toward Santa Catarina. During the day he learned from Major Tompkins that Villa had not appeared at Namiquipa. On March 28, he led his men toward El Rubio, where Villa was last reported. Brown then dispatched Major Evans and his squadron to Tepehuanes and continued on to La Quemada. There Brown nearly captured one of the Villistas. He did, however, recover seven Seventh Cavalry horses that had been taken in the Columbus raid.

Intelligence at La Quemada indicated that Villa had been there six days earlier. Brown camped near the village and sent out patrols. He soon learned that Villista General Pablo López might be nearby. He sent a message advising Dodd of López's location, then proceeded to El Rubio to confer again with Evans.

On returning to La Quemada, Brown learned that his message to Dodd had not been delivered. Dodd had moved on toward Guerrero. On March 30, Brown decided to march to San Diego del Monte, where he found out that Carrancista troops had recently fought Villistas at the village of Guerrero. Brown also heard that Villa had been wounded in the leg in the confrontation. On March 31, Brown remained in camp, trying to communicate with Pershing or Dodd. Because it was snowing heavily, however, moving about or finding allies was extremely difficult.[13]

The column under Major Evans had met Brown's men at El Toro on March 23 but had accomplished little. Evans had kept his men on the train until the evening of March 21, when, near Música, two cars overturned. The wreck injured eleven men, whom medics transported to

Música. On the morning of March 22, Evans arrived at Las Varas, where he talked with Colonel Maximiliano Márquez of the Constitutionalist army. Márquez, who probably wished to distance the United States troops from his position, told Evans that Villa was near Namiquipa.

On March 24, Pershing ordered Evans to Babícora. Seven hours later, Brown ordered Evans to meet him at El Toro. The two columns remained at El Toro until March 28. By March 31, Brown had concentrated his command at San Diego del Monte, where he awaited orders from Dodd or Pershing.[14] On March 31, the U.S. columns were unaware how close they were to Villa.

Dodd's Seventh Cavalry was not far behind the fast-charging Villistas. Dodd raced through the Santa María Valley after the enemy and by March 25 was in the high sierra. To keep warm in the frigid night air the men piled hay upon one another. Dodd had heard that Constitutionalist troops were in position to block Villa's escape, but instinct told him they would not.[15] On March 28, Dodd arrived at Bachiniva, where he learned that Villa was at Guerrero, only thirty-six miles away. As Dodd prepared to head in that direction, Lieutenant Herbert A. Dargue, one of the First Aero Squadron's flyers, landed, bringing an order from Pershing for Dodd to return to Namiquipa. Dodd sent back a message saying he would return, but thought it wise to pursue the immediate lead first.

This was not the first use of airplanes in the Punitive Expedition. The aero squadron had arrived on the border shortly after Villa's raid on Columbus. By mid-March a squadron of eight Curtiss JN-2 (Jennies), under command of Captain Benjamin D. Foulois, was in service for Pershing. The aircraft had no machine guns—pilots had to fire pistols or rifles from the cockpit. Artillery shells supplied by the army ordnance department were used as bombs. The Jennies were so underpowered that they could not climb through the high mountain passes of northern Mexico. Pershing could use them only as couriers in low altitude areas. They provided some communications for a couple of months, but accidents and mechanical failures limited their use. By May 1916, Pershing stopped using them.

On the morning of March 27, Villa attacked Guerrero, successfully defeating a Constitutionalist garrison.[16] During the battle, Villa was shot in the right leg below the knee, fracturing the bone. Although painfully wounded, Villa stayed in command and ordered a detachment to attack General José Cavazos across the valley. Cavazos was ready for the assault and drove the Villistas back to Guerrero. On the evening of March 29, Villa withdrew from Guerrero. Dodd had hoped to catch the guerrilla leader before he left. On the morning of March 29, leading a force of 370 officers and men, Dodd headed for Guerrero. His maps of the countryside were vague, however, and civilians along the way were uncooperative. Dodd drove his men all night covering fifty-five miles in seventeen hours before he arrived at Guerrero at 8 A.M. Villistas were still there and tried to slip away as Dodd's men entered the village. Villa evidently was present when Dodd arrived, but was quickly escorted out of town while other Villistas remained to slow down the American troopers.[17]

The Villistas fled to the security of bluffs on the eastern bank of the Río Papigochic. En route, they encountered Lieutenant Colonel Selah R. H. Tompkins of C Troop and his men. In the ensuing fight, Private T. P. Brown was wounded at the first volley. As the United States troops poised for attack, Sergeant Daniel Heaton made ready for the charge by cutting a barbed-wire fence. A Villista held up a Constitutionalist government flag, however, and the Americans hesitated just long enough to allow the guerrillas to escape. Five Americans were wounded, but Dodd's men killed fifty-six of the enemy and wounded others. The Americans captured thirteen horses and twenty-three mules. The battle proved to be the closest Pershing's men would come to Villa during their foray into Mexico.

While Dodd pursued Villa, Pershing moved his headquarters temporarily to San Gerónimo and awaited word from Dodd and others. The weather was generally nasty—cold, windy and snowing off and on. Newspaper correspondent Frank B. Elser remarked in a column that:

> five hundred yards from the tent in which I write, our
> artillery is parked, and 500 yards north of the guns, the
> dough boys (infantry) are lying flat on their bellies in their
> dog tents. They are seeking shelter from the sand driven

before a north wind of sixty-miles-per-hour. It is mingled
with snow now, and it cuts like a knife filling the eyes and
hair and mouth, filtering through the clothing and into boots
and shoes.[18]

While Pershing camped at San Gerónimo, he heard of Dodd's fight
at Guerrero. He also received a visit from Carrancista commander
General Luis Herrera, who, escorted by 200 men, demanded to know
why Pershing was still in Mexico. Herrera gestured wildly and shouted
at Pershing, then led his men out of the area. Pershing ordered his troops
to continue marching south. Along with most members of his staff, he
assumed that they would receive no help from the Mexicans in the quest
for Villa. One newspaper correspondent reported that "Villa has disap-
peared in a way which, considering the relentlessness of the American
pursuit, seems mysterious. The American troops have not encountered
any natives who will even admit they have seen Villa."[19]

Early in April, Pershing sent the Tenth, Eleventh and Thirteenth
Cavalry in four columns slicing southward, deeper into Mexico. Colonel
Dodd's Seventh Cavalry, rested and refitted after the fight at Guerrero,
headed southwest into the rugged sierra. Pershing correctly sensed that
Villa was disorganized and he pressed his commanders to move with
dispatch to block the enemy escape. Brown had an opportunity to catch
the enemy late in March and early in April, but he was out of touch
with Pershing much of the time and too indecisive to trap any of the
hard-riding Villistas.

During the last two weeks of March, while most of the Tenth
Cavalry was with Brown and Evans, Troops I and K were assigned to
Major Frank Tompkins and the Thirteenth Cavalry. On March 21,
Tompkins had marched toward Galeana, passing by Nuevo Casas
Grandes. Constitutionalist troops stationed there were unfriendly;
Tompkins avoided further contact with the Mexicans. He arrived at
Galeana early on March 22. Approximately one hundred of Dodd's men
and three officers joined Tompkins long enough to pass on supplies and
inform him of recent actions.[20]

Dawn brought a howling wind, heavy dust clouds and a message flown in by the aero squadron. Pershing ordered Tompkins to El Valle twelve miles away. At mid-day, March 24, Pershing and his aide Lieutenant George S. Patton, Jr., arrived nearby and requested that Tompkins come to his headquarters close to Las Cruces.[21] After Pershing met with Tompkins, he led his men to Namiquipa, and on March 26 he was rejoined by I and K Troops of the Tenth Cavalry. Tompkins left the Tenth at Namiquipa and led the Thirteenth Cavalry to Providencia, fifty-seven miles away.

During the first week of April, while units searched various sectors for Villa, Colonel Brown and his command of Tenth Cavalry headed toward Agua Caliente. On arrival, Brown found approximately 150 Villistas. Hearing of the approach of the Americans, the Villistas headed south and east toward Major Charles Young (one of three African-American officers in the army) in command of H Troop. Young and his men killed two Villistas in a brief fight.[22] United States troops pursued the Villistas until dark, then established a defensive camp.[23]

The day after the fight at Agua Caliente, Brown led his units fifteen miles to Napavéchic. He later reported that "the people are sullen and inhospitable and the place poor. Water is bad and scarce and fuel, forage and food only obtainable in negligible quantities."[24] Brown had divided his column, sending Major Young and fifty men along a different route. Brown ultimately found the Villista trail, but was still uncertain about Evans' location. On April 3, Brown marched to San Antonio and was able to telegraph Pershing of his activities. Pershing responded, telling Brown to send his wounded to headquarters along with a pack train to retrieve requested supplies. On the morning of April 5, Brown traveled to Cusihuiriáchic to talk with Carrancista officials about marching south.

In the early days of April, Major Frank Tompkins anxiously pressed his pursuit of Villa. Pershing gave him permission to take two troops, mules and supplies and to venture into the mountains near Parral. Tompkins assumed correctly that Villa—who had strong local support in the area—would be nearby. Early in the afternoon of April 2, Tompkins left with his command from Bachiniva, riding more than eighty-five miles through rugged country. At Cusihuiriáchic, Tompkins and his men talked to local Mexicans, who told them that Constitutionalist troops were forty-five miles south. On April 3, the United States soldiers arrived

Charles Young (United States Military Academy Archives, West Point, New York).

at the camp of General Cavazos, who informed Tompkins that Villa was dead. Tompkins refused to believe Cavazos and led his men to Santa Rosalía de Cuevas the next day. The Americans stayed a few days, replacing horse shoes and preparing to continue the chase.

On the evening of April 10, a Carrancista officer, Captain Antonio Mesa, arrived at the U.S. bivouac to tell Tompkins that he would call ahead to Parral and officially arrange for the troops to enter the city. Telegraph lines were down, however, so the Mexican said he would send a messenger. On the morning of April 11, 1916, Tompkins led his men toward Parral, expecting a formal reception by the local commander.[25]

Pershing also pushed hard in early April, shifting his headquarters deeper into Chihuahua at Satevó. Pershing reported that at one point his men were fired on by soldiers believed to be Constitutionalists. His men returned fire and the Mexicans fled. Later that evening Pershing established camp and prepared to lead his troops toward Parral. Pershing also talked with Constitutionalist General Luis Herrera. In the meeting, a journalist had the opportunity to observe the Mexican troops. Correspondent Frank B. Elser described them as "armed only as Mexicans can arm, with double rows of cartridges where an American has one, spurred only as Mexicans can equip their heels, and riding pinto, roan, gray, black, sorrel, and bay mounts cruelly bitted and weighted down with accoutrements."[26]

Meanwhile, just before noon on April 12, Tompkins finally entered Parral. The tired cavalrymen had been in Mexico almost a month, and this was the first major settlement that they had reached. No Mexicans greeted the column. Tompkins talked with Carrancista General Ismael Lozano, who was hostile about the presence of the yanquis. Lozano told Tompkins that he knew of no invitation for the United States troops to enter Parral, and, to the best of his knowledge, Villa was to the north near Satevó. Tompkins then asked the Mexican commander to show him where to establish camp. While Tompkins and his men moved toward a bivouac on the outskirts of town, Mexican civilians and perhaps some Carrancista soldiers fired at the troopers.[27] In the exchange, two of Tompkins' men died and several others were wounded. Tompkins was also wounded, but he led his men in a fighting retreat toward Santa Cruz de Herrera where they took up protected postions. The Mexicans attacked again, and forty-two of their number died in the shooting.[28] Tompkins remained in his position for the time being.

On April 6, under orders from Pershing, Colonel Brown (who had been camped near Parral) moved out to reinforce Tompkins. On the afternoon of April 8, Brown's command reached Satevó, where the men and animals rested. The Americans then took up a sixteen-mile march to Tres Hermanas, where Brown met with a local Carrancista officer who commanded 200 troops. The Constitutionalist dispatched an officer to accompany Brown toward Parral. On April 11, the U.S. force reached Valle de Zaragosa and continued on to Sapien the next day. On the evening of April 12, Brown received a message from Tompkins that he was under attack. Brown immediately led his Tenth Cavalry to reinforce Tompkins. Brown's arrival at Tompkins' encampment strengthened the United States position sufficently. Nevertheless, Carrancista troops were nearby and occasionally shots were exchanged between patrols. Brown and Tompkins waited for orders from Pershing about the next move. Brown later advised Pershing that he did not believe the United States troops could catch Villa without going deeper into Chihuahua. Pershing, however, already realized that the task at hand was going to be more difficult than he had first thought. He told General Funston that the local "inhabitants without exception aided Villa's escape."[29] Pershing did not want to retreat north and asked Funston for more troops to allow him to move south. Pershing also drafted a strong note to General Gutiérrez, blaming the Mexicans for the conflict at Parral and calling for punishment of the perpetrators. The Carranza government remained impervious to requests or threats from the U.S., and a spokesman for the Constitutionalist government blamed the confrontation on "the commander of the American detachment for entering Parral in alleged violation of 'instructions' not to occupy Mexican towns."[30]

With Constitutionalist generals acting more and more hostile toward the Punitive Expedition, Pershing recognized the dangers of his command being dispersed and being isolated from supplies at Columbus.

Consequently, he moved his headquarters and most of his men north to Namiquipa. He justified the move after assessing the dangers posed by 15,000 Carrancista troops at Monterrey, Nuevo León.[31] Once at Namiquipa, Pershing sent General Funston a lengthy message stating that the pursuit of Villa was at a standstill.

Pershing kept Brown, Tompkins and others scouring central Chihuahua for Villa, but supply problems, particularly for flying columns, a hostile population, and the desert and mountain landscape made success unlikely. To resolve supply difficulties, Pershing ordered Brown to move his command to Satevó, a march he completed by the morning of April 22. From there, Brown led his men to Carretas, which is near the international border. During the first week of May, Brown transported his troops by rail part of the way north to San Antonio de los Arenales, Chihuahua. By this time, Pershing had ordered Evans and his men to bivouac near Namiquipa.[32]

Wilson recognized the deteriorating conditions in Mexico and dispatched General Hugh L. Scott, army chief of staff, to San Antonio, Texas, for a strategy meeting with Funston. On April 22, the two advisers told Wilson that Pershing should be given permission to move farther south. They suggested that the alternatives included moving north to the border or getting out of Mexico altogether. The final decision was to move Pershing's headquarters to Nuevo Casas Grandes, deep enough into Mexico to protect the border but not so deep as to be dangerous to United States units.

On April 22, Pershing's men caught up with Villistas again. Colonel Dodd's Seventh Cavalry—175 men and fifteen officers—met Villa's troops near the village of Tomóchic, a small, impoverished hamlet of Mexicans and Tarahumara Indians located in a valley surrounded by high mountains. The previous day, Dodd had learned that about 200 Villistas under command of Candelario Cervantes were headed for the village. Dodd led his men on an all-night ride from Yoquivo, arriving early in the morning. At 3 P.M. he advanced downhill toward Tomóchic. Villistas were already there. Dodd positioned his machine guns to support his troops and at 4:30 P.M. ordered his men to charge the enemy position.

The Villistas put up a fight but ultimately were defeated in deadly close-quarter combat. Under cover of darkness, the Villistas withdrew. Dodd reported that his men had killed thirty of the enemy and wounded at least twenty-five more.[33]

Both Mexico and the United States recognized that the Punitive Expedition and the attitude of Mexicans could ultimately provoke a wider confrontation. Accordingly, Wilson requested that Carranza send his top military advisor to meet with General Scott at El Paso. Wilson told Scott to try to obtain Mexican cooperation for capturing Villa. He was to ask that Mexican troops drive Villa north so the United States forces could deal with him. Scott and Funston also wanted to tell General Alvaro Obregón, Carranza's representative and now secretary of war and marine, that "depredations on American soil and the loss of lives of American citizens cannot be tolerated."[34] In the event that Obregón refused to cooperate, United States representatives were to insist that only the president, in conjunction with Carranza, could make any decision about withdrawal of American troops from Mexico.

On April 30, 1916, Generals Scott, Obregón and their staffs met on the international bridge at Cuidad Juárez. Obregón, under orders from Carranza, insisted that the Punitive Expedition withdraw before any meaningful discussion would take place. Both sides dug in and the meeting ended. A short time later, Scott and Obregón met in a hotel room in El Paso and signed an agreement about border security. Carranza, on hearing of this, reiterated that without the United States first agreeing to get the Punitive Expedition out of Chihuahua, there would be no agreement of any kind.

On May 3, Wilson approved the document, although the move settled nothing. Carranza refused to sign.[35] He had decided that yanqui meddling in Mexico's internal affairs was a violation of Mexican sovereignty. Carranza's strong nationalist stand precluded any compromise with the United States.

CHAPTER 5

THE CONSTITUTIONALIST ARMY

▼▼▼▼▼▼

President Woodrow Wilson, General John Pershing and others in the United States government erred greviously in thinking that the Carranza regime did not make a serious effort to find and defeat Francisco Villa. Secretary of State Robert Lansing even accused Mexico of "protecting, encouraging, and aiding bandits." He also charged that Villa was "operating without opposition ... a fact well known all along to the Carrancista authorities."[1]

At the same time that U.S. troops campaigned in Chihuahua, Constitutionalists were very much on the trail of the enemy. In fact, before the attack on Columbus, Carranza's Constitutionalist army had pursued Villa vigorously and continued to do so long after the U.S. troops left Mexican soil. American criticism that the Carranza forces did not cooperate with Pershing's army was accurate. Despite the possibility of war with the United States, Carranza insisted on protecting Mexican sovereignty. The actions of the Constitutionalists before and after the Columbus raid clearly indicated that Carranza was more concerned about Villa than about the presence of United States troops in Chihuahua. The confrontation at Parral in April between Carrancista troops and United States forces also demonstrated how intensely hostile Mexicans were about the presence of American forces in their country and levied public pressure on Carranza to focus his rhetoric against the United States. Even so, Carranza did not want to escalate the tensions caused by the Punitive Expedition.

Both Carranza's advisors and U.S. authorities were surprised by the attack on Columbus. Wilson and Carranza both faced political pressure at home that forced them to respond strongly. On March 10, Carranza ordered General Luis Gutiérrez to deploy his troops to block Villa's path to Durango and away from the western sierra of Chihuahua.[2] With 2,500 men, Gutiérrez launched a vigorous search for the elusive guerrilla. Carranza also advised Wilson that he was concentrating more than 3,000 troops to block Villa's escape southward.[3]

Some of Carranza's commanders and most civilians were indeed concerned about the arrival of the Punitive Expedition. From Empalme, Sonora, General Manuel M. Diéguez volunteered to bring 13,000 troops to fight the American invaders. Carranza told Diéguez that, if at all possible, he hoped to avoid armed confrontation. He placated Diéguez by ordering him to be ready to destroy railroad tracks leading south from Sonora should the United States launch a general invasion.[4] Diéguez apparently remained anxious to attack the Punitive Expedition in Chihuahua.[5]

General Plutarco Elías Calles of Sonora promised 14,000 more troops and offered to lead an invasion of Arizona within a few days. The First Chief told Calles, as he had Diéguez, to be calm and to be prepared to block a United States invasion into his region.[6] Carranza—not certain about American intentions—remained cautious. He ordered General Agustín Millán, commanding at Jalapa, to march to Veracruz immediately "and take all precautions in case United States Marines tried to land." If they did so, he ordered Millán "to fight them."[7] Millán was a dedicated Carrancista and followed orders precisely.[8]

On March 12, Carranza sent a letter to all Mexican governors and military commanders—often they were the same man—telling them that the situation between the United States and Mexico was delicate and dangerous. While Carranza did not want war with the United States, he recognized that his nationalist position and other forces at work between the two countries might lead to hostilities. He prepared Mexicans psychologically and militarily should war break out. He advised his representatives in the U.S., consular and covert agents, to supply details about the attitude north of the border and to report any unusual preparations that the United States might be making.

General Diéguez, like many other Mexicans, remained adamantly hostile toward the United States. Diéguez telegraphed Carranza more than once, urging that Mexico declare war on the gringos. Diéguez asked to meet personally with Obregón and the First Chief. Carranza ordered him to report to Querétaro, where the First Chief advised Diéguez to keep his composure. He told the general that Mexico faced dire problems, and that the United States was only one of them.

Diéguez was not alone in his outrage about the intervention of the United States. In Puebla and Tampico, among other cities, Mexicans had scuffled occasionally with American citizens, leading to a few injuries. In a nationalistic outburst, Mexicans volunteered themselves and their sons to fight the invaders. The Brotherhood of Locomotive Machinists, for example, offered to spill their blood to protect their "beloved country."[9] Carranza publicly continued his rhetoric against the United States, but he focused his efforts on getting control of the country from factions like those of Villa. His communications with General Treviño in the northeastern frontier and Treviño's replies show Carranza's goals as well as the tactical and strategical difficulties Treviño faced before and after the raid on Columbus.

Villa tried to avoid the American forces and, at the same time, harrass Constitutionalist units. On March 13, only four days after the raid into the United States, Villa appeared at Galeana and ordered his ardent supporter, General Nicolás Fernández, to scout toward El Rubio and to attack Constitutionalist forces wherever he found them.[10] Fernández encountered a Constitutionalist force at Las Animas on March 19 and fought for several hours in an indecisive battle. Both sides withdrew temporarily.

General Francisco Murguía, still in Durango, clearly recognized all battle reports as estimates or even exaggerations. Murguía had considerable reservations about many of his fellow commanders and expressed his doubts publicly. He believed, for example, that General Petronilo Hernández, campaigning at Milpillas in mid-March, essentially lost a skirmish through lack of skill.[11] He was correct, in part, but the Constitutionalist military problems went much deeper.

On March 20, Luis Cabrera, a Carrancista government official and close confidant of Carranza, advised Charles A. Douglas, Carranza's legal counsel in the U.S., that Mexico regretted that the United States did not understand the difficulties of having American troops in the country while facing the ongoing threat from Villa. Cabrera told Douglas that Constitutionalist troops were doing all they could to capture Villa, that Mexicans were better able to pursue him than American soldiers and that Villa was "too smart to be caught by United States troops."[12]

On March 18, James Linn Rodgers was named Woodrow Wilson's special agent to the Carranza government, taking the place of John R. Silliman. The next day Rodgers officially asked Carranza to allow the Pershing Expedition to use Mexican railroads to move supplies, arguing that U.S. troops had used the rails earlier. Carranza adamantly refused. Negotiations continued while Constitutionalist troops engaged the Villistas several times before the end of March.

Although the Villistas encountered bad weather, their leader demonstrated his ability of eluding both U.S. and Constitutionalist forces while remaining a threat to Carranza. On March 15, 1916, Villa led his men to San Miguel de Babícora, then on to Las Cruces and ultimately to Namiquipa, where, on March 19, he attacked and destroyed a government column under command of Colonel Enrique Salas. At Namiquipa, Villa captured several hundred pounds of government supplies and a number of men, whom he recruited for his army.[13] On March 20, Villa marched to El Rosal, en route passing through La Cartuchera. (It was on March 18 that more than 600 men of the United States Seventh Cavalry began their journey from Colonia Dublán to Babícora.)

Skirmishes also broke out near Santa Rosalía de Cuevas. General Domingo Arrieta clashed with Villistas on March 21, killing three of them, capturing three horses and six rifles along with considerable ammunition. The next day, Arrieta fought a small party and captured two more Villistas.[14] On March 22, Villistas defeated a Carrancista garrison at La Quemada, then moved on to El Rubio, where they stayed until March 25 when reinforcements under General Nicolás Fernández arrived. At dawn, Villa headed for San Diego del Monte and, without rest, on to Agua

Caliente. From there he headed south and west toward San Isidrio, where, on March 27, Villa readied to attack General José Cavazos' government troops at Guerrero.

The day before the main party arrived at Guerrero, a few Villistas had engaged Constitutionalists under General Ignacio Ramos near Sierra del Samoso. Intense combat lasted for more than an hour, when the Villistas finally retreated from the field, leaving behind sixteen dead and others wounded. Constitutionalist troops did not rest. Shortly after the battle, they encountered Villistas trying to burn a railway bridge at Concordia, between Torreón and San Pedro. Carrancistas claimed they killed all of the raiders.[15] On March 26, Eliseo Arredondo, Mexican minister in Washington, incorrectly advised his government that since March 15 more than 12,000 American soldiers had crossed into Mexico.[16]

The Battle of Guerrero began when Villa sent a line of skirmishers to an arroyo in front of the government troops. Villa, leading additional forces, advanced on foot. As the fight raged, the Villistas almost broke and ran. At the critical moment, however, Villa personally led the final charge. His brash attack routed the Constitutionalists. Although Villa won the confrontation, he was badly wounded in the leg.[17] In excruciating pain and unable to continue the campaign, Villa named his longtime associate, General Francisco Beltrán, overall commander of the Villistas.

Villa's personal escort carried him to the home of Dr. L. B. Raschbaum in Guerrero. Raschbaum treated the wound and told Villa that the bullet had to be removed, but Villa refused to stay for the surgery. He must have known that United States troops were not far away and he needed to move quickly. In fact, Colonel Dodd and his cavalry were approaching Guerrero at the time.

Villa gathered approximately 150 men and, with the help of General Nicolás Fernández, headed south (the only direction open to him) toward Parral. The Villista party got to Porvenir at dawn on March 29 and continued south, arriving at Hacienda La Cieneguita around 5 A.M. the next day. By this time, Villa's leg was infected and he was in considerable pain. When the owner of the hacienda resisted Villa's efforts to rest there, Villa ordered the hacendado and his wife shot. Fernández then carried Villa to a cave near Sierra de Santa Ana, where he hoped to recover. Villa told Fernández that he would be out of contact for a couple of months and to spread the word that the guerrilla leader had died from his wounds at Guerrero.

Although Villa was out of the action, his men continued their offensive. On March 29, guerrillas attacked a Constitutionalist garrison at Namiquipa, but were beaten back. They scattered into the surrounding sierra.[18] Facing increasing opposition from Villistas, on March 13, 1916, the First Chief had appointed General Alvaro Obregón secretary of war for the Constitutionalist government and General Cándido Aguilar— Carranza's trusted son-in-law—secretary of foreign relations. Trust in Obregón, however, was another matter. Long jealous of Obregón's military successes and his support in Sonora, Carranza appointed him only after Villa attacked Columbus. It was a move of desperation; Carranza wanted Villa neutralized in some fashion at any cost. He believed Obregón was the only man who could accomplish the task. Carranza recognized Obregón's talents but distrusted his ambitions. He also hoped that Obregón could resolve difficulties within the Constitutionalist army and enhance its effectiveness as a fighting force.[19]

Obregón, however, could not easily solve the problems because Carranza was the very architect of many of the army's difficulties. The origins of the woes stemmed from decisions made by First Chief in 1914 and 1915. He had restricted the army's use of the telegraph and railroads and had suspended recruiting. Obregón, as secretary of war, now had more challenges to face than capturing Villa or confronting U.S. troops in Mexico. Early in March, Carranza and Obregón had ordered Constitutionalist troops under General Pablo González to take the offensive against Zapatista rebels in Cuernavaca. Carranza also sent General Joaquín Amaro's Fifth Division and General Pedro Morales' Eighth Division to the northeastern frontier to reinforce troops in Chihuahua. A primary concern for Carranza and Obregón revolved around continuing supply problems. General González told the First Chief, for example, that over the last ten days of March, González did not have guns and ammunition for his recruits. Because he could not supply his soldiers or pay them, some of his men were deserting and joining the Zapatista movement.[20]

During the first week of April, Constitutionalist troops continued to pursue Villa. Also that week, Major Frank B. Tompkins and men of the Thirteenth United States Cavalry arrived at Parral, where General Ismael López, under the overall command of General Cavazos, was in charge. It was López who advised Tompkins to move his men no farther south and to leave as quickly as possible.[21] Before Tompkins could move out, gunfire between his forces and the Mexicans broke out.[22] U.S. officials later stated that they knew Constitutionalist soldiers had been involved in the incident. They also said that Tompkins was invited into Parral, then fired on.[23]

While Carranza dealt with the incident at Parral, Villistas took the offensive. By the end of the first week of April, Villista General Beltrán and 150 men were in Santa María de las Cuevas and Ciénega de Ladrones; General Fernández with 120 men was in Santa Ana, San José del Sitio and at Valle de Zaragoza. Villa, his staff and fifty men were near Gavilana. In fact, nearly 320 Villistas harassed Constitutionalist positions. Bitter fighting broke out at San Borjas on April 3 and at Cieneguita the next day. Skirmishing continued for another week.[24]

On April 15, 1916, Treviño advised Obregón of the status of the frontier. Treviño commanded the First, Third and Fifth Divisions of the Army of the Northeast. As a general of division, Treviño was overall commander in charge of six generals and about forty-one other commissioned officers. About 300 men, including civilian employees, were at Treviño's headquarters. The First Division included some 1,590 enlisted men and commissioned officers in three regiments and two brigades. The Third Division had twelve brigades, two regiments and a battalion of railroad engineers. Total strength of the Third was 7,191 men, all military, no civilians. The Fifth Division included six brigades, five regiments, one battalion and administrative personnel. Treviño had 10,231 soldiers under his immediate command. When troops under General

Gabriel Gavira and others who campaigned on the Chihuahuan frontier were included, the Constitutionalist forces numbered 21,308 men. It is doubtful, however, that Treviño could actually field this many fighters and correspondence clearly shows that the government could not supply them. Treviño included in his report only regular troops, many of whom had served under his command for as long as three years and had been recruited from areas distant from the frontier. Treviño believed they were dependable. He also reported that while his men were armed, they did not have any reserve ammunition. He told Obregón that he had approximately 1,400 auxiliaries, but said nothing about their state of readiness. Treviño also admitted that communications between his headquarters and field commanders were often poor. Field commanders frequently and urgently asked for more ammunition, food, money to pay troops and materials to repair the telegraph lines.[25]

In addition, conflicts continued between commanders, and troops often disobeyed orders. General González complained early in March that he had suffered the insubordination of his troops more than once.[26] A month later, General Murguía experienced similar disobedience from both officers and enlisted men. He found it necessary to disarm some of General Domingo Arrieta's men who refused to obey an order.[27] Finally, Murguía told Carranza and Obregón that Arrieta was unqualified because of the "incapacity of his generals and disorderly" behavior of his troops.[28]

On April 28, Obregón advised Carranza that General Scott was to arrive in El Paso that night and the "alarmist American press predicted additional problems with Mexico." Obregón also reported that he had visited an arms factory in Chihuahua and placed orders for artillery supplies and other war materials the day before.[29]

On May 16, 1916, Mexican raiders again crossed the United States border, this time attacking Glenn Springs, Texas. U.S. troops pursued the raiders south of the international line, and, predictably, Carranza was irate at another violation of Mexican sovereignty.[30] On the same day, Treviño moved his headquarters to Chihuahua in response to Carranza's order to deploy closer to the center of Villista activity.[31] Obregón told Treviño that

Carrancistas on the move near El Valle. Members of the Punitive Expedition look on. (Arizona Historical Society, Tucson, photo #51532).

the military commander near Glenn Springs, Major Timoteo Rodríguez, headquartered at Esmeralda, Coahuila, should be told to prepare to fight the Americans if they did not leave Mexico at once.[32] Carranza clearly hoped that this would be unnecessary, but he was compelled to act.

Treviño advised Obregón the next day that not only had he given the order to Rodríguez, but he had also stationed troops between the United States forces and the border, thereby preventing any more Americans from entering Mexico uncontested and placing those Americans south of Glenn Springs in a precarious position.[33] Rodríguez, after receiving orders from Treviño, told the commander of the American troops who crossed from Glenn Springs that they must leave Mexico. The United States officer stated that he had entered Mexico under authorization from border-crossing reciprocity agreements and that he was in pursuit of bandits who had attacked an American town.[34]

The Third Military Sector commander, General Ignacio Ramos (in charge of the contested area), advised Treviño that he had made it clear to Rodríguez that he should confront any United States soldiers entering Mexico. He also advised Treviño that stopping the Villista raids along the frontier was the only way to prevent United States incursions. Ramos reported that he was mounting a "tenacious and energetic pursuit of the bandits that would in the end leave his region free of bandits."[35]

Meanwhile, General José Cavazos advised Treviño that United States troops were nearing San Antonio de los Arenales. He wanted instructions on whether or not to challenge them.[36] Fortunately, before a skirmish occured, the Americans withdrew.[37] The next day in a coded message, Obregón advised Treviño of the possibility of Mexican troops engaging the Americans. Treviño was to keep this in mind when deploying his troops.[38] Villa used the presence of United States troops to his advantage by telling Mexicans that Carranza had allowed the entry of the gringos into Mexico. Carranza and Obregón were aware of such propaganda and knew that the situation with the United States was dangerous. Obregón advised Treviño to be prepared for fighting with the U.S. forces if America did not "categorically [state] its attitude."[39]

In late May, Villista General Francisco Beltrán circulated a manifesto accusing the Carranza regime of encouraging the United States deployment of troops in Mexico. Beltrán called for war against the United States and a cooperative effort by Sonora, Durango and Chihuahua citizens against both Carranza and the U.S.[40] Carranza knew of the circular and its potential effect, and he was well aware of the deteriorating situation along the international border. Carranza authorized Obregón to transfer more troops to the area as soon as possible to be in position to deal with the United States Army, should it be necessary, and to be ready to pursue the Villistas.[41] In accordance, Jacinto Treviño sent a message that General Apolonio Treviño personally delivered to Domingo Arrieta in Durango, telling him that rail transportation would be available to bring his troops to Ciudad Chihuahua. He suggested that Arrieta concentrate his forces and prepare to use the rails to get to Chihuahua as quickly as possible.[42]

On May 26, Treviño authorized General Gabriel Gavira to meet with United States authorities at Nuevo Casas Grandes, Chihuahua. Gavira was to tell the Americans that they should not go near any Mexican villages or Constitutionalist garrisons and that they should not move any farther south. Treviño also ordered Gavira to place his troops in the positions from which the United States forces withdrew.[43]

Pershing, on receiving a communiqué from Gavira concerning Mexican troop placement, advised the general that he feared that Mexican troops were too close to United States positions. To avoid an explosive situation, Pershing also urged Gavira not to station Mexican troops along the flanks of the United States positions.[44] Gavira responded to Pershing's headquarters that he was now in command of the Galeana and Guerrero districts, that Constitutionalist troops were taking up positions to defend the villages and that U.S. troops should avoid the Constitutionalist units. Pershing replied that there were no bandits operating in the Galeana district at present, and, in fact, there had not been any between Bachiniva and Colonia Dublán recently. Villista General Candelario Cervantes was known to have been operating near Namiquipa, but had been killed on May 25, and his band had temporarily dispersed.

Villista activity in late May was concentrated south of the Mexico-North Western Railroad beyond Temosáchic, the southern limit of Gavira's command.[45] Constitutionalist troops under Gavira were stationed at haciendas Alamos de Peña, El Carmen and San Lorenzo. In the Bravos district, fifty soldiers manned each garrison. Other garrisons—with 400 men per outpost—had been established along the Carmen River and along the North Western Railroad. Pershing advised Gavira that he would notify him as United States troops evacuated an area so Mexican troops could take up the position.[46] On learning of events on the border, Carranza ordered Treviño to deploy his troops in response to any difficulties along the line. Treviño quickly organized a brigade of 1,000 cavalrymen under General Francisco González to provide rapid reaction along the Chihuahua-United States border.[47]

While Constitutionalist commanders—Treviño specifically—tried vainly to convince Pershing that Carranza's forces had sufficient determination and resources to control the frontier, the truth was less optimistic. The same supply problems, lack of discipline, desertion and inadequate leadership continued to plague the Mexican army. On one occasion, General Enríque R. Nájera, who commanded troops in Durango and was municipal president of Cuidad Durango, advised Treviño that he was so frustrated with problems with discipline and poor leadership that he wanted the general to remove some high-ranking commanders. If not,

Nájera believed success against Villa would be limited, and the Mexicans would not be able to confront American troops. Nájera threatened to resign his command if nothing was done.[48]

Other difficulties contributed to inefficiency. On June 2, 1916, General Apolonio Treviño told Jacinto B. Treviño that General Domingo Arrieta (who also led troops in Durango) was not an aggressive leader, and his men were not well organized. After waiting a full day for Arrieta to load his troops on a twenty-car train, Nájera got angry with the delay. Treviño could do little more than ask Arrieta and other generals to cooperate. Officers like Arrieta were actually local *jefes* who recruited from their home region, acted independently and ignored the chain of command. Most often, local troops owed their loyalties to the *cabecilla,* not to Carranza.[49] Adding to the woes, United States-Mexican relations became more complex on June 12, when Constitutionalists arrested about ten United States soldiers near Casas Grandes. The local Carrancista commander claimed the men were at a house of prostitution. When Mexican troops arrived at the scene, both sides opened fire. One Mexican soldier was wounded. Mexican troops surrounded the Americans and demanded their surrender. They detained the men a short while, then released them. The confrontation underscored the Mexicans' anger at United States troops—this time for visiting a Mexican village.[50]

By mid-June, reports placed Villa and his men at Janos, seventy-five miles south of the international border.[51]

On June 15, Carranza directly ordered Treviño to keep U.S. troops in Chihuahua from moving any direction except north, even if it led to armed confrontation. The following day, Treviño notified his commanders along the frontier of the First Chief's order.[52] General Ignacio Ramos was at Río Florido, General Domingo Arrieta at Camargo, General Luis

Herrera at Parral, General Matías Ramos at Villa Aldama, General M. P. López near Camargo and five other generals were at Chihuahua. Colonel Carlos Carranza was at Cusihuiriáchic, Colonel Franciso Bórquez at Guerrero, Colonel Arnulfo Ballesteros at Matóchic, and General Carlos Zuazua at Santa Isabel.[53] Treviño also warned General Pershing of Carranza's orders.[54] Pershing was not intimidated and replied that same day that his government had not issued orders about the deployment of his troops; he would position them according to sound military tactics.[55]

On June 21, 1916, in the midst of the difficulties of pursuing Villa and confronting United States troops, tempers finally boiled over. At Carrizal, Chihuahua, a violent battle broke out between men of the Punitive Expedition and Constitutionalists. After the confrontation, the two countries appeared poised on the brink of declared war. It quickly became apparent, however, that neither Wilson nor Carranza wanted to broaden the conflict.

CHAPTER 6

CONFRONTATION AT CARRIZAL

▼▼▼▼▼▼

Pershing blatantly ignored Mexican requests to stay put or move north. Although the American general had deployed most of his men in secure defensive positions in the final weeks of April, he also sent columns south to scout for the Villistas. Major Robert Howze took the Eleventh Cavalry to San Francisco de Borja, between Chihuahua and Parral.[1] Howze already had led his men on forty-two days of campaigning, marching almost 700 miles and perhaps coming as close as any U.S. unit to trapping Villa.[2] On April 11, Howze and his men had attacked guerrillas at the small village of Santa Cruz de Nerrera, north of Parral. After a brief fight, the enemy slipped away in the darkness. Howze did not pursue. His men had been in the saddle for three straight days. For the remainder of April, Howze searched the region near Guerrero and Parral but did not engage the Villistas again. On the morning of May 4, Pershing ordered Howze to march on Cusihuiráchic. Howze sent Lieutenant James A. Shannon, with Apache Indian scouts guiding him, ahead of the main column. Shannon entered the small town several hours later and encountered the remnants of a Constitutionalist force that was headquartered at nearby Rancho Ojos Azules. The Carrancistas claimed that they had fought the Villistas all day but had suffered no casualties and had killed no bandits. The United States troops said the Mexicans smelled of tequila and were uncooperative. At this point Howze, who had arrived with the main column, wasted an opportunity. He was again near the Villistas, but he stalled, claiming that he did not know the region and needed someone to guide his troops.

When Howze left Cusihuiráchic, he led his men on a hard ride of more than thirty-six miles to Ojos Azules. As the troops approached the rancho at 5:45 A.M., they saw a red glow from fires burning brightly. The Villistas had taken up defensive positions about 900 yards away, and they opened fire on the Americans. A newspaper correspondent reported that the Apache scouts were firing wildly at the Mexicans and "shrieking shrill, weird war whoops."[3] Some of the Villistas tried to gather their horses in the midst of considerable confusion, for the troops had "charged so suddenly that the bandits bolted for the mountains," according to the reporter.[4]

About forty Villistas decided to make a stand from new positions on the rooftop of a building. Between the American position and the Villista escape route was a barbed-wire barrier. Lieutenant A. M. Graham led a few cavalrymen down the road directly toward the village. En route, his men had to turn sharply left to avoid the packed mass of cavalry horses. They could not go to the right because of the barbed wire. Graham had no choice but to take his men into the buildings and into close-order fighting. The Villistas abandoned the buildings and fled up a hill as the U.S. troopers pursued. The fight at Ojos Azules lasted only twenty minutes, but Pershing's troops killed forty-two Villistas near the rancho and nineteen more on the chase. There were no American casualties. The men of the Pershing expedition also freed four Constitutionalist soldiers whom the Villistas had captured earlier.

On May 5, 1916, relations between the United States and Mexico further deteriorated when Villistas crossed into Texas and attacked Boquillas and Glenn Springs, tiny settlements in the Big Bend country of Texas, a 708,000-acre mountain and desert wilderness.[5] Historically, Glenn Springs was a well-known watering spot in the foothills of the 8,000-foot-high Chisos Mountains. In 1916 it was the site of a wax extraction works, a few tin buildings for the factory, scattered adobe huts and the tents of eight men of Troop A, Fourteenth Cavalry. During the late-night hours about a hundred Villistas crossed the international border near San Vicente, upriver from Glenn Springs. Immediately, the column split: one heading for Glenn Springs, the other toward Boquillas.

Just after 11 P.M. the first group galloped into Glenn Springs, firing their rifles and pistols into the huts.

A few soldiers of the Fourteenth, who were staying in the shacks, returned fire. The Villistas then set the grass roofs of the huts on fire, forcing the soldiers to take cover. In the fight, the Mexicans killed a civilian and three troopers and wounded two more. The Villistas raided the general store and remained until almost dawn. They carried off their wounded, but left one dead man dressed in a Constitutionalist uniform. He might have been a captive who was shot by the raiders. About the time the raid at Glenn Springs ended, the other Villistas attacked Boquillas, twelve miles down river. The raiders broke into the general store for food and ammunition and captured store owner Jesse Deemer. At about 10 A.M. the Villistas who had struck Glenn Springs arrived. Together the parties returned south, taking Deemer and his assistant as hostages.

Across the river was a small Mexican village also called Boquillas, where there was an American silver mine.[6] The Villistas looted the company store and captured four more Americans. By this time, the raiders had so much booty that they had to use an old mining truck to carry the load. The Mexicans also captured Dr. Homer Powers, the mining company physician. He and the three other company workers were loaded into the truck and the group headed south. Eventually the truck stalled and had to wait for repairs while the balance of the column moved on south. There were only three Mexicans left to guard the vehicle and the prisoners. The hostages managed to overpower the guards, restarted the truck and headed back toward the border, with the Mexicans walking in front tied together.[7]

The attack into Texas and the crossing of United States troops into Mexico near Boquillas in hot pursuit led to further diplomatic conflict. Woodrow Wilson authorized 4,000 additional men to the border in the event that hostilities widened.[8] Carranza's orders to his commanders made it clear that he would not tolerate more United States soldiers in Mexico. He instructed Obregón to take whatever measures necessary to block the entry of Americans and sent an ultimatum to the United States to remove all men from Mexico. Carranza wanted to communicate plainly to the

American government, as he had done so many times before, that he could not countenance additional United States troops entering Mexico for any reason.

On learning of the ultimatum, General Scott informed Wilson and others in the administration that he believed that the Mexicans were only stalling for time to bring enough forces to the frontier to push the U.S. troops out of the country.[9] Scott further advised Wilson to send more men to the border. Secretary of War Baker and Wilson agreed. Wilson issued orders for the National Guard of Texas, New Mexico and Arizona to be called to active duty. In West Texas, a reporter wrote on May 9 that "all day today there was a hint of war in the atmosphere of El Paso."[10] The National Guard units did not respond well; Texas sent only 3,003 men, Arizona 990, and New Mexico 1,128.

During this period Obregón and Scott also met to discuss the problems along the border. They adjourned on May 11, having settled nothing. The mood in Mexico was tense, and one United States representative in Mexico advised his government that local Mexican leaders were organizing "citizens for defense, treating the question of war as a certainty but not yet declared."[11] Although Carranza postured against the United States, his communications to his generals remained focused on capturing Villa.

The men of the Eighth United States Cavalry were not greatly concerned with diplomatic maneuverings. They were intent on the pursuit of Villistas, especially those who had attacked Glenn Springs and Boquillas. Most men of the Eighth had remained at Fort Bliss when Pershing first led troops into Mexico, but now they had a chance to join the pursuit. On the morning of May 8, 1916, Troops A and B arrived at Marathon, Texas, just north of the Big Bend country. They immediately disembarked from their train and with four trucks, some mule-drawn wagons and other supplies headed south after the raiders. In about two weeks they covered some 200 miles in Mexico.

When the troops crossed the border, they saw no Constitutionalists. The Mexican military, according to United States sources, did not wish to defend the frontier against the Villistas. Truthfully, Carranza's troops were dispersed throughout the region, usually in pursuit of the Villista bands that threatened various key towns and rail centers. Still, because the Constitutionalist troops posed a potential threat to the United States forces, on May 9, 1916, General Funston cabled General Pershing to withdraw his main body north to Colonia Dublán, where he could be supplied easier and reinforced if necessary. Pershing was not quite ready to pull back that far north, so he convinced Funston to allow him to establish his base at Namiquipa. From there he could probe the surrounding countryside.[12]

Funston was adamant about the danger the Constutitionalists posed, but Pershing complied only in respect to establishing a fall-back location at Colonia Dublán. He moved his headquarters to Namiquipa and sent his best cavalry twenty-five miles south to Providencia and the San Gerónimo Ranch, where they would have quick access to Guerrero. The United States troops still did not know the enemy's location, but they thought the Villistas were south of Parral. Newspaper reporters recognized the situation in Mexico as serious. One wrote that because of the threat of the Constitutionalists and the rumors that Villa was raising a huge army, "the American expedition has been withdrawn entirely from the Parral region."[13]

Except for an occasional meeting with a Carrancista detachment and a rare encounter with a small band of Villistas, the Americans suffered through largely boring duty. After May 16, mapmakers assigned to the Second Engineering Battalion traveled about Chihuahua charting the terrain, a task that at least gave them something to do. Villista General Candelario Cervantes and his men were reported in the hills near Namiquipa, but the U.S. forces had not even come close to finding the elusive guerrillas.

On May 25, engineers of the Second and Seventeenth Infantry left Las Cruces (about twelve miles north of Namiquipa) to study the Santa María Valley. Six miles south of Las Cruces, Sergeant James M. Mayson, in charge of the party, had his men map Alamía Canyon. He ordered two men to begin walking to the canyon; two soldiers were to remain with the supply wagon; six others hunted for pigs. Just as the men began beating the brush for the pigs, two of the group saw Mexicans suddenly appear on the horizon, riding furiously toward them. Approximately thirty Mexicans opened fire on the United States troops, wounding several. Mayson sent one trooper to Las Cruces for reinforcements. The fight intensified when the United States troopers were pinned down. Only Mayson and Corporal Earl Phillips were not wounded in the first volley. One soldier, still mounted and unhurt, rode off for help. In thirty minutes he arrived at Las Cruces, and two detachments from the Eleventh and Thirteenth Cavalry rode to the rescue, arriving at the canyon just as the Villistas retreated. Villista commander Candelario Cervantes—a close confidant of Villa—was killed in the battle.[14] According to one writer, Cervantes was "one of the most important Villistas and had been a will o' the wisp of this northern country, repeatedly eluding cavalry drives through the mountains near Namiquipa."[15]

Approximately a week later, Pershing journeyed to Colonia Dublán to talk with General Gabriel Gavira, commanding at Ciudad Juárez. Pershing still did not want open war, and he sought a solution to the problems of joint occupation in Chihuahua. In the discussion, Pershing agreed to have the Mexicans deploy a limited number of troops along the United States Army's left flank. Pershing also agreed to inform the Mexican commander when American units withdrew from any location. Gavira said he would send troops to protect any areas that Pershing's troops abandoned.

Unfortunately, often the agreements between field commanders do not please their governments. Such was the case in this instance. On the day that Pershing and Gavira signed their agreements, Carranza sent a terse note to Secretary of State Robert Lansing about United States troops remaining in Mexico. A reporter who saw the message said that the Mexicans did not set a time for the withdrawal of United States troops from Mexico, but "the sharp manner in which the de facto government presents the situation as viewed through Mexican glasses, threatens to precipitate a new crisis in the Mexican situation."[16] Adding to the already tense conditions was a note from General Luis Herrera, commanding Constitutionalist troops at Parral, to the local citizens "promising the people of northern Mexico that if the American forces did not evacuate Mexican soil within two weeks they would be driven across the border."[17]

Lansing did not respond at once to any of the notes from Mexico. Instead, he focused on other concerns. He had received intelligence reports about the "Plan of San Diego," which involved an attack on the United States from south of the border. Immediately, he asked civilian authorities in Texas for information about the plan.[18]

The Plan of San Diego originated on February 20, 1915, at the small South Texas town of San Diego and further complicated relations between the United States and Mexico at a critical time. Organizers signed a document calling for a general revolt that would bring independence of Texas, California, New Mexico, Colorado and Arizona. Ultimately, the group would propose that part of the newly conquered territory be annexed to Mexico. The scheme called for a rebellion of Mexican Americans, Japanese Americans, African Americans and Native Americans, all of whom had suffered at the hands of the white majority. Under a banner of equality and independence, the members of the rebellion proposed killing all white males sixteen years of age or older. The scheme was so far-fetched that it had no chance of succeeding. It illustrated, however, the anger felt by minorities that had grown out of long-lasting Anglo discrimination against citizens of Mexican heritage.[19]

Who concocted the plan remains unknown. It is certain that the organizers issued several manifestos designed to recruit followers from both sides of the border who would join raids into the United States after July 1915. Luis de la Rosa, a one-time Cameron County, Texas, deputy sheriff, apparently was one of the leaders. When fifty riders, about half from Mexico and the others from north of the border, attacked the King Ranch on August 8, 1915, local authorities were convinced that Carranza's government or at least Carrancista commanders in the northeastern frontier supported the movement. Violence continued until October 21, 1915, two days after the United States extended de facto recognition to Carranza's government.

In effect, the raiding simply added to the problems for Mexican Americans in the lower Rio Grande Valley. They suffered increasing discrimination and harsh treatment at the hands of Anglos. In early 1916, the Plan de San Diego fell apart. Several of the raiders, whom Texas authorities had arrested during the previous few months, were tried, jailed or hanged. After the retaliation, the Plan de San Diego no longer seemed a threat.

Villa's raid on Columbus, New Mexico, in early March 1916, prompted a resurrection of the scheme. Luis de la Rosa began recruiting again in northern Mexico, hoping to cross the border into Texas and carry out the original strategy. The fact that he was able to move about freely to recruit has convinced some scholars that, at least during 1916, Carranza supported the effort. During most of 1916, however, Carranza's control of the country was so tenuous that it is doubtful that he had complete authority so far from his center of government in Mexico City.

During 1916, Estéban Fierros, superintendent of the Mexican railroad at Tampico, was possibly one of the organizers and most important military commander of the plan at this time. He scheduled an invasion of the United States for June 10, 1916. The raid never took place because the authorities north of the border discovered it. Nevertheless, between June 10 and 15, 1916, the conspirators periodically raided into Texas from Mexico. On June 15, more than a hundred Mexicans, perhaps supporters of the Plan de San Diego, crossed the international border and attacked San Ignacio, Texas, about thirty-three miles below Laredo. One hundred and fifty men of the Fourteenth United States Cavalry were nearby and in position to repel the attack. In the ensuing fight, the Americans killed or captured several of the raiders. The next day, the Fourteenth crossed the border in pursuit of the remaining attackers but did not intercept them. One of the battle dead was identified as a Lieutenant Colonel Villareal of the Constitutionalist army. A captured Mexican claimed that he was not a member of any plan nor a Villista, but a Carrancista soldier who was just obeying orders. This might not have been true. Carrancista General Alfredo Ricaut, commander at Nuevo Laredo, apparently led a vigorous pursuit of the Mexican raiders. The Mexican troops eventually captured forty men. De la Rosa, however, escaped to Monterrey where local authorities refused to surrender him to United States agents.[20] With Carrancista troops controlling much of the northeastern frontier after mid-1916, the Plan of San Diego collapsed.

No matter which faction was responsible for raids north of the border, conditions between the United States and Mexico became increasingly tense. Carranza again warned the Wilson government that all United States troops should immediately leave the country and that Mexico would tolerate no further intrusions. On June 15, *El Pueblo,* a newspaper in Mexico City, predicted "war between Mexico and the United States."[21] Under pressure to respond more strongly, on Sunday, June 18, 1916, Wilson announced that the National Guard—at least 150,000 men—soon would be called up for duty against Mexico. A few days later he issued orders to begin the mobilization. The National Guard, however, was ill-prepared, and it would be twelve days before any units began arriving at the border.

A feeling of imminent confrontation was also present in Mexico. Carranza advised his military commanders along the frontier to oppose any extension of United States forces south from their present positions in Chihuahua. Carranza adamantly told the United States that its troops must move only north toward the border.[22] He was tough and direct, but he did not use inflamatory language. He wished to avoid an escalation of problems with the United States. On June 17, official newspapers throughout the country carried a message to the Mexican people and to the United States. Carranza said that he was "absolutely certain that the American people do not want war with Mexico ... but there are nevertheless strong American interests and strong Mexican interests determined to procure a conflict between the countries." He insisted that "the Mexican government firmly desires to maintain peace with the American Government, but in order to [reach this goal] it is [imperative] that the American Government explain frankly its true intention towards Mexico."[23]

Lansing received copies of Carranza's messages; nevertheless, he remained critical of Mexico and its continuing civil strife. He stated the concerns of the United States government when he offered that

for three years the Mexican Republic has been torn with
Civil strife; the lives of Americans and other aliens have been
sacrificed; vast properties developed by American capital and
enterprise have been destroyed or rendered nonproductive;
bandits have been permitted to roam at will through the territory contiguous to the United States and to seize, without
punishment or without effective attempt at punishment, the
property of Americans.[24]

Lansing reiterated that the United States would not withdraw its
troops from Mexico until the Mexicans were willing to take some action
to protect United States citizens and property, especially in northern
Mexico. The two countries seemed to be at an impasse. Carrancistas used
the diplomatic embroglio for propaganda purposes. Members of the First
Chief's government urged all "Mexicans to unite in 'driving out the
gringos.'" The Carrancistas called for all able-bodied Mexicans to volunteer for "military service against the 'invaders from the north.'"[25]

Pershing was aware of the diplomatic tensions and worried about
his troops at Namiquipa, deep in Constitutionalist territory.
Consequently, he moved his headquarters to Nuevo Casas Grandes. He
continued to dispatch units to search for Villistas near Namiquipa. On
one patrol, soldiers of the Thirteenth Cavalry managed to capture a
Villista, Pedro Luján, but otherwise the U.S. units had little success.
Pershing was aware that several thousand Constitutionalist troops were
stationed at Villa Ahumada, less than seventy-five miles from his headquarters, and he was concerned about their activities.

On June 16, 1916, Pershing ordered Major Ellwood W. Evans of
the Tenth Cavalry to send an officer with strong diplomatic skills on a
scouting expedition toward the Mexican position. Ellwood sent Captain
William T. Boyd.[26] What Pershing told Boyd is uncertain—there
were no written orders. Pershing later reported that he told Boyd to
avoid trouble with Mexican Constitutionalist troops. Boyd had in his
command sixty men of Troop C, Tenth Cavalry, when he headed for
Villa Ahumada on the morning of June 18. Pershing also sent Captain
Lewis S. Morey and about forty men of K Troop, Tenth Cavalry, with
the same orders, but Morey departed from a different location and

traveled a separate route.[27] The two columns were to meet at Rancho Santo Domingo.

The trip was slow and difficult, and, according to survivors of the column, Boyd became irritable and impatient. Finally, the captain sent his supply wagon back to camp because it slowed his progress. At Rancho Santo Domingo, Boyd and Morey consolidated their forces. Boyd, as senior officer, assumed command of both columns and headed toward Villa Ahumada as soon as the horses and men were rested. An American citizen named W. P. McCabe, who was the ranch foreman, warned Boyd on June 20 not to lead troops through the town of Carrizal (about halfway between the ranch and Villa Ahumada); McCabe had heard there were about 400 Constitutionalist soldiers in or near the village.[28] Boyd said he would not bypass Carrizal no matter how many Mexican troops were deployed there. Boyd implied to McCabe that Pershing had told him to enter all towns as he advanced.

At 4 A.M. on June 21, Boyd led his command toward Carrizal. About a mile from the village, the troopers dismounted and surveyed a grassy clearing that lay between them and the edge of town. The logistics for battle were hopelessly in favor of the Mexicans. There was no cover for 600 yards, and in the distance the Americans could see the Constitutionalists taking defensive positions. Boyd paused long enough to send a note to the Mexican garrison commander advising him that he wished only to pass through Carrizal on his way to Villa Ahumada. The Mexican commander sent a party under a white flag to discuss the matter. After seeing the size of the United States force, the Mexicans adamantly refused to allow them to pass. Boyd, possibly disobeying Pershing's orders, signaled his men to advance. Finally, General Félix Gómez, in charge of the Constitutionalist troops, rode out to meet with Boyd. He told Boyd that his orders from General Treviño were not to let any United States units pass through Mexican towns. Boyd refused to listen. Gómez returned to his defenses. Boyd also refused to heed advice from other officers in his command who suggested that they simply bypass Carrizal. Boyd may have told one Mexican messenger to Gómez to "tell the son-of-a-bitch [Gómez] that I am coming through." Pershing later forwarded an explanation that "during [the] Conference Mexican[s] moved troops toward [the] American flanks." Pershing suggested "that if Boyd saw this, he should have known Mexican intentions. . . . Dismounting his troops in the face of mounted Mexican forces suggests that Boyd did not appreciate [the] gravity of [the] situation."[29]

As the United States troopers marched across the grassy field, the Mexicans laid down a barrage of machine gun and rifle fire, wounding nearly all the men in C Troop. Lieutenant Henry M. Adair, who had opposed the action, was shot in the chest and died almost immediately. Boyd's C Troop formed the left of the skirmish line, while Morey's comprised the right. When the shooting began, C Troop had advanced about 250 yards toward the Mexican position. Eventually, the troopers captured the machine gun position, but Sergeant Will Hines of C Troop was killed in the process. Men of the Tenth Cavalry fought bravely, killing many of the enemy; but according to one report, when they ran out of ammunition, they got "cut to pieces." Boyd was wounded in the left shoulder and arm before getting to the safety of an irrigation ditch. He died nearby. C Troop had advanced slightly toward the Mexican positions, but K Troop, outflanked by the Mexican cavalry, had to retreat. Morey was hit in the shoulder by rifle fire during the manuever. One trooper, Corporal H. C. Houston of K Troop, later gave his version of the attack, saying that the Mexican cavalry actually moved around both flanks of the United States position.

Mexican tactics and numerical superiority proved decisive. In describing the battle later, another soldier wrote that "by that time bullets were falling like rain and the Captain ordered all of us to look out for ourselves."[30] Corporal William Hogue of C Troop later remembered Captain Boyd shouting, "Don't any man fire a shot until you are fired upon. If you do, it will take me fifty years to explain why." Hogue said Mexican machine gun bullets were "knocking up so much dust in front of us that we could not see the Mexicans, so we moved forward." Boyd was shot and then shouted again, "go on boys; don't pay any attention to me. You've got them on the go." When Hogue saw Boyd a few minutes later, he had been hit again, "because he was bleeding from the shoulder [and] from the upper part of the right leg." A few minutes later, Hogue saw Boyd stand near Hogue's position, put his pistol in its holster and wave his hat. A Mexican sniper killed him while he was urging his men to attack. By that time, Hogue recalled, there were "only four men of my platoon that were not killed or wounded."[31] Constitutionalist officer Daniel González, who participated in the battle, also described the action. As U.S. troopers approached the Mexican position, General Gómez shouted to fire. At that moment Gómez died from a bullet to the forehead. González said the Mexicans were frightened but nevertheless won the battle.[32]

The Mexicans did not press their advantage and pursue the retreating Americans.[33] They did, however, capture a number of men, some of whom were wounded. The captives were sent by rail to Ciudad Chihuahua, where they were marched through the streets to the state jail.

Morey and four troopers had escaped from the field by retreating to a lime kiln 2,000 yards west of Carrizal. From there Morey sent one of the men to report to Pershing. In his note to the general, Morey related that he and others were in desperate straits, as they were "hiding in a hole two yards from [the] field."[34] After dark, Morey and the others with him slipped away, heading toward Pershing's headquarters. He and a few men had survived the worst disaster the United States troops had suffered to that point in Mexico. The Constitutionalists had killed twelve men, wounded ten and captured twenty-four.[35]

The next day, survivors from the confrontation arrived at the ranch where McCabe worked. Word also came in that about 1,000 Constitutionalist troops were approaching the ranch. The men moved on quickly to avoid another fight. Once news of the fight reached Pershing's headquarters, Major Charles Young asked to take all the men he could and attack any Constitutionalist soldiers he could find. Pershing refused, fearing a general outbreak of war.

Pershing advised Funston of events at Carrizal and awaited orders. Wilson and Lansing recognized the sensitivity of this matter and sought more information. Pershing did not know many details until Sunday, June 25, when Captain Morey's messenger with the letter explaining Carrizal arrived. Pershing was shocked at Boyd's actions but still blamed the Mexicans. General Funston advised Pershing, however, to await further orders from Wilson. Newspaper correspondent Frank B. Elser praised the men of the Tenth Cavalry for their bravery: they were "out-numbered, surrounded, and leading a forlorn hope, the two troops of the Tenth Cavalry, attacked by Carrancistas near El Carrizal on Wednesday morning, fought and died game, according to the best traditions of the American Cavalry."[36] The clash caused Wilson considerable concern. He, like Pershing, feared a wider conflict might develop. Before Wilson knew the full details of the fight, he had planned to request that Congress give him permission to send the army in sufficient force into Chihuahua to clear out all Mexican military units. Carranza's quick release of the prisoners, Wilson's hesitancy to get into a war and Pershing's report defused the situation.[37]

General Treviño, still commanding the northeastern frontier, learned about the battle when General Francisco González informed him, telling of the loss of General Gómez and the capture of the American troopers.[38] Gómez later became known as the "Hero of Carrizal." Captain Daniel González, who wrote of the conflict later, said that his unit had been stationed eighteen leagues south of Carrizal at Hacienda El Carmen when he was ordered to take his men to Carrizal. He reported that he had about 300 men, all badly mounted and provisioned. On June 18, General Gómez had arrived from Casas Grandes to take charge. Two days later, a small Constitutionalist detachment encountered United States troops a few miles from Carrizal. The Americans detained the Mexicans for a few hours then released them. They reported to Gómez, who wanted to attack the United States troops. Gómez telegraphed his superior in Ciudad Juárez, who told him to hold his position.

When Gómez talked with Captain Boyd, he said that the captain told him that he was searching for bandits and a soldier who had desert-ed. Gómez replied that his orders were to stop any United States troops from passing through towns. González recorded that when Boyd's men attacked, Gómez sent troops to flank the Americans and then opened fire with the machine gun. According to González's account, all of Boyd's men were either killed, wounded or forced from the field.[39]

Although tension between the United States and Mexico escalated, neither Wilson nor Carranza sought to widen the affair. For days Wilson and Lansing had worked to establish a plan regarding Mexico. On June 28, Wilson received a note through the Mexican minister in Washington, Eliseo Arredondo, in which Carranza blamed the United States for trouble on the frontier and insisted on withdrawal of the United States forces.[40] Wilson advised Carranza that the captured troopers and all their equipment must be returned to the United States immediately before any further actions would be taken.

On learning of the incident at Carrizal, Treviño notified all frontier commanders and alerted them to the possibility of additional confrontations with the United States.[41] Carranza was aware of the potential for more violence but took measures to avoid it by telling his generals to be calm and by ordering the release of the United States prisoners.[42] Andrés G. García, Mexican consul in El Paso, Texas, informed United States authorities that neither the Mexican government nor its people desired war. If a conflict should erupt, however, then the responsibility for it should fall on the United States.[43]

Treviño had taken some action to prepare for a fight with the United States. His command included a special group that supplied intelligence about the American troops. Ramón Arías, who reported directly to Treviño, headed the unit. On June 21, Arías advised Treviño that he recently had traveled by train from Namiquipa to the station at Santo Tomás. He noted where and how the United States troops were deployed. He also reported on U.S. strength: approximately 800 soldiers, four large artillery pieces, twenty-five machine guns, four airplanes and ten automobiles. He added that the force appeared well organized, supplied and disciplined.[44]

When the Mexicans heard of the fight at Carrizal and realized the serious nature of the clash, they volunteered by the thousands to fight the gringos. Again members of the Brotherhood of Locomotive Engineers vowed to Treviño that they were ready to die for their country.[45] A medical doctor offered his services in case of war.[46] The military governor of Zacatecas proposed a solution to the problem, suggesting to

Treviño that in case of wider hostilities with the United States, the Mexicans should seek an alliance with the "Negros who have been so badly treated by the whites." Mexico should offer to create a black republic across the southern part of the United States—including California—to be called *República Para la Raza de Color*.[47] Such unifying sentiment was evident when Pershing's expedition entered the country in March and became stronger after episodes like confrontations at Parral and Carrizal. On the frontier, the conflicts might also have helped Villa to recruit. Both Villa and Carranza used the United States presence in Chihuahua to help raise armies.

While Carranza recognized the value of patriotic rhetoric, he knew that he could not win a war against his northern neighbor, and he acted to pacify the United States. He ordered Treviño to release the prisoners taken at Carrizal, and on June 29 the men marched to freedom across the international bridge at El Paso. A correspondent for the *El Paso Morning Times* wrote that the troopers were "ragged and gaunt, but happy, thirsty, hungry and tired."[48] The crisis passed.

The fact that war between the two countries was avoided was a credit to both Carranza and Wilson. Wilson refused to allow public

After their release by Mexico, Tenth cavalrymen captured durting the confrontation at Carrizal pose for a photo (Arizona Historical Society, Tucson, photo #28354).

Lieutenant Henry Adair, killed at Carrizal in June 1916, is brought home. His casket can be seen on the railroad car. (El Paso Public Library).

pressure to provoke him into rash behavior in Mexico. In a speech on June 30 before the Press Club of New York, Wilson explained his position. He offered:

> The easiest thing is to strike. The brutal thing is the impulsive thing. No man has to think before he takes aggressive action; but before a man really conserves the honor by realizing the ideals of the Nation he has to think exactly what he will do and how he will do it.

> Do you think the glory of America would be enhanced by a war of conquest in Mexico? Do you think that any act of violence by a powerful nation like this against a weak and destructive neighbor would reflect distinction upon the annals of the United States? Do you think it is our duty to carry self-defense to a point of dictation into the affairs of another people?

Finally, Wilson added,

> And I have constantly to remind myself that I am not the servant of those who wish to enhance the value of their Mexican investments, that I am the servant of the rank and file of the people of the United States.[49]

Wilson's refusal to be stampeded into war with Mexico was related to the worsening situation in Europe, his upcoming fall reelection campaign, pressure for peace in the United States, the release of Captain Lewis Morey's letter showing that American troops provoked the Carrizal fight and Carranza's release of the prisoners. Carranza did not want war either, but he was willing to do whatever was necessary to protect Mexico from United States intervention. Carranza knew that the United States would probably join the fighting in Europe, and he used this to his advantage. The Germans were also interested in brewing trouble for the United States in Mexico, so Carranza exploited the threat of German influence to pressure Wilson to remove the Punitive Expedition. Despite the advantages and disadvantages of both sides, Wilson and Carranza were eager to resolve their differences.[50]

CHAPTER 7

THE JOINT COMMISSION: A MEXICAN VIEW

▼▼▼▼▼▼

The fierce battle at Carrizal between Pershing's Tenth Cavalry and General Félix Gómez's Constitutionalist forces demonstrated to both Mexico and the United States the need to make special efforts to resolve border difficulties. Carranza recognized that both American domestic affairs and international pressures influenced Woodrow Wilson's dealings with Mexico. Some businessmen, Republican politicians and the pro-Republican press sought to make Wilson look weak in his role of protecting U.S. interests in Mexico. And political advisers wanted Wilson to intervene militarily in order to curtail the nationalistic direction of the Revolution. At the same time, Wilson also had to deal with deteriorating conditions in Europe as World War I claimed more casualties and as German U-boats sank more ships of both combatants and neutral countries.

On July 3, 1916, a few days after the Carrizal confrontation, the Carrancista government sent a diplomatic note to the United States asking again for the withdrawal of United States troops to prevent another armed confrontation.[1] Lansing received the note and replied that the most important problem between the two countries remained Carranza's inability to control his side of the international border.[2] He suggested that perhaps additional high-level discussions might resolve the dilemma.

On July 11, 1916, Cándido Aguilar, acting on Carranza's orders and in response to recent diplomatic exchanges, suggested that the two nations form an international commission to discuss mutual grievances.

Speaking for Carranza, Aguilar emphasized, however, that before meaningful discussions on border-crossing reciprocity could take place, the question of withdrawal had to be settled. Aguilar also suggested that Mexico wanted a "frank and cordial" conversation that would bring the two countries to a mutually beneficial agreement.[3]

On July 28, 1916, the United States formally agreed to the creation of a joint commission. The agenda in which the United States was interested, however, did not give priority to the withdrawal of its troops. Rather, the United States suggested a desire for a "wide and friendly discussion over matters all along the border." In truth, American officials hoped to force the Mexicans to back away from the strong nationalistic provisions of the Revolution and to protect U.S. citizens and their property. Carranza reiterated that he wanted the negotiations to focus on the "withdrawal of American troops then in Mexico" and establish an immediate date for their departure.[4]

Despite obvious differences in the positions of the two governments, Carranza moved ahead with the appointment of his commission members. He named his representatives on August 3; Wilson announced his appointees five days later. Carranza selected a blue-ribbon panel including Luis Cabrera, a close confidant and an intellectual of the Revolutionary period, and engineers Alberto J. Pani and Ignacio Bonillas, both of the First Chief's inner circle. Juan B. Rojo and Fernando González Roa, both university trained, were to assist the commissioners. Carranza selected Cabrera as the president and primary spokesman for the Mexican delegation. Carranza felt that he could depend on Cabrera to take a hard-nosed approach toward negtiations.

The Mexican commissioners were familiar with the politics and customs of the United States and all spoke English with varying degrees of fluency. Alberto Pani, the most sociable of the Mexican team, got along well with his American counterparts. Ignacio Bonillas had spent a considerable amount of time in the United States and understood American politics better than the other Mexicans. Luis Cabrera—the First Chief's hard-liner—had studied U.S. mores and had translated the diary of President James Knox Polk into Spanish. Mexican representative in Washington, D.C., Eliseo Arredondo, Carranza's nephew, would follow the proceedings closely and give Carranza updates on the progress of the meetings.[5]

Wilson appointed Franklin K. Lane, secretary of the interior; Dr. John R. Mott, one of his confidants; George Gray, an attorney; and L. S. Rowe, a student of Latin American history and politics to his commission. Rowe, the only member with some knowledge of Spanish, was named secretary. The staff of the United States team included two other men who were acquainted with Mexico and its recent history. Although the United States commissioners were qualified in some respects, in general they were not as informed about the problems facing the two nations as were their Mexican counterparts.

On August 3, 1916, Carranza telegraphed instructions to his commissioners. With adamant resolve, he told them that the "principal" objective was to obtain "the withdrawal of United States troops from Mexico." Only then could they discuss other issues concerning the border region. He added that all information on tentative agreements "must be telegraphed" to him, and he alone could "approve or reject the agreement."[6] The Mexican commissioners journeyed to Washington, D.C., had a brief meeting with Wilson, then traveled to the Hotel Griswold in New London, Connecticut. On September 6, 1916, the first of fifty-two meetings began.

Because the American commissioners knew little Spanish, the Mexicans agreed to hold the proceedings in English with simultaneous translation. At the end of the day the various staffs, working with translators, printed the proceedings in both languages. During the first two sessions, the commissioners discussed general conditions in the border region. At first, neither side seemed ready to tackle specifics. On the third day, Luis Cabrera formally demanded that the United States immediately withdraw its troops from Mexico. The Americans refused to address the subject, insisting that other items merited discussion.[7]

The stubborn positions assumed by both sides during the third day set the tone for the duration of the deliberations and cloaked the entire proceedings in confrontation. On September 9, the Mexican commissioners demonstrated that they were aware of the political problems that the United States faced. In fact, the commissioners advised Carranza that their counterparts were beseiged with "complaints from radical Americans in Mexico or those who had interests there." These Americans wanted the commission to address a satisfactory financial agreement to preserve their interests. Newspapers, primarily those in the Hearst chain, also ran numerous stories about the lawless conditions along the international boundary. The Mexicans believed that such news coverage was a distraction, "creating difficulties for the commissions and making it impossible to focus discussion on troop withdrawal."[8] The Mexican commissioners advised Carranza that some of the articles were clearly pro-Republican and slanted to reflect badly on Wilson just before voters went to the polls. The Mexican consul in New York City, who had been carefully following the newspaper coverage of Mexico during the months preceeding the joint meeting, warned Carranza that "bastard" interests in the United States were provoking conflict between the countries.[9]

Wilson met with the joint commission on September 12 for an hour but dealt with nothing specific. As the meetings continued, the Mexican commissioners explained conditions in Mexico and the status of foreign residents and investments. The United States delegates countered that Mexico had promised protection of foreigners and their property, had guaranteed religious toleration and had agreed to the creation of another joint commission to settle U.S. claims against Mexico. The Mexican commissioners viewed the proposal as meddling in the internal affairs of their country and refused to entertain it seriously.

The United States press and special interests continued to attack Mexico, painting bleak portraits of the predicament of foreigners south of the border and of the Mexicans' inability to provide a safe environment for any citizen, foreign or national. Some newspaper editors suggested that only a full-scale intervention would solve the problems. Various American companies with investments in Mexico sent agents to the Hotel Griswold to pressure the United States delegates to pursue claims against the Mexican government and to obtain guarantees allowing them to operate in Mexico as they had before the Revolution. The Mexican commissioners believed that the lobbyists were trying to make certain that the commission failed in its deliberations. They were convinced of a plot when they learned that each member of the U.S. delegation received a copy of Francisco Bulnes' book, *The Whole Truth About Mexico*. The Mexican author defended the Porfiriato and harshly criticized his country, suggesting that Mexico would wallow in poverty, ignorance and violence without United States intervention.[10]

To Carranza and his commissioners, the presence of United States troops on Mexican soil remained a national humiliation. The discussions would resolve nothing—Carranza insisted—until Mexico had its self-respect restored by forcing the withdrawal of the Pershing Expedition from Chihuahua.[11] The Americans, however, refused to discuss the withdrawal of troops, and the negotiations stalled. Juan B. Rojo advised Carranza that the conference would continue, "but that the American delegates did not sufficiently understand Mexico's situation." Rojo remained somewhat optimistic when he added that "we believe soon we will be able to renew concrete discussions over the withdrawal of troops and protection of the frontier. The American delegates, it appears, are receiving a great number of complaints from American citizens who reside in Mexico."[12]

On September 27, Carranza reminded Cabrera not to deviate from his orders. Before anything else could be discussed, the United States must set a date for troop withdrawal. Carranza also seemed perplexed. He told Cabrera,

> it is strange to me that in more than two weeks of conferences with the American delegation you have not resolved the point of withdrawing the United States forces that are in Mexican territory and I declare to you and your companions in the delegation that you cannot treat any other point in the conference without results relative to the withdrawal of American troops.[13]

At the end of September the commissioners decided to leave New London and resume meetings at the Hotel Traymore in Atlantic City,

New Jersey, hoping a change of venue might prompt progress.[14] The logistics of moving, finding office equipment and returning to negotiations proved trying. On October 2, 1916, after some difficulty solving these problems, the delegates met again. In the second encounter, John R. Mott proposed that the commissioners consider not only the removal of Pershing's troops from Mexico, but also general matters that would lead to cordial relations on the frontier. The "general matters" differed little from earlier United States proposals.[15]

On October 6, Luis Cabrera restated Mexico's position. The next day, he heard from Carranza, who stubbornly refused to change his demands.[16] The position of the two governments had not changed from the first meeting, but on this occasion the Americans agreed that a discussion of troop removal would be part of the agenda for the meeting.[17]

After this exchange, Cabrera advised Carranza that the situation in the negotiations was delicate and in danger of ending with no accomplishment because Wilson's commission only wanted to talk about the "lives and property of foreigners in Mexico."[18] On October 11, Commissioner Lane advised the Mexicans that before any discussion about troop withdrawal could begin, the two parties must discuss the details of protecting both sides of the international border. Lane insisted that the talks include mutual use of national railroads to pursue bandits, complete exchange of information and permission for U.S. Army patrols to advance up to ten miles into Mexico when necessary. The United States commissioners offered to remove the troops as rapidly as the security of the frontier could be guaranteed but added that they would not be completely out of Mexico until March 15, 1917, and then only as long as no additional Villista raids occurred within 100 miles of existing American positions. The United States would reserve the right, moreover, to send troops to Mexico for up to ninety days when such action protected the international frontier.[19]

The Mexican delegation adamantly refused, and Cabrera angrily denounced the proposal by the United States as "an affront to Mexico's sovereignty and dignity as a nation."[20] He demanded, furthermore, that the United States remove its troops from Mexico by December 16;

meanwhile, Pershing should take all his men north to Colonia Dublán. Once the United States troops retreated northward, as Carranza had suggested previously, the Mexican commander of the region would have his men occupy the evacuated positions. When the United States finally withdrew, both countries could establish a system of reciprocal border crossings to protect the frontier. The Mexicans insisted that the United States would also have to make a sincere effort to stop the activities of filibusters, who for decades had organized on the north side of the border to invade northern Mexico.

In October, Aguilar had also asked Juan B. Rojo to give his opinion of the progress of the joint meeting. In his first report Rojo told him that in his judgment, the United States had never before been engaged in such a bitter presidential election, with the Republicans using the European war and the situation with Mexico against Wilson. The Republicans, in his opinion, wanted to influence Mexican society and politics, and, he said, "they are frankly against the Revolution." Rojo added that "not a day passes that the Hearst press does not inflame public opinion against Wilson and Mexico."[21] On October 27, the United States officially refused Mexican pleas for the evacuation of troops. Mexico would have to accept terms affecting internal conditions in Mexico before troops would be withdrawn. The American delegates added a demand that Mexico eliminate disease and starvation in their country.[22] The Americans clearly hoped to force Mexico to make changes in its government and society that exceeded the scope of problems with Villa and along the border. Carranza again refused to accept, citing the need for a firm date for troop withdrawal before further discussion.

On November 1, 1916, the heads of the respective delegations recognized that a concensus could not be reached at the time, in part because the United States election was a few days away. Each side then appointed one member to work on a plan for the pullback of U.S. forces, as well as other issues regarding the border region. Commissioners John Mott and Alberto Pani were assigned the task.[23]

The Mexicans showed considerable understanding of the pressures that dictated both the attitudes and activities of the U.S. delegates. The

commission advised Carranza of the problem, referred to the "efferves-
cence of politics that reigned in the United States," and told him that at
the moment it was virtually impossible to accomplish anything. They
further informed Carranza that the Republican press in the United States
continually used "the Mexican case" to attack Wilson, inferring that he
was "weak and vacilating, and urging him to take strong action to protect
American lives and investment in Mexico." The press also portrayed Villa
as the commander of thousands of well-armed men who were winning
the battle against Carranza. One reporter attacked Luis Cabrera, suggesting that he was the "most obstinate and obstructionist member of the
commission."[24] To newsmen, Cabrera was the main problem. Because of
the imminent elections, the delegates adjourned.

Meetings resumed on November 16, with American representatives
insisting that protecting the international border was essential. The
American commissioners suggested that each country should be responsible for its own frontier, but that the United States would retain the right
to pursue bandits into Mexico without restriction. When possible, U.S.
forces would cooperate with Mexican troops. On November 17, the
United States delegates advised the Mexicans that they wanted to post-
pone the meetings to go to Washington to talk with President Woodrow
Wilson.

On their return to Atlantic City, the Americans advised the
Mexican commissioners that the United States would eliminate most of
the restrictions it had placed on the removal of troops from Mexico. Not
mentioned were the sticky questions of border-crossing reciprocity and
the precise date for American troop withdrawal. Pani and Mott continued to work on a plan that both sides could accept.

While the dialogue progressed, the press continued attacks on Mexico
and its commissioners. The *New York Times* carried a piece suggesting that
the "best way to deal with the Mexican commissioners was to pay them
off as had been done before to grease a deal with the Mexicans."[25] Luis
Cabrera replied to the *Times* editor, denouncing the allegation.

On November 21, Mott and Pani agreed on a basic plan. The accord
called for an American withdrawal as soon as practical, but not more than

forty days after the agreement. The pullback would go slowly in order to protect United States troops, then Mexican forces would take up the positions evacuated by Pershing's men. Wilson notified the Mexican delegation that the United States reserved the right to enter Mexico when necessary to protect American citizens and property.

On receipt of this protocol, the Mexican commission unofficially accepted some of the provisions, then sent Alberto Pani to Mexico to deliver the plan to Carranza. The First Chief did not deliberate long: he would accept no agreement until the United States got its troops out of Mexico, suggesting as well that the protocol insulted Mexico's sovereignty. Carranza was willing, however, to continue the negotiations.[26] Alberto Pani later wrote that the First Chief asked him what would happen if Mexico did not accept the plan. Pani replied that "at any rate the United States will have to get its troops out." Carranza told Pani that he agreed and said "in this case, I prefer not to ratify it."[27] Mexican secret agents in the United States had apprised Carranza and Pani of the increasing U.S. involvement in Europe and realized that it was simply a matter of time before Pershing would have to pull out.

By this time the commissioners realized that no accord would be reached. Both sides agreed, however, that another change in location might revitalize discussions. The proceedings moved to Philadelphia, where on December 18, 1916, members resumed talks. The Mexican commissioners handed their American counterparts a statement that included Carranza's point of view. Carranza told the delegates that Mexico's acceptance of the protocol would be tantamount to admitting that the United States had a right to place troops in Mexico whenever it wished.

On December 19, 1916, the Americans—claiming that they had changed their position considerably since the deliberations had begun—demanded that the Mexican commissioners accept the plan as offered or the meetings would be terminated.[28] The Americans accused the Mexicans of being inflexible because they limited their negotiations to the U.S. troop withdrawal. Despite this rigid public stand, the United States was already preparing to pull back the Punitive Expedition. Luis

Cabrera advised Carranza that the newspapers were preparing the public for the withdrawal. Cabrera also believed that Mexico had sent a clear message that interventionism would not be acceptable under any terms. Carranza reiterated that no further discussion would be held until United States troops were out of Mexico. On December 27, 1916, the Mexican commissioners notified the United States commissioners of Carranza's position. The joint commission was dead. On January 15, 1917, the commissioners met and informally agreed to end the proceedings.

Though it is doubtful that the joint meetings contributed to an understanding between the two nations, the commission was not a complete failure. At least the meetings allowed time for both sides to cool down after the battle at Carrizal. Throughout the sessions the Americans naively thought that they could force Carranza, by the presence of the Punitive Expedition in Mexico, to alter his economic and social policies. They were mistaken. Wilson was dismayed with Carranza's intransigence, but had few options and none without serious repercussions for the United States, Mexico and those involved in the carnage of World War I.[29]

CHAPTER 8

CARRANCISTAS VERSUS VILLISTAS

▼▼▼▼▼▼

High-level negotiations and joint commissions notwithstanding, the Revolution raged on in Mexico. Constitutionalist troops continued their dogged pursuit of the Villistas, and troops of the Punitive Expedition continued patrols.

During the months after Pershing entered Mexico, most of Carranza's communications to frontier commanders had not concerned the United States; rather they addressed the activities of Villistas and others who opposed the First Chief. In several hundred messages to officers, Carranza mentioned the United States intruders few times before June 1916; afterward he advised his frontier commanders only to block any southward movement by the Americans. He related no order of battle and issued no orders that allowed offensive action against Pershing's forces. For the next several months, Constitutionalist troops trailed and fought Villistas in Chihuahua, Coahuila and Durango.

General Jacinto Treviño, still in charge of the northeastern frontier, had taken additional steps to enhance Constitutionalist chances of finding Villa. On May 16, a little more than a month before the incident at Carrizal, Treviño moved his headquarters to Ciudad Chihuahua to be closer to Villista activities. Carranza had suggested that Treviño's command near the international border placed him too far away from the action.[1] During May and June, Carrancistas pursued bands of Villistas, encountering them only briefly. The Villistas, meanwhile, used the time to recruit and to supply a force that could challenge the Constitutionalists for control of major cities. On June 26, Treviño ordered General Ernesto García to Parral and General Jacinto Hernández to El Rosario to pursue Villistas. He sent General Ignacio Ramos to Jiménez to secure that town. On June 27, Ramos' troops briefly combined with the others and engaged small parties of Villistas near Namiquipa and south of Casas Grandes. The Villistas fled into the desert.

During July, the Villistas, their strength increasing, renewed offensives against Constitutionalist troops across the state of Chihuahua. On July 2, General Ramos deployed his troops above Las Lomas and notified Treviño that a large concentration of the enemy was south of Hacienda de Zapata not far from his position. Treviño, on hearing of this potential confrontation, ordered Generals Hernández and García to move near Canutillo, where they were to concentrate with Ramos for an attack on the Villistas. Ramos, however, had already taken his men to Hacienda de Corrales, where he ordered them to prepare defensive barricades and trenches in case of an attack. At 4:30 A.M., July 3, the 800 Villistas attacked Ramos, but the Constitutionalists forced them to retreat after heavy losses. Though Ramos and several of his men were severely wounded, they maintained position. By 6 P.M., the battlefield was littered with bodies, and the Constitutionalists were running low on ammunition. Ramos reluctantly retreated toward Jiménez, where he hoped to find reinforcements.

Ramos had advised Treviño of his situation at the start of the battle, and Treviño reinforced him by sending General Maclovio García, heading a column of fifty men, toward Jiménez. García encountered Villistas outside Hacienda de Jalapa, where his troops fought for three hours. García was wounded in the leg and was forced to withdraw. Treviño also sent Lieutenant Colonel Agustín Maciel with the Sixth Brigade (under the overall command of Colonel M. P. López in Camargo) to Jiménez to support Ramos. On July 4, Treviño notified Colonel Emiliano Triana, in charge of government troops at Jiménez, that the Villistas were nearby and that he was to supply the remainder of General Ramos' men with arms from the ammunition train at Jiménez. At the same time, Treviño urgently requested that General

Domingo Arrieta, commander in Durango, march rapidly toward Jiménez. He also ordered General Francisco R. Bertani, at Villa Ahumada, to take his soldiers toward the town. The stage was set for a full-scale fight over Jiménez.

Villista forces also marched toward Jiménez, with Villa—still suffering from his leg wound—in command. Villa attacked early on July 5. The Constitutionalists made a strong stand, but when Ignacio Ramos died of a massive wound, his men retreated in disarray. Villistas occupied Jiménez on July 6 and remained for two days. Victories, even temporary triumphs, probably helped Villa recruit. Early in July, General Gerónimo Ortega led his hundred-man Constitutionalist detachment to Escalón by train and disembarked to the cries of "Viva Villa." He turned his command over to Villa.[2] Treviño reacted to the loss of Jiménez and to Ortega's desertion by sending columns of 1,000 under General Matías Ramos and 800 under Generals Ismael Lares and Ernesto García to recapture Jiménez. No battle was necessary this time. Government troops marched in unopposed at 3 P.M. on July 7, 1916.

Government troops quickly began repairing the railroads and telegraph facilities that Villistas had destroyed north of Jiménez.[3] On learning of the Villista withdrawal from Jiménez, Treviño ordered General Domingo Arrieta, then at Jiménez, to form a cavalry column of 500 of his best men to pursue Villa and fight him wherever an opportunity occurred. Treviño also ordered General Ernesto García to form a similar column and head toward Río Florido. Also on July 7, Treviño received a telegram from García, who was then at Parral, that General Jacinto Hernández had fought Villistas at San Salvador, defeating them and killing Villista General José de Jesús Contreras and his two sons. Government forces suffered wounded, including Colonel Leandro Hernández. On the same day, Treviño ordered General Matías Ramos, who was then at Santa Isabel, to lead his troops to Jiménez and to take command of other soldiers from Durango who were at the village.[4] The Constitutionalist cavalry skirmished with small bands of Villistas on July 9 and 10, then attempted unsuccessfully to cut off the Villista retreat and to envelope the main enemy force near Ciénega.[5] In brief fights with the

Villistas, Constitutionalist troops claimed to have killed several and pursued the remaining fighters until they dispersed.[6]

Frustrated with Villista activity in Chihuahua and Coahuila, Treviño made command changes in June and July that included sending the Segunda División de Oriente to Coahuila and replacing General Francisco Coss with General Pilar R. Sánchez. He sent General Arnulfo González from Durango to replace General Murguía as chief of staff of the division.

On July 9, 1916, Constitutionalist troops again fought Villistas near Parral. General Luis Herrera pursued Villistas until they took up strong positions south of Parral. As darkness fell, Herrera dug in, taking defensive positions that he held until the Villistas attacked again the next morning. Herrera tried to envelope the Villistas, opening a vicious fight during which government troops captured 200 Villista horses and killed approximately eighty-five of Villa's men. Constitutionalists suffered eleven wounded and five killed.[7] Because of the threat to Parral, Constitutionalist forces reinforced the village with more than 200 additional troops.[8]

Carranza—aware of Villa's resiliency—understood the limited progress being made against the enemy. Treviño, however, exaggerated Constitutionalist successes and underestimated Villista strength. On July 30, 1916, he announced that the recent campaigns had reduced Villa to no more than thirty effective fighters and that the guerrilla leader's power was broken. Treviño was sorely mistaken. Villa's men numbered many more than Treviño suggested, and, while Villa's wound had hampered his mobility, it had not curtailed his ability to recruit even more troops. Soon after the July confrontations, Villa decided to have his leg operated on again. A Dr. José de Lille removed bullet fragments from his leg, slowing him down for a couple of months. It did not deter his lieutenants, however, from raiding government outposts, trains and isolated villages.

Carrancista troops also remained active. In August, Generals Luis Herrera, Matías Ramos and Ismael Lares concentrated a major force at Parral. Villistas, meanwhile, attacked Hacienda La Ciénega, killing members of General Herrera's family and others who opposed them or sympathized with the Carrancistas.

Treviño continued to face command difficulties, supply problems, desertions and bad weather. Heavy rains washed out railroad beds and bridges across the northern frontier of Chihuahua.[9] During late August and early September, Colonel Dario F. Cortes, of General Domingo Arrieta's staff, advised Treviño that Arrieta's men often did not have sufficient food and ammunition. Cortes suggested that Arrieta reorganize his troops but noted that it would take about 50,000 pesos monthly to supply the division's needs.[10] Colonel Ysidrio Cardona of the El Rayo Brigade advised Treviño that his men were exhausted by the constant pursuit. The soldiers needed a rest and many had families they wanted to visit. During the past year Cardona had lost more than 300 to desertions and more men would leave soon if nothing were done to help them. He suggested a three-month leave. Cardona also thought that Villista power was broken in the region at the time.[11]

Additionally, Treviño had to cope with the presence of United States troops. He told Obregón on one occasion that Americans caused trouble in every village they neared, that they often confiscated supplies without paying for them and that U.S. troops wreaked havoc in taverns and brothels. Locals were afraid and asked Treviño for protection.[12]

In September, Villa returned to the field to lead his men. He initiated a series of skirmishes aimed at testing Carrancista strength. Villa also detailed units to continue attacking isolated government outposts. On September 8, his men attacked a work train under command of Colonel J. Gutiérrez between stations Nopalera and Picháchic on the Kansas City-Mexico and Eastern Line. A squadron of thirty Constitutionalists were protecting the train when approximately fifty Villistas attacked. Gutiérrez was gravely wounded and several government soldiers were killed. A few Villistas reportedly died as well.

Treviño, fearing that Villa was planning to attack Ciudad Chihuahua again, prepared his defenses.[13] In his approach to the city, Villa fought and defeated government troops at Hueráchic, forty kilometers from the capital. The day of the attack, Villa sent Treviño a message, telling the general that he was on his way and expected to shake hands and that Treviño should have a hearty meal ready. On September 15, Villa slipped into the city to take stock of the defenses and to visit family and friends. He returned to his troops that night and organized for the next morning's assault. Approximately 4,000 Villistas invaded at 2:50 A.M. One group attacked the railroad station on the northeast side; while some of Villa's men quickly severed electric power to most of the town; others occupied the governor's palace, captured some government workers and took over the state penitentiary. The raiders released the prisoners.[14]

Treviño had assigned General José Cavazos with his 2,000 men to defend Ciudad Chihuahua. Although Treviño was in the city when Villa attacked, he was not at the Governor's Palace and escaped capture. Treviño rallied the troops, who rained artillery fire on the Villistas near the palace. About 120 Villistas were killed and several were captured. The captives were shot. Treviño's losses were also heavy and included a number of desertions during the fight.[15] Most Constitutionalists remained loyal, however, and at 4 P.M. Treviño telegraphed Obregón of the victory, saying that the Villista's had been "completely annihilated."[16]

On learning of the attack, Carranza decided that Villa's activities had no real military significance, but were strategically planned as fodder for American newsmen who clamored for large-scale intervention. On September 16, on Carranza's orders, Obregón ordered Treviño to declare martial law in Chihuahua and to execute anyone who took up arms against the government.[17] Treviño had already served notice on the Villistas by executing his prisoners. When news of Villa's attack reached the United States, Wilson's government made it clear to Carranza that because of his inability to defeat Villa, the Punitive Expedition would remain in Mexico.

After the setback at Chihuahua, Villa turned his efforts to smaller Constitutionalist detachments. He headed for San Andrés with 200 men and on September 19 engaged and defeated a government force of thirty under Colonel Carlos Zuazua, who died in the battle. The Villistas captured all of the survivors and executed them.[18] Treviño's next chance to deal with the Villistas came when part of General Cavazos' troops under Colonel José V. Elizondo and General Ignacio Ramos engaged Villistas at Cusihuiriáchic. Villa soundly defeated the Constitutionalists, killing or capturing almost all of them. On September 23, Treviño apprised Obregón of the skirmishes and insisted that his forces had suffered the defeats because of ammunition shortages.[19] In an extended battle, slaughter was inevitable.

Obregón and Carranza were aware of chronic ammunition short-ages, production-quality complications and delivery problems. These combined to make it almost impossible for Carranza's troops to maintain a steady flow of ammunition to the various armies in the field.[20] While ammunition reports list the type and quantity shipped to various units, they do not reflect shortages or other munitions difficulties.[21]

Adding to the woes, on September 22, 1916, fifty Villistas attacked twenty government troops under command of Major Timoteo Rodríguez at Sierra Mojada. The Villistas, under command of Porfirio Rodríguez, captured seven government troopers, sacked the village and rode off toward Escalón.[22]

During the last week of September, Constitutionalist General Matías Ramos headed by rail through San Andrés en route to attack Villa, but Villa had left the village the day before, systematically destroying railroad tracks and bridges to slow Ramos' advance. Ramos eventually arrived in the area of Cusihuiriáchic. A fierce five-hour fight followed, during which Ramos received a nasty leg wound and Villa's troops suffered heavy casualties. The Villistas again withdrew, fleeing into the mountains and leaving behind more than eighty dead and a large cache of supplies. Ramos did not pursue. Instead he concentrated his command at Santa Isabel. Other government detachments fought small groups of Villistas with mixed results between September 28 and 30.[23]

On October 4 Obregón queried Treviño whether Carrancistas or Villistas occupied Cusihuiriáchic. He also asked if anyone else could take over while Ramos' wound healed. Obregón's message had a tone of despair or, at least, impatience.[24] On October 6, Treviño responded that the Villistas had evacuated Cusihuiriáchic and government troops had again occupied the village. He also noted that he intended to name General Carlos Osuna to take Ramos' command. He continued that it was not plausible to engage Villa in battle without resupplying his munitions.[25]

Villa continued his offensive in October, chosing the time and place where he would strike government troops. He believed that in an area so large with such difficult terrain, he could isolate Constitutionalist units and defeat them. Small victories would help his cause among Mexicans, as well as, he hoped, provoke the United States into a full-scale invasion.

Villa's tactics were simple. Most often he did not have sufficient numbers to confront large Constitutionalist forces, so he attacked detachments, then quickly dispersed only to unify again. He often concentrated on destroying railroad track, telegraph lines, generally isolating government units from their central commands in Ciudad Chihuahua or Ciudad Juárez. As he had since the beginning of 1916, Villa waged a guerrilla war in a territory he knew well and where local residents were either sympathetic, neutral or afraid of him. Villa's successes during September and October 1916 forced Carranza to reevaluate his strategy. Clearly, it was not going well.

Obregón, meanwhile, spent much of October encouraging his troops and trying to put together a more cohesive force in Chihuahua and Durango. He also spent time attempting to find out more about Villa's actions. He repeatedly asked Treviño where Villa was, how many men he had and what Treviño intended to do.[26] Treviño—constantly complaining that he did not have sufficient munitions or men—had no specific answer. On occasion Obregón ordered troops to join Treviño, but, at least in one instance, General Domingo Arrieta and General Luis Herrera either did not get the message or chose to ignore it. They continued to march north rather than going to Treviño's assistance.[27]

In addition to general logistical problems and difficulties with troop commands, the Constitutionalists continued to lose men who either fled to join Villa or to return to their families. Throughout the Mexican Revolution, family members often traveled with the soldiers and fought alongside them. Soldaderas—under the most difficult of conditions—played an important role, carrying out domestic chores, taking care of the wounded and providing general support. Some women even joined in combat, leading troops into battle.[28] Even with families by their sides, many soldiers simply wanted to get away from the fighting and deserted.

Vascilating loyalties, insubordination and desertion were the result of numerous problems, including the murky chain of command and the inability of the Constitutionalist government to supply and pay its troops. In October Consul Andrés G. García passed on the litany of problems to Carranza and asked if he could report directly to the First Chief.[29]

In addition to the myriad problems that Carranza faced across Mexico, he had to contend with hostile attitudes, both official and unofficial, in the United States. In October, the American press suggested that Villa controlled western Chihuahua, that the Constitutionalist troops had not energetically pursued the guerrillas, and that Obregón was at fault because he did not send ammunition to Treviño.[30] Carranza was well aware of the issues along the frontier. In mid-October he again tried to convince United States bureaucrats of his dedication to stopping Villa. Eliseo Arredondo passed a note from Carranza to Luis Cabrera (then at Atlantic City, New Jersey, meeting with the joint commission) that the Constitutionalists intended to destroy all Villista resistance completely.[31]

Following the Villista defeat of Cavazos, in mid-October Treviño detached another column of 3,000 men under General Osuna to confront Villa. On October 20, Villa, after losing an initial skirmish, stood his ground at Santa Isabel and in a bloody six-hour battle that commenced at 4 A.M., soundly defeated the government force. Osuna maintained that his men had fought valiantly, but that they ultimately had to withdraw when almost all their ammunition was gone. Osuna claimed that his men killed several Villistas, but among his own losses was Colonel Martín Salinas, commander of the Osuna Brigade.[32] In the wake of the Villista success, Villa issued a manifesto calling the Constitutionalist government traitorous for allowing the gringos to invade the country.

Fearing the collapse of his forces, Treviño retreated to Ciudad Chihuahua, telegraphed Obregón that he needed reinforcements (suggesting they be sent from Sonora), and began to consolidate troops. Treviño feared that Villa's next target would again be Ciudad Chihuahua. On October 22 he advised Obregón that he had begun to fortify positions at the edge of the city, and that he was confident that he could hold his position. He repeated his request for more arms and ammunition. He also encouraged Obregón to send Generals Fortunato Maycotte and Jesús Novoa and the Arrieta brothers from Durango to Chihuahua.[33] Obregón advised Treviño that he could not immediately resolve the ammunition problem, but would send reinforcements.[34] Obregón suggested that Treviño give General Maycotte some of his ammunition, but Treviño responded that he had none to spare.[35]

On October 26, Obregón demanded of Treviño just who—Villistas or government troops—controlled the railroad northeast of Ciudad Chihuahua. Treviño should send details about Osuna's defeat at Santa Isabel. Finally, Obregón wanted an appraisal of Treviño's chances of holding Chihuahua.[36] The next day, pressured by Obregón's insistence upon an accurate update of events in Chihuahua, Treviño reported the previous five days' troop actions. While his troops had fought regularly with Villistas, Treviño feared that Ciudad Chihuahua was again Villa's next target.[37] On the same day that Obregón asked Treviño for information, Villistas headed toward the capital. En route 1,500 of the enemy attacked Constitutionalists under the command of General Marciano López Ortíz at Estación Díaz near Camargo and north of Jiménez. After heavy losses—approximately 160 killed, wounded or missing—disorganized government troops retreated. The Villistas again occupied Camargo.[38] Whether Villa was present can only be conjectured, although Arrieta insisted Villa had indeed led the forces into Camargo.[39] Moreover, by October 27, Fortunato Maycotte had probably left Torreón and was heading for Chihuahua.[40]

On October 28, Obregón advised Treviño that government forces should seize the opportunity and attack any concentration of Villistas. If Villa's troops attacked first, Obregón thought the government troops could not sustain a defense of Ciudad Chihuahua.[41] Treviño's troop deployment had left much of the state of Chihuahua unprotected, giving Villa control of the countryside. Obregón, therefore issued the orders for General Maycotte to join Generals Arrieta and Herrera to concentrate government troop strength at Camargo. Treviño still feared that he did not have sufficient ammunition. On October 30, as Arrieta and Maycotte combined their forces, Treviño again warned Obregón of the grave and

Left: Francisco Murguía (Archivo Fotográfico, Centro de Estudios de Historia de Mexico, Condumex). Right: Fortunato Maycotte (Archivo Fotográfico, Centro de Estudios de Historia de Mexico, Condumex).

worsening supply problems.[42] Obregón had wired Maycotte that "we have no ammunition to send you." He also ordered him to attack the Villistas despite the situation.[43]

Fortunato Maycotte arrived at Estación Díaz late in the day of October 30, expecting to find government troops under General Ismael Lares. Together they could confront the Villistas—all well armed and provisioned and now numbering around 3,000 fighters. Lares, unfortunately, had started for Camargo, leaving Maycotte to face the Villistas alone. Maycotte, angry at being left in a precarious position, directed his troops toward Santa Rosalía where he hoped to catch up with other Constitutionalists.[44]

Before Constitutionalist troops could concentrate, Villa took the offensive. His goal was to isolate Ciudad Chihuahua by cutting railroad and telegraph lines and occupying Jiménez and Santa Rosalía. At Santa Rosalía, Domingo Arrieta's troops had abandoned their railroad cars after the Villista attack and had left thousands of rounds of ammunition and other supplies. Government troops retreated in such disarray that they demoralized Maycotte's approaching troops. From Escalón on October 31, Arrieta telegraphed Treviño that his troops had been badly beaten. General Francisco Murguía was not surprised. He reported to Obregón that poor strategy and disorganization had led to the defeat. Leadership and discipline broke down, and the battle was over in ten minutes.[45] Obregón did not delay long before dispatching a three-man board of officers to the frontier to investigate.[46]

Villa hoped to isolate Constitutionalist forces at Chihuahua, then send the majority of his army south to capture Torreón. He knew that he still enjoyed a good deal of popular support in the area, and he counted on his popularity to threaten Treviño. Villa also thought that he might be able to recruit in Ciudad Chihuahua from some of Treviño's command. He might then control the railroads completely, and rail was the best way to move large numbers of men and supplies. Villa also constantly waged a war of rhetoric against the Constitutionalist government, trying to discredit it by charging that Carranza had sold out to the United States. As a recruiting gimmick, on one occasion in November 1916, Villa reputedly rode through Parral on horseback yelling, "Let's go kill gringos."[47] Townspeople who did not volunteer to ride with Villa were rounded up and forced into service.

General Arrieta warned Carranza on November 2, 1916, that Villista propaganda was effectively turning some of the frontier citizens against the Constitutionalist government. He also reported that in the recent battles with Villistas near Santa Rosalía he had lost about seventy men killed, wounded or missing and that he had no idea of the losses inflicted on the Villistas.[48]

By November 1, the Constitutionalist military situation in Chihuahua had deteriorated considerably, and it worsened daily.[49] In addition, Villa's strength was increasing. Obregón was clearly aware of the dilemma. On November 3 he suggested to General Treviño that Villa was headed back to Ciudad Chihuahua. Francisco Murguía, having journeyed to Mexico City to meet with Carranza, had been absent from the frontier during much of October, but he arrived back at his command at the end of the month. Obregón now advised Treviño that Murguía was leading his 6,000 men from Torreón towards Chihuahua.[50] Obregón also took the opportunity to relay a message from Carranza to Treviño expressing the First Chief's displeasure with Treviño's efforts. Carranza

Opposing forces: *below,* Generals Benjamín Hill and Alvaro Obregón with Constitutionalist officers (Archivo Fotográfico, Centro de Estudios de Historia de Mexico, Condumex). *Bottom,* Officers of Villa's Division of the North (AHUNAM, Archivo Octavio Magaña Cerda).

suggested that Villista victories had nothing to do with supply problems. Carranza railed that government troops had not been well commanded and had been surprised by the Villistas in every instance. If government troops were short on ammunition, they should be more vigilant yet more aggressive. They should, wherever possible, take the offensive. The failure of General Osuna at Santa Isabel could and should have been avoided. It made no sense to Carranza or Obregón to divide forces when facing an enemy as Osuna had done when he sent one column to Namiquipa and the other to Santa Isabel. Carranza proposed that "it is not my intention to censure your military operations. Perhaps in your position I would have committed equal or worse errors, but I want to suggest that it was not the shortage of ammunition that caused any of the defeats."[51]

Treviño did not quietly accept the criticism by Carranza and Obregón. On November 4, he responded, saying that it was the first time he had encountered such a complex situation. Mountains and deserts were difficult terrain in which to locate and fight a guerrilla force, and supply shortages were a factor in failures. He advised both Carranza and Obregón that he fully understood their criticisms, but they should realize that ammunition shortages had caused grave sacrifices.[52] He reminded them that he had not plagued them with constant complaints. He pointed out that he had ordered the two columns to split to attack different objectives. Treviño argued that Osuna's column was numerically stronger than the Villistas and Osuna failed only as a consequence of actions by incompetent field officers. Finally, he reported that much of Villa's success came as a result of the United States troops in Chihuahua.[53]

Unfortunately for Villa, General Francisco Murguía, who was apparently more competent than many government generals and had an army of approximately 6,000 to 7,000 men with adequate ammunition, was eager for a confrontation and had occupied Torreón early in November. In discussions with Murguía, Obregón warned him of Villista tactics. In every instance, Obregón advised, guerrillas had attacked stronger government troop concentrations by drawing them into an envelopment. A force of Villistas would attack, then withdraw. Government troops would pursue enthusiastically and would be caught in a crossfire. Obregón suggested that Murguía use the same strategy.[54]

On learning that Murguía had occupied Torreón, Villa turned north to attack Ciudad Chihuahua again. On November 5, 1916, he

General Jacinto B. Treviño (AHUNAM, Archivo Octavio Magaña Cerda).

struck Parral and occupied the town. In early November, Villistas also fought government troops commanded by Generals Maycotte, Riza, Arrieta and Rosalío Hernández (an ex-Villista) at Camargo. Villistas won the fight at Camargo with a strong cavalry charge that sent the government troops running from the field. Villa pursued them for forty kilometers, killing many. The defeat was so serious that government troops had to evacuate Parral and Jiménez. Treviño, aware of Villa's approach to Chihuahua, asked for reinforcements from General Francisco González in command of some of the troops in Juárez. González, however, feared an attack on his position and refused to send help. Facing tenuous communications, among other problems, Treviño advised Obregón on November 10 that "in view of the difficulties of communication" he had stopped sending daily reports to Mexico City. In the future—if communications allowed—he would send one report every five days.[55]

General Pershing, meanwhile, grew more concerned daily about Villa's increasing strength. He reported to General Frederick Funston in San Antonio that Villa had attacked Chihuahua City with 1,700 men, and that despite the 6,000 Constitutionalist troops in the city, Villa enjoyed considerable success. Pershing also added that he had heard that several hundred Constitutionalist soldiers had deserted and joined the enemy. Despite the Carrancistas' deteriorating situation, the Americans were looking for a way to withdraw from Mexico, yet save face. Carranza surely realized this. Early in October, Eliseo Arredondo had stated "emphatically" that international matters "between the United States and Mexico were going well," but Carranza still "energetically defends the interests of Mexico."[56] Mexican sources in the United States reported that Wilson had stated that conditions in the Mexican frontier were improving.[57]

Luis Cabrera, head of the Mexican delegation, and Arredondo, both still in Washington, told the U.S. representatives that Mexico would continue its efforts against Villa vigorously.[58] By this time Obregón and Carranza believed that Treviño was not up to the task of fighting Villa, and they decided to replace him with Francisco Murguía. Obregón ordered Murguía to move north toward Ciudad Chihuahua to take command. In fact, by November 6, 1916, Carranza had named Murguía chief of operations for the state of Chihuahua. He also would have overall command of the northeastern frontier, where his primary responsibility was to stop Villa.[59]

In reports to his superiors, Pershing often commented about the effectiveness of Mexican troops. He once advised General Funston that even Treviño's personal escort had abandoned his headquarters and joined Villa. Funston was somewhat skeptical of the report, although the rumor was often reinforced by other sources. What Pershing sensed, and Carranza probably knew, was that Villa was gaining success and prestige in Chihuahua. Constitutionalist General José Cavazos also believed that Villa was readying for another attack on Ciudad Chihuahua. Pershing believed this, too. He advised Funston that the Carranza government was "completely incapable of suffocating the bandits in the state of Chihuahua."[60]

In truth, Villa's army was growing. Recruits were joining, either because they believed Villa would eventually succeed or to protect their families and villages from his wrath. It was apparent to frontier dwellers that the Carranza government was incapable of sending sufficient numbers of troops to protect the villages. Thus many believed that they had no choice but to support Villa. Surely, some supported Villa's efforts, but that alone would not account for the size of his army. Furthermore, both Villista and Constitutionalist troops had abused local villagers, taking what they wanted without paying for it and attacking and raping local women.

By early November 1916, despite Murguía's successes, Villa's army loomed as a greater threat to Carranza's government and to the United States than it had at any time during 1916. Pershing and other American military leaders believed that the only real option for the United States was to move toward general occupation of Chihuahua, focusing on points from Ciudad Chihuahua to the international border.

CHAPTER 9

THE PUNITIVE EXPEDITION AND THE CONSTITUTIONALIST ARMY: SUCCESSES AND FAILURES

▼▼▼▼▼

The confrontation at Carrizal prompted General John J. Pershing to act more cautiously in deploying elements of the Punitive Expedition. He established his headquarters at Colonia Dublán, and the National Guard troops, called up by Woodrow Wilson to protect the United States border, remained north of the international line awaiting word on the negotiations of the joint commission.

Pershing's troops spent much of their time after July 1, 1916, in camp at Colonia Dublán, cleaning weapons, drilling and playing poker.[1] The army did not officially sanction gambling, drug use or prostitution, but Pershing understood his men sufficiently to allow many things civilians in the United States would not have condoned. The general recognized that drilling the men daily did not keep up morale; other diversions were necessary. In fact, Pershing not only allowed his men to visit prostitutes, he actually organized and policed the service with military physicians. Venereal disease was always a problem, but the general knew that lonely young soldiers isolated from regular society needed an occasional release. The women—Mexican, Chinese and American— were screened by army medical staff. Medics also examined newly arriving soldiers for infection. Although the cases of VD rose during the fall of the year, without Pershing's efforts the problem surely would have been worse.[2]

Despite the fact that the Pershing Expedition was largely idle, Carranza continued to demand immediate withdrawal. He sincerely wished, however, to resolve all "conflict between both countries."[3] Pershing, who had no faith in Carranza's ability to stop Villa, remained committed to the idea that the Americans should occupy Ciudad Chihuahua (and, perhaps, all of the state) in an attempt to stabilize the frontier. He advised General Funston that "in view of the conditions it certainly does not appear probable that the Carrancistas can restore anything like order."[4] Villa's successful attacks on major cities during the fall of 1916, including Ciudad Chihuahua, prompted Pershing to advise Funston on December 9 that Villa probably had 6,000 men in Chihuahua and that the United States should attack him at once. Others shared similar convictions. Consul Alonso Garrett at Laredo suggested that the Villistas were "gaining strength and activity and it looks like they would soon have control over northern Mexico."[5] Although the news was not what President Wilson wanted to hear, he did not order Pershing's Expedition deeper into Mexico.

Villa had recruited a sizeable army by this time, in part through propaganga against American troops in Chihuahua. In October, from San Andrés, Chihuahua, Villa released a manifesto that read, "in order to oppose the unjustified invasion by our eternal enemies, the barbarians of the North, we ought to unite in imitation of that host of valiant men who sacrificed their lives, calmly and smilingly, in behalf of the beloved country which gave us birth."[6] Villa called for all Mexicans to join him in the fight. Actually, he dedicated most of his resources to war against Constitutionalist forces and religiously avoided confrontation with Pershing's men.

Although neither Villa nor Carranza was aware, Wilson had decided by December to withdraw the Punitive Expedition. The United States did not expect to stay out of the European war much longer and needed to be ready for hostilities on land and sea. In the first week of January 1917, Constitutionalist troops defeated Villistas at Torreón, giving Wilson the opportunity to announce that Carranza had the situation on the border under control. The United States prepared to pull out of Mexico.[7]

On January 12, Wilson ordered Pershing to begin the withdrawal. A week later, the army dispatched 170 trucks from Columbus, New Mexico, to retrieve Pershing's equipment. On January 31, 1917, Wilson extended full diplomatic recognition to the Carranza government.[8] On the same day, the European war escalated as Germany announced the resumption of unrestricted submarine warfare. On the morning of February 5, 1917, Pershing—then at Palomas, Chihuahua—began the crossing. With the returning army of 10,690 men were 9,307 horses, as well as 2,030 Mexican, 197 American and 533 Chinese refugees. At the peak of the expedition, 130,000 men were posted along the border to stop Villista raids into the United States and in Mexico. Men of the Punitive Expedition killed about 125 Villistas and wounded another eighty-five after the Columbus raid. Pershing suggested that of the 485 Mexicans who had attacked Columbus, as many as 203 had been killed, 108 wounded, 19 captured. If Pershing's goal was to capture Villa, however, he had failed.

Despite military successes and failures, Wilson lost the war of nerves and time with Carranza. In the process, Carranza probably solidified his

U.S. camp, San Antonio, México, 1916, after the active pursuit of Villa (U.S. National Archives, Washington, D.C., photo #111-SC-81531).

standing among many Mexicans as a result of his posture against the United States.

Complicating matters, on February 25, 1917, British intelligence services passed the infamous Zimmermann Telegram along to Wilson's government. German foreign secretary Arthur Zimmermann had offered Carranza an alliance with Germany. On the defeat of the United States, Mexico could recover territory lost to the Americans during the previous century. Carranza knew, however, that the Germans were bogged down in Europe and would be of little help to Mexico. The First Chief chose to remain neutral. Carranza simply had too many problems at home to get involved in a European conflict.

Early in April 1917, because of Germany's belligerent stance, the Wilson administration declared war. U.S. involvement in the European conflict meant that the threat of war with Mexico was over.

▼▼▼▼▼▼

In Mexico, meanwhile, the Villistas and Zapatistas remained a direct threat to the First Chief's government. Carranza maintained pressure on the northern commanders to be more aggressive against the Villistas. Treviño, in charge of the northeastern frontier until Murguía arrived to assume command, continued to have ammunition, supply and command problems. On one occasion in the fall of 1916, he had asked Obregón for 10,000 serapes—his men were cold and without protection from the elements. Obregón told him he could not help. Treviño told his superior that his ammunition shortages were so severe that his forces were paralyzed and could not launch any offensive actions. On November 2, 1916, Treviño, fearing another Villista assault on Chihuahua, advised Obregón that in spite of shortages he was concentrating troops to defend the state capital. He told Obregón that he had 224 commissioned officers, 1,441 noncommissioned officers, and 4,937 soldiers in Chihuahua. He also reported that there were seventeen officers, 137 noncommissioned officers and 540 troops in Ciudad Juárez. Madera and San Buena Ventura were bases for five officers, seventy-nine noncoms and 445 troopers, making a total of 246 officers, 1,647 noncommissioned officers, and 5,937 troops in his command.[9]

While Treviño planned the defense of Ciudad Chihuahua, Villistas left Santa Rosalía, heading by rail toward Jiménez. General Maycotte in Juárez had already evacuated Jiménez, saying it was of no strategic importance. Maycotte concentrated his men with those of General Murguía at Escalón, where the Constitutionalists maintained a train loaded with light cannon in order to be able to respond quickly.[10]

Murguía was en route to take over command, which made matters worse for Treviño. On November 17, 1916, Treviño had asked that Obregón relieve him at once. Obregón ordered him to remain in command until Murguía arrived, then submit to Murguía's orders. Treviño was humiliated; Obregón was exasperated.[11]

General Murguía began his march north toward Ciudad Chihuahua on November 9, 1916, taking his artillery and infantry by rail and his cavalry overland. He had approximately 7,500 men, about 1,000 of them cavalry. The Villistas had so completely destroyed the tracks south of Chihuahua that Murguía's progress was snail-paced. As of November 20, Murguía also learned that the Villistas nearest to him— just outside Jiménez—numbered about 100 infantry and 1,500 cavalry and four supply trains. Murguía advised Treviño of the situation and urged him to prepare to defend Ciudad Chihuahua again.[12] Murguía reached Rellano on November 19 but was still about forty-eight hours from Jiménez, considering the pace at which his crews were rebulding the railroad. While at Rellano, Murguía learned that the Villistas had broken camp and were heading directly for Chihuahua, destroying more track as they moved north. On November 21, Murguía occupied Jiménez without a fight and rested his troops for two days while crews repaired the track north.[13] Murguía had complained to Obregón the day before that his progress was discouraging, but he was moving as quickly as possible.[14]

Other government columns pursued Villistas in various sections of the frontier. General Carlos Osuna led his men to the area of Casas Grandes, northwest of Ciudad Chihuahua, where another column under

Pancho Villa (mounted at left and facing the camera) watches units of his army ride by (AHUNAM, Archivo Octavio Magaña Cerda).

Colonel Ricardo Cantina was to join him.[15] The combined forces, however, were too far from the capital to help defend the city.

Villa launched his attack during the early morning hours of November 23, but Constitutionalist troops held throughout the day. At 7 P.M., Villa broke off his assault. Treviño felt he had readied for anything, establishing a fourteen-kilometer defensive perimeter around the city with barbed-wire barricades and machine guns and artillery at critical points. Additionally, some of the commanders assigned to defend the city had received their training at the Colegio Militar and Treviño trusted them to be aggressive and competent.[16] When the Villistas pulled back at nightfall, Treviño advised Obregón of his success. On November 24, the secretary of war and marine congratulated him for his defense of the city. Obregón also asked for a complete report on the killed and wounded on both sides.[17]

After the fight, Villa headed north temporarily, while Treviño prepared for a renewed attack. General Murguía, still at Jiménez, learned of

Villa's assault and was ordered to start overland at once to assist in the defense. Obregón told Murguía that, as commander of the northeast region, he should take control from Treviño as soon as possible.[18] Murguía abandoned the rail lines and led his cavalry and 4,000 infantry overland toward Ciudad Chihuahua, leaving 2,500 men under Arnulfo González to complete repairs on the tracks. The column moved slowly and did not reach Santa Rosalía until November 25, then moved on to La Cruz station that afternoon, still several hours south of their destination.

Villa's local intelligence network warned him of Murguía's approach, and on November 24, he launched a vigorous charge on Chihuahua. Treviño, fearing that Villa would encircle the city, withdrew by train on November 27. Meanwhile, on November 26, Murguía moved to Ortíz, about sixty-five kilometers to the south. At Ortíz, he received information from Obregón that Treviño had evacuated. Murguía was to halt his advance until further notice. Obregón advised Carranza that the situation in Chihuahua was extremely grave.

Carranza did not need Obregón to tell him about the gravity of the situation. He had been aware as early as November 22 that conditions were worsening. Carranza reminded Obregón that only 800 men defended Ciudad Juárez and that if Villa captured Chihuahua, he might take his troops by rail to attack the border city. Carranza advised Obregón of the trouble an assault on Juárez might cause with the United States.[19] Treviño had been in communication with Obregón during the battle for Chihuahua, insisting that his men had fought valiantly for four days to defend the capital, and not until they had exhausted almost all of their ammunition did he give the order to abandon the city. Treviño felt that General Carlos Osuna's troops north of the city could keep communications open to the border and preclude Villa from moving that direction.[20] Obregón remained critical of Treviño for abandoning Ciudad Chihuahua. In Obregón's opinion, expressed many times, the reason for the loss was Treviño's unwillingness to take the offensive.[21]

Treviño's retreat from Ciudad Chihuahua once again demoralized his troops and was costly in matériel and real estate—he had abandoned considerable supplies and a city critical to the Constitutionalists.[22] The

Villistas, moreover, had executed the municipal president and other wealthy individuals who did not give them money when they demanded it. Carranza advised Murguía on November 28 and 29 that he should establish headquarters in Santa Rosalía until further notice. Carranza hoped that Generals Treviño and Murguía could soon combine their forces and, together, have sufficient strength to confront Villa. The First Chief also ordered Obregón to send General Luis Herrera, then at Tepehuanes, to occupy Parral and prepare to move to Jiménez. Obregón had anticipated Carranza's orders to move Herrera and had already begun the deployment.

At approximately the same time, Obregón received a message from General Francisco González in Juárez that General Carlos Osuna was organizing a force of some 2,000 men at El Saúz railroad station with the intent of joining Murguía in the south and attacking Villa, who remained in or near Ciudad Chihuahua. González feared that Osuna did not have enough ammunition to contribute strongly to Murguía's effort. González recommended that money be sent from Juárez to Osuna to buy more ammunition from any available source. Obregón approved and advised González to proceed. He also told the First Chief that because he had little control over Osuna, he recommended extreme caution.[23] By this time, Murguía, Osuna and other Constitutionalist commanders had learned that Treviño was thirty-four kilometers north of Chihuahua.[24] Rumors prevailed among the Constitutionalist forces that Villa commanded about 4,000 men. Murguía was not certain of the number, but he claimed that at the time Villa had just over 3,000 men who were widely dispersed, occupying various rail and village areas.[25] Murguía also heard rumors that Villa was intending to continue north to Juárez. On the advice of Murguía, Obregón ordered Treviño to concentrate at Juárez to defend the city and the border.[26]

After the fall of Chihuahua, personal problems—including petty jealously—between Murguía and Treviño led to conflict. Treviño believed that Murguía had not made a sufficient effort to help him during the attack on Chihuahua. Murguía, however, claimed that he had done all he could to move an army by rail, at the same time rebuilding track. His progress north was naturally slow. Murguía also was unhappy that railroad workers had not cooperated with him. He believed the majority were "enemies and obstructionists who had no feelings of patriotism and were only self interested."[27] Murguía again expressed his lack of confidence in Treviño when he advised Obregón that everything Treviño's commanders said or did reflected the discouragement and disorganization of the Army of the Northeast.[28] In later years, Treviño wrote that those responsible for many of the defeats included not only Murguía but also Obregón for not sending reinforcements at critical times.[29]

The animosity between Treviño and Murguía was serious enough to interfere with operations on the frontier. The conflict extended into 1917, when the two men exchanged terse notes. Treviño was aware of Murguía's comments to Obregón and Carranza about Treviño's alleged incompetency. Treviño accused Murguía of "great flippancy in your references to me." Treviño told him, "I have never considered you capable from a military point of view, of estimating the labors of a soldier, who like the undersigned, has always known how to comply with his duty." Treviño accused Murguía of being,

> guided by the first impressions of the moment, believed erroneously, that your capabilities were almost supernatural, and you permitted yourself to be misled by the adulation of a few fatuous fools who surround you, and who, I have been told, have publicly compared you with Napoleon the Great, a thing which has caused much hilarity among all those who heard it.

Finally, Treviño charged that Murguía had a habit of depositing money in United States banks, telling him that Treviño had never

> stained his name with assassinations or despoliation of property; who has been able to remain poor, but worthy, a thing which unfortunately cannot be said of many of his companions in arms....[30]

Murguía angrily replied to Treviño's hostile note:

> considering the vulgarity and reproaches contained [in the message], my first impression was that it was not conceived during

a normal "condition of mind." I should have arrived at the conviction that the said letter was exclusively the result of your tardy pretention to justify your acts, in the complete decadence of your social, political, and military prestige; from your vain attempt to reconquer a false and elusive bombastic prestige, and from the maneuvers of your adulaters and satellites.

To Murguía, Treviño's losses in Chihuahua clearly showed

the scant intrinsic value of your personality from these three points of view, political, social, and military, which you pretend to magnify through salaried writers, who narrated ridiculous and imaginary heroisms.[31]

Despite the infighting, Murguía led his cavalry north.[32] On November 30, 1916, Murguía joined Treviño at Estación Bachimba and advanced toward Ciudad Chihuahua.[33] On that same day, Carranza took steps to alleviate the ammunition shortages that had plagued the northern army. A train from Veracruz headed north carrying 200,000 7 mm and 200,000 30-30 cartridges destined for several frontier commanders. Additional supplies were sent by train from Mexico City.[34] At the same time, Obregón moved to increase troop strength in Chihuahua when he ordered General Manuel M. Diéguez in Guadalajara to send 1,500 infantry and cavalry to the state.[35] On November 30, Obregón also advised Carranza that Diéguez would add troops to those from Sonora and that Sonoran General Plutarco Elías Calles agreed to send men to the troubled state.[36] Finally, Obregón advised Carranza that the production of badly needed cartridges had hit a high of 100,000 in a twenty-four-hour period in Mexico City.[37] While the increase in supplies would help Murguía, the news that Treviño probably lost 4,000 men killed, wounded or missing defending Ciudad Chihuahua and that he had abandoned his artillery and most of his supplies to Villa was disheartening.[38] Murguía learned later that the defeat was not as bad as early reports indicated. Obregón cautioned Murguía that most of Treviño's artillery had, in fact, been taken to Juárez and that troop losses were under 2,000 men.[39]

Murguía remained aggressive against the enemy. On December 1, 1916, his forces fought Villistas at Estación Horcasitas. Murguía's troops first contacted the Villistas at 1 A.M., when units under command of Generals José C. Murguía, Rómulo Figueroa, Helidoro T. Pérez, Pedro Favaela and Colonel Cruz Maltos (often spelled "Maultos") held off a Villista attack in the center and left flank of the government lines. Constitutionalists responded, forcing the Villistas to flee the field. In the six-hour battle, the government troops captured weapons, supplies and 300 Villistas, whom they quickly executed. Murguía claimed that his troops killed approximately 800 of the 3,000 Villistas. Constitutionalists losses were thirty-five dead and 170 wounded. Murguía split his forces, sending some to pursue the Villistas and taking the rest toward Chihuahua.[40] Other minor skirmishes between Constitutionalists and Villistas continued.[41] Villa, with about 400 men, retreated to San Andrés to reorganize.[42] At San Andrés, Villa captured another locomotive and several cattle cars, loaded the artillery taken from Constitutionalist forces in Ciudad Chihuahua and prepared to advance.[43]

Meanwhile, on December 2, 1916, Constitutionalist troops under Colonel Humberto Barros of the Sixth Brigade occupied the capital. Two days later, Murguía arrived with his column. Treviño continued to defend his evacuation of the city and said that he knew nothing of Murguía's approach from the south. Obregón again suggested to Treviño that he should have taken the offensive before running low on ammunition. Reinforcing Obregón's attitude was a message to the secretary of war and marine from Murguía, charging that Treviño unneccessarily evacuated the city. He suggested that Carranza send an investigating committee to look into Treviño's activities. Treviño retorted to Obregón that he had received a message on November 26, stating Obregón would reinforce him later that day. Treviño realized that this was impossible—Murguía was still more than 200 kilometers away. Murguía could not have arrived at the city until November 28 and, by that time, Treviño's troops in Ciudad Chihuahua would have been killed or imprisoned and waiting to be shot. Treviño did not have sufficient ammunition or organization to take the offensive. He could only hope to hold the city until reinforcements arrived.[44] In criticizing Treviño, Murguía and Obregón did not consider crucial political factors. It was critical for the Constitutionalist forces to hold Ciudad Chihuahua to prove to local citizens that the government could provide protection. Treviño did the only thing he could under the circumstances.

After the fight at Horcasitas, Murguía found himself low on ammunition. He incorrectly assumed that Villa was between him and the city of Chihuahua, perhaps advancing south toward Torreón, destroying the rails behind to keep the Constitutionalists forces from following too closely. Villa's plan, however, was to capture Torreón and live off its large government warehouses. He changed his plans and headed northeast out of Chihuahua, recruiting as he moved.

Murguía had an efficient network of spies in the Chihuahuan countryside and learned from them that Villa was concentrating near Cañon de Bachimba to launch a new assault on Chihuahua. Murguía realized that it was urgent to resupply quickly with ammunition and to keep Villa from completely destroying the rails between Torreón and Chihuahua. Carranza responded to Murguía's pleas for ammunition by sending General Miguel M. Acosta to escort an ammunition train from Querétaro at dawn on December 5, 1916. Acosta had 300 men, 2,000,000 cartridges and 1,000,000 pesos to deliver to Murguía. Obregón warned him to travel only by day in the region surrounding Torreón. In the evening of December 7, Acosta arrived at Torreón and prepared to head north.[45] After several fights with Villistas, he ultimately delivered the ammunition.[46]

Unlike Treviño, Murguía was in control of his troops and apparently maintained morale. By early December, Murguía claimed that each day Treviño received requests from his generals to be retired from the army. In Murguía's opinion, this underscored how bad morale was under Treviño. Treviño's men, Murguía thought, were "demoralized and disorganized."[47]

General Severiano Talamantes, who commanded approximately 2,000 men at Torreón, advised Obregón in December that Villa and several hundred men were headed toward the town. Constitutionalist Colonel Juan Gualberto Amaya entered Torreón just before Villa's attack. He found an agitated Talamantes, who asked Amaya to keep his men and artillery there to fight the Villistas. But Amaya had orders to go on to Saltillo. Amaya wrote later that although there were sufficient government troops at Torreón, they were not well led or correctly deployed. Before Amaya could leave, however, he and his detachment were caught in the rapid advance of the Villistas.

Several other Constitutionalist generals were in or near Torreón: Fortunato Maycotte commanded approximately 1,000 cavalry, Luis Herrera had 500 men and Carlos Martínez led several hundred more. All told, there were about 3,000 Constitutionalist troops in the area. Obregón had ordered Murguía south with a column of 500 men.[48] If Murguía received the order, he did not respond. By then Villa was near Bermejillo, moving toward Torreón. On December 20, the commanders in Torreón decided to send General Luis Herrera to Bermejillo to confront the enemy. If the column were successful, it would be at the center of Villista activity. If Herrera were unsuccessful, he would return to Torreón and join other government forces. Problems began at once for the Constitutionalist forces, however. That same day Villa cut all communications between Torreón and Monterrey, Nuevo León, and between Torreón and Durango. General Martínez assisted Herrera at Bermejillo, but the Constitutionalists were forced to retreat. Villa decisively won the battle.

Next, Villa attacked Gómez Palacio, and on December 23, he assaulted Torreón from three directions. In a fierce battle that began at 5 A.M., Villistas killed Constitutionalist Generals Luis Herrera and Carlos Martínez. Villa occupied Torreón when General Talamantes withdrew in disarray. Amaya was caught in the middle of the fight and had to abandon his artillery. Amaya later said that Talamantes awakened him at 3 A.M. on December 22 and warned him that Torreón was almost completely surrounded. There had been a few shots fired during the night, but Amaya was surprised at the debacle that developed. Amaya told Talamantes that the only alternative was to take the initiative and attack the Villistas. Talamantes agreed but told him that General Maycotte would not respond to any request that Talamantes sent. Amaya suggested that even without Maycotte, Talamantes should have taken the offensive.[49] Talamantes did not take Amaya's advice, retreating instead toward Viesca on December 23. He waited two days, then marched to Parras, Coahuila, joining forces with Generals Eugenio Martínez, Pablo Quiroga and Juan Carrasco. Amaya narrowly escaped capture by the Villistas and blamed the government defeat on Talamantes' incompetency.

Talamantes reported to Obregón on December 24, 1916, that— running out of ammunition after fifteen hours of hard fighting—he had abandoned Torreón. Much of the ammunition he had was of poor quality and unreliable, which discouraged and frustrated the men. Talamantes indicated that he planned to recapture Torreón as quickly as he could regroup. Obregón recognized the difficulties and sent General Luis Gutiérrez and his men to assist in retaking the town. Obregón also ordered General Manuel M. Diéguez and his command to join the offensive, placing Diéguez in charge of the military district around Torreón. Obregón then appointed an investigating committee to determine why Generals Maycotte and Arrieta—both of whom he believed incompetent and careless—suffered repeated disasters at the hands of the Villistas.[50]

It was also at this time that General Jesús Herrera, brother of Luis Herrera who was killed at Torreón, advised Carranza that Talamantes was so inept that he was a military liability. Murguía agreed with the charges, accusing Talamantes of "notorious failure of spirit and energy." Murguía told Obregón that he would soon advance from Torreón to Santa Rosalía and Jiménez, where he expected to confront Villa.[51]

Carranza ordered Obregón to look into the charges against Talamantes. Shortly afterward, the governor of Coahuila, Licenciado Gustavo Espinosa Mireles, advised Carranza of Talamantes' incompetence. Carranza decided to call Talamantes to Mexico City. Before he could send the order, however, he learned that Talamantes had committed suicide. Talamantes left a note in which he claimed that General Maycotte had suggested the evacuation of Torreón. Obregón stopped the investigation.[52]

The command problems extended beyond the local level. By the end of 1916, the long-standing difficulties between Carranza and Obregón were becoming more serious and disrupting Constitutionalist military and political unity. Since 1913 Carranza had suspected that Obregón had ambitions to succeed him as president. Carranza needed

Obregón, however, from 1914 to 1916, when the First Chief faced military threats from Villa, Zapata and the United States. As 1917 opened, Carranza prepared for a May presidential election. When the First Chief became consitutional president on May 1, 1917, Obregón resigned as secretary of war and returned to Sonora.

By late 1916 and early 1917, however, the struggle against Villa was far from over. When Murguía learned of the fall of Torreón in December, he dispatched 4,000 men to Santa Rosalía to block Villa from again attacking Ciudad Chihuahua. Murguía then traveled south by rail to inspect the situation at Jiménez. Finally, he sent a column under General Eduardo Hernández, with the help of General Espiridión Rodríguez and Colonel Humberto Barros, to northeastern Chihuahua to deal with the Villistas who had captured government matériel when they occupied Chihuahua on November 27, 1916. The Constitutionalists succeeded in catching up with the Villistas and recovered both the artillery and the locomotive taken from the capital. By the end of December 1916, however, Villa appeared stronger than he had been in the preceding months. His successes had helped him to recruit and he may have had as many as 5,000 fighters.

Amaya wrote later that Maycotte's refusal to cooperate with other commanders was often the reason for government failures. On one occasion, Amaya declared that Murguía, upon learning of the Talamantes episode, said that such "reprehensible" behavior was normal for Maycotte.[53]

On January 2, 1917, the Constitutionalists under Generals Eugenio Martínez, Maycotte and Ernesto García launched an attack against Torreón, Lerdo and Gómez Palacio. Villa evacuated Torreón and the surrounding area and, using the railroad machinery captured in Torreón, moved his men to Jiménez. He then sent the trains to Parral. Next he led his troops overland to confront Murguía, who was advancing south from Santa Rosalía. Villa had approximately 4,000 soldiers, including the hard-fighting Madero Brigade commanded by General Jerónimo Padilla. On January 3, 1917, the two armies collided at the La Reforma rail station. From 9 A.M. to 4 P.M., a bloody battle raged. Several times during the fighting it appeared that the Villistas were on the verge of winning. In the end, they lost the confrontation with as many as 1,500 killed, wounded or missing in action. Villa resorted to a series of cavalry charges against entrenched government troops. Victory was unlikely. Villa's forces were stretched too thin and could not bring sufficient numbers at any critical point to turn the tide. Although Murguía also suffered heavy casualties, his troops occupied Torreón again. Villa fled by train for Parral.

Murguía did not rest on his laurels; he quickly pursued. On January 8, he occupied Parral, capturing Villa's locomotive, rail cars and considerable supplies. Murguía was relentless, sending General Pablo González and his men toward Santa Rosalía, where at approximately 2 P.M. on January 11, 1917, they met and defeated 1,500 Villistas. Villa fled toward Satevó and into the northeastern sierra of Chihuahua. Murguía knew the direction Villa was heading and dispatched two columns of 2,500 men north toward Guerrero. He led one of the columns; General Eduardo Hernández led the other. Hernández traveled by rail directly toward Guerrero, while on January 26, Murguía led his column toward Santa Inés, Mala Noche, Santa Clara and Namiquipa.

Villa again retreated, this time into the Sierra de San Andrés. Murguía ordered General Eduardo Hernández to follow. Hernández's rapid pursuit allowed him to overrun Villa's supply depot where the government troops captured 500,000 cartridges—ammunition that Murguía badly needed. Carranza watched Murguía's progress closely, hoping that the Constitutionalists could finally take control of Chihuahua.

Early in February, Carranza ordered Obregón to move more government troops from Sonora to Chihuahua to reinforce Murguía. Two thousand men under General Guillermo Chávez left Agua Prieta, Sonora, and headed toward Ciudad Juárez. The detachments arrived at Sabinal rail station on March 9, 1917, then moved on to Juárez.

Murguía occupied Parral again during early March, then headed toward El Rosario with 1,800 men because Villa was reportedly there. The two armies met on March 11, 1917. In a battle lasting from 11 A.M. until 4 P.M., Murguía forced Villa from the village, but it was a short-lived victory. Murguía then heard that Villa was expecting reinforcements that would give him an advantage of 4,000 men compared to the Constitutionalist's 1,800. Murguía, recognizing that he faced a serious problem, decided to risk a night withdrawal. Discipline broke down as the government troops marched toward Parral, and Murguía lost as much as one-half his force and much of his supply train. Murguía continued his withdrawal, moving on to Jiménez, then Santa Rosalía and ultimately back to Ciudad Chihuahua, where he prepared to defend the city. Reinforcements from Sonora arrived shortly afterward. Villa's attack came on April 1, 1917. This time Murguía deployed his troops more carefully. He repulsed the attacks and took some 200 Villista prisoners. He immediately ordered these men hanged from trees along Avenue Colón.

Murguía was finally enjoying some consistent successes. The Villistas retreated into western Chihuahua, where they assumed they would be safe. Murguía recognized that he must pursue, however, and on April 18 and 19, concentrated his troops for an attack. Murguía surrounded the Villista camp and in the fight that followed, Villista Generals Francisco Beltrán and Lucio Contreras were killed. Villa escaped by shooting his way through the Constitutionalist lines. He then fled into Durango, where he went into hiding.

Between 1917 and 1920 Villista strength grew at times, but Villa more and more frequently encountered increasing Constitutionalist forces. He finally accepted government peace terms in exchange for hacienda life and an armed bodyguard. Although he was retired from revolutionary activities after 1920, he remained a potential threat to Alvaro Obregón and Plutarco Elías Calles, both of whom aspired to the presidency.

CHAPTER 10

END OF AN ERA

▼▼▼▼▼▼

Although neither the Punitive Expedition nor Constitutionalist forces were able to eliminate Pancho Villa in 1916 and 1917, both Woodrow Wilson and Venustiano Carranza remained dedicated to bringing security to the border region. The attention of both presidents, however, would be focused on growing national and international problems after 1917, and both nations would face considerable violence before the decade ended. By 1920, the United States emerged as a major world power, while Mexico still struggled to consolidate the ideological nationalism prompted by the Revolution.

Carranza faced a difficult agenda, including taking control of the country by eliminating his opposition, shaping the text of the Constitution of 1917 and managing domestic and international affairs. He also hoped to limit, as Douglas Richmond has written, the "individualistic independence" of the army.[1] It would be a struggle for the future president of Mexico. The framers of the constitution met in Querétaro where they approved the document on February 5, 1917. Carranza, however, was not happy with the final draft. The First Chief was not a soldier and cut financial support for the army. He tried to reduce its size by dropping both officers and enlisted men from the active rosters, in the process creating strong antagonism within the military. Alvaro Obregón, who had long enjoyed support of the army, was ultimately the benificiary of a growing revolt against Carranza among the troops.

Carranza also encountered considerable opposition to his policies from the Sonorans—Obregón, Plutarco Elías Calles and Adolfo de la Huerta. The northerners refused to recognize Carranza's declaration concerning water rights and rivers of Sonora, for example. In April 1920, Carranza sent troops to Sonora to seal off the United States-Sonoran border and to enforce his dictates. Obregón, a 1920 presidential candidate, was supported by Calles and de la Huerta, vigorously contesting Carranza's action. Early in April 1920, Carranza tried to jail Obregón, who was in Mexico City to defend himself against charges that he was involved in a conspiracy against the government. Obregón escaped, however, and fled south. De la Huerta and Calles remained in Sonora where they issued the Plan de Agua Prieta, formalizing a revolt against the government. The scheme, which repudiated recognition of Carranza and his regime, effectively established Sonora's independence.

Carranza faced other difficulties. Foes outside of Sonora, as well as the military, continued to oppose him. His enemies accused him and his entourage of enriching themselves through extensive corruption. In 1920, when Carranza tried to place his close confidant Ignacio Bonillas in the presidency, his fate was sealed. With much of the army in revolt, Carranza announced that he would reestablish his government in Veracruz. Escaping Mexico City aboard his private train in early May 1920 and carrying a considerable share of the national treasury and governmental records with him, he headed toward the coast. Unfortunately, he was unable to escape the wrath of his adversaries. They destroyed railroad tracks, attacked his train and forced him to take refuge at Tlaxcalantongo, Puebla. In the early hours of May 21, Rudolfo Herrera, once part of the opposition but now pledged to support the Carrancistas, again turned against Carranza and led an attack on the camp. Carranza died in the gunfight that followed. Some Mexicans accused Obregón and Calles of orchestrating the assassination.

Emilio Zapata, who had never supported Carranza, faced increasing Constitutionalist strength after 1917. Although Carranza's troops never managed to defeat the Zapatistas entirely (they forced them to hide in the mountains), Carrancista Colonel Jesús Guajardo managed to deceive and assassinate Zapata in April 1919.

Pancho Villa, meanwhile, was nearing his end. De la Huerta, who briefly served as president upon Carranza's death, convinced Villa to retire

Left: Venustiano Carranza in death, 1920 (Archivo General de Nación).

Below: A crowd gathers to look at the aftermath of Pancho Villa's assassination, 1923 (AHUNAM, Archivo Octavio Magaña Cerda).

to a large hacienda in Durango. The veteran guerrilla accepted the terms, which included a sizable force of personal bodyguards. As long as Villa remained alive, however, he was a threat to many, particularly to the Sonorans, who thought he would be a major player in the election of 1924. Villa did not have the opportunity. In 1923, while driving his Dodge touring car out of Parral with some of his favorite troops, several men (who later claimed that Villa had shot members of their families), killed him and his guards. The Sonorans must have been relieved.

Alvaro Obregón, who had returned to Sonora in May 1917 when Carranza became president, resigned from the army, strengthened his financial and political power base, concentrated on his business interests and planned his campaign for the presidency of 1920. Duly elected president in 1920, Obregón set out to institute change. One of the organizations he hoped to reform was the army. He tried to professionalize it by eliminating many generals. He also made some progress at implementing the revolutionary Constitution of 1917 but faced resistence from several private sectors. Obregón also learned during his presidency, as Carranza had, how presidential succession could complicate his regime. He wanted to name Calles as his successor, but de la Huerta, former governor of Sonora (then serving as secretary of the treasury), believed he was the logical choice. As a result, de la Huerta led a revolt in 1923 during which approximately 7,000 people died. In the end, Obregón and Calles won. De la Huerta fled to the United States, ultimately settling in Los Angeles. Calles served as president until 1928, when Obregón won election again. On July 17, 1928, José de León Toral, a supporter of the Cristero or Catholic Church rebellion against anticlerical legislation that Obregón had enforced, assassinated the president as he ate dinner at the San Angel Inn in suburban Mexico City.

Other participants in the campaigns of 1916 and 1917 suffered similar fates, while some survived long after the revolution. Francisco Murguía remained loyal to Carranza and continued to fight Villistas though 1918. He was with Carranza in 1920 when Carranza fled Mexico City, and defended him in fights at Aljibes and Tlaxcalantongo. On Carranza's death, Murguía escaped to the United States, but returned to

Mexico in 1922 to fight against Obregón. Obregonista forces captured him at Tepehuanes, Durango, that year and executed him.

Jacinto B. Treviño fought Villistas until Carranza sent him to Europe in 1919 to study the French, German and Spanish armies. In May 1920, he joined Carranza's opposition and retired from the army in 1927. Upon Mexico's involvement in World War II, President Manuel Avila Camacho recalled him as general of division. He held numerous governmental posts until his death in 1966.

While Mexico persevered through the throes of revolution, the attention of Woodrow Wilson and the United States Army focused on the war in Europe. On April 6, 1917, the United States entered the Great War. Wilson named General "Black Jack" Pershing, who had just returned from Mexico, commander of the American Expeditionary Force. For the next few months the United States faced bitter fighting in France, then treaty negotiations with a defeated Germany and finally the start of a post-war isolationist period. Wilson suffered a devastating stroke during the fall of 1919 and, although he recovered sufficiently to walk with the help of a cane, he never returned to full presidential duties before his administration ended in 1921. The voters elected Republican Warren G. Harding president and for the next twelve years the Republicans steered the country on a conservative, isolationist path.

Pershing returned from Europe as leader of the victors. He rose to the rank of general of the armies in 1919 and in 1921 became chief of staff of the army. He retired on September 24, 1924, and died at Walter Reed Hospital on July 15, 1948. Colonel Herbert J. Slocum, who led units of the Punitive Expedition, served in World War I and retired from the army in 1920. Major Frank Tompkins, who campaigned under Slocum, also served during World War I. He retired at the rank of colonel after the war. Tompkins wrote a great deal about his experiences in *Chasing Villa: The Last Campaign of the U. S. Cavalry.* That work remains the most insightful account of the Pershing Expedition. Colonel William C. Brown fought in World War I, retiring after the war. Lieutenant George Patton, although not of note in the pursuit of Villa, was easily the most famous of the officers who accompanied the

Americans into Mexico. Patton remained in the army, served in both world wars and became famous for his aggressive armored campaigns during World War II. In 1945, he died in an auto accident while still in Europe. Many of the other officers and thousands of enlisted troops who had been in Mexico during the 1916–1917 campaign also served in World War I.

NOTES

▼▼▼▼▼▼

ABBREVIATIONS USED IN THE FOLLOWING NOTES:

AGJB: Archivo del General Juan Barragán Rodríguez; Ramo: Ejército Constitucionalista; Subramo: Operaciones Militares, Centro de Estudios sobre la Universidad, Universidad Nacional Autónoma de México

AHSRE: Archivo Histórico "Genaro Estrada" de la Secretaría de Relaciones Exteriores

AJBT: Archivo del General Jacinto B. Treviño: Ramo: Ejército Constitucionalista, Subramo: Operaciones Militares, Centro de Estudios sobre la Universidad, Universidad Nacional Autonóma de México

FAPEC: Fideicomiso Archivos Plutarco Elías Calles y Fernando Torreblanca

FDRM: Isidro Fabela, *Documentos de la revolución mexicana*

INAH: Instituto Nacional de Antropología e Historia

NYT: New York Times

OAR: *Official Army Register*

Per. Ofic. Chi.: *Periódico Oficial del Estado de Chihuahua*

RDS: United States Department of State, *Papers Relating to the Foreign Relations of the United States, 1913-1921*

VCD: Documents, Manuscritos de don Venustiano Carranza, Centro de Estudios de Historia de México, Fundación Cultural de Condumex

VCT: Telegrams, Manuscritos de don Venustiano Carranza, Centro de Estudios de Historia de México, Fundación Cultural de Condumex

PREFACE

1. Some disagreement exists about Pershing's goals. See James A. Sandos, "German Involvement in Northern Mexico, 1915-1916: A New Look At The Columbus Raid," *Hispanic American Historical Review*, 50 (February,

1970), 70-88; Friedrich Katz, "Pancho Villa and the Attack on Columbus, New Mexico," *The American Historical Review*, 83 (February, 1978), 101-130. Wilson probably wanted Villa eliminated. He had decided that only Carranza could bring stability to Mexico. Some United States Army leaders—with the exception of General Hugh Scott, who admired Villa—also wanted to eliminate Villa.

2. See Robert Freeman Smith, *The United States and Revolutionary Nationalism in Mexico, 1916-1932* (Chicago: University of Chicago Press, 1972).

3. See Alan Knight, *The Mexican Revolution*, 2 vols. (Cambridge: Cambridge University Press, 1986) and Alan Knight, *U.S.-Mexican Relations, 1910-1940: An Interpretation* (San Diego: University of California, 1987). See also Charles H. Harris, III, and Louis R. Sadler, *The Border and the Revolution: Clandestine Activities of the Mexican Revolution, 1910-1920* (Silver City, New Mexico: High-Lonesome Books, 1988). This work contains several excellent articles analyzing Carranza's participation in raids and plans involving Mexican invasions of Texas from 1915 to 1917. The authors contend that Carranza orchestrated the activities during both years, first to force U.S. recognition of Mexico before October 1915 and after the Villista attack on Columbus, New Mexico, in March 1916, as a method of keeping pressure on the United States to get the Pershing Expedition out of Mexico. Douglas Richmond agrees in his article, "La Guerra de Texas se Renova: Mexican Insurrection and Carrancista Ambitions, 1900-1920," *Atzlán*, 11 (Spring, 1980), 1-32. This may be an accurate assessment of Carranza's involvement. No specific documentation in Mexico supports the theory. See also James Sandos, *Rebellion in the Borderlands: Anarchism and the Plan of San Diego, 1904-1923* (Norman: University of Oklahoma Press, 1992). Sandos does not believe Carranza orchestrated the movement, but that it was a Mexican-American movement organized north of the border.

4. Mark T. Gilderhus, *Pan American Visions: Woodrow Wilson in the Western Hemisphere, 1913-1921* (Tucson: University of Arizona Press, 1986).

5. Gilderhus, *Diplomacy and Revolution: U.S.-Mexican Relations Under Wilson and Carranza* (Tucson: University of Arizona Press, 1977), 46. This work is an excellent analysis of Wilson's ideology as it pertained to Mexico.

6. Luis Muro y Berta Ulloa, *Guía del Ramo Revolución Mexicana, 1910-1920, del Archivo Histórico de la Defensa Nacional y de otros repositorios del Gabinete de Manuscritos de la Biblioteca Nacional de México* (México, D.F.: El Colegio de México, 1997).

7. Juan Barragán Rodríguez, *Historia del ejército y de la revolución constitucionalista*, 3 tomos (México, D.F.: Instituto Nacional de Estudios Históricos de la Revolución Mexicana, 1985-1986). See also Federico Cervantes, *Francisco*

Villa y la revolución (México, D.F.: Instituto Nacional de Estudios Históricos de la Revolución Mexicana, 1985).

1: CARRANZA, VILLA AND THE UNITED STATES

1. At the time, the army had an authorized strength of 25,000 men. Officers usually reported forty percent more men present for duty than actually were there. The officer in charge got a per diem for each man and could pocket remaining funds. See Edwin Lieuwen, *Mexican Militarism: The Political Rise and Fall of the Revolutionary Army, 1910-1940* (Albuquerque: University of New Mexico Press, 1968). See also David G. LaFrance and Errol D. Jones, eds., *Latin American Military History: An Annotated Bibliography* (New York: Garland Publishing Co., 1992); José María Dávila, *El ejército de la revolución: contribución histórica del ejército mexicano* (n.p., 1938); Luis Garfias M., *Breve historia militar de la revolución mexicana*, (México, D.F.: Secretaría de la Defensa Nacional, 1981); Jesús de León Toral, *El ejército mexicano* (México, D.F., Secretaría de la Defensa Nacional, 1979); Alvaro Matute, "Del ejército constitucionalista al ejército nacional," *Estudios de historia moderna y contemporánea de México*, 6 (1977), 153-183; and Elizabeth Salas, "Soldaderas in the Mexican Military: Myth and Mythology," unpublished Ph.D. dissertation, University of California, Los Angeles, 1987 (published as *Soldaderas in the Mexican Military: Myth and History* [Austin: University of Texas Press, 1990]).

2. A number of books treat the Mexican Revolution. See, for example, Douglas Richmond, *Venustiano Carranza's Nationalist Struggle, 1893-1920* (Lincoln: University of Nebraska Press, 1983); Linda B. Hall, *Alvaro Obregón: Power and Revolution in Mexico, 1911-1920* (College Station: Texas A&M University Press, 1981); John M. Hart, *Revolutionary Mexico: The Coming and Process of the Mexican Revolution* (Berkeley: University of California Press, 1987); Friedrich Katz, *The Secret War in Mexico: Europe, the United States and the Mexican Revolution* (Chicago: University of Chicago Press, 1981); and Friedrich Katz, *The Life and Times of Pancho Villa* (Stanford: Stanford University Press, 1998). For studies of the frontier, see Michael C. Meyer, *Mexican Rebel: Pascual Orozco and the Mexican Revolution, 1910-1915* (Lincoln: University of Nebraska Press, 1967); William H. Beezley, *Insurgent Governor: Abraham González and the Mexican Revolution in Chihuahua* (Lincoln: University of Nebraska Press, 1973); Peter V. N. Henderson, *Félix Díaz: The Porfirians and the Mexican Revolution* (Lincoln: University of Nebraska Press, 1981). Ciudad Juárez and the general border area are treated in Oscar J. Martínez, *Border Boom Town: Ciudad Juárez Since 1848* (Austin: University of Texas Press, 1975);

Oscar J. Martínez, *U.S.-Mexico Borderlands: Historical and Contemporary Perspectives* (Wilmington, Delaware: Scholarly Resources, 1996); Oscar J. Martínez, *Fragments of the Mexican Revolution: Personal Accounts from the Border* (Albuquerque: University of New Mexico Press, 1983); Don M. Coerver and Linda B. Hall, *Texas and the Mexican Revolution: A Study in State and National Border Policy, 1910-1920* (San Antonio: Trinity University Press, 1984); Charles C. Cumberland, *The Mexican Revolution: The Constitutionalist Years* (Austin: University of Texas Press, 1972). For a recent collection of documents, see Douglas W. Richmond, ed., *La frontera México-Estados Unidos durante la época revolucionaria, 1910-1920: Antología documental* (Saltillo: Consejo Editorial del Estado, 1996). See also Daniel Cosío Villegas, *Historia moderna de México*, 10 vols. (México, D.F.: Editorial Hermes, 1953).

3. *New York Times*, March 29, 1914 (hereafter cited as *NYT*).

   For additional information about Villa, see Martín Luis Guzmán, *Memoirs of Pancho Villa*, Virginia H. Taylor, trans. (Austin: University of Texas Press, 1965). It is of interest to read what Luz Corral de Villa said about this work when she was interviewed by INAH.

4. Interview, Gonzalo Franceschi with doña Luz Corral de Villa, Chihuahua, Chihuahua, 1973, Pho 1/23, Oral History Collection, Instituto Nacional de Antropología e Historia (hereafter cited as INAH). This manuscript and many others exist as part of the collection. It is of note that among Mexicans who lived through the Revolution, and many who have studied it, there is a difference of opinion about Villa. For an extremely critical view, see Celia Herrera, *Francisco Villa ante la historia* (México, D.F.: Costa Amic Editores, S.A., 1989, originally published in 1939).

5. Arturo Langle Ramírez, *El ejército villista* (México, D.F.: Instituto Nacional de Antrolopogía e Historia, 1961).

6. For the best treatment of the Veracruz occupation, see Robert E. Quirk, *An Affair of Honor: Woodrow Wilson and the Occupation of Veracruz* (New York: W. W. Norton, 1967; first published by the University of Kentucky Press, 1962).

7. In his attempt to build an effective army, Carranza received advice from many sources. Sherburne G. Hopkins of the United States told the First Chief that proper organization was the key. Hopkins counseled that military history had proven that successful armies required leaders with considerable technical knowledge—men who paid strict attention to detail. Hopkins suggested that Carranza create a general staff to study the problems. Carranza was undoubtedly receptive to the idea, but did not wield sufficient control of the Constitutionalist forces to make such a system work. See Sherburne G. Hopkins to Venustiano Carranza, June 21, 1914,

Washington, D.C., in Archivo de General Juan Barragán Rodríguez, Ramo: Ejéricto Constitucionalista; Subramo: Operaciones Militares, Centro de Estudios sobre la Universidad, Universidad Nacional Autónoma de México, México, D.F., Caja 2 (3), hereafter cited as AGJB. Almost 60,000 pieces are in this collection. In many instances copies of telegrams found in other archives are included in this archive. I have chosen to cite primarily the Treviño, Carranza and Obregón collections rather than duplicates in this file. In instances where a significant telegram is in the Barragán collection, I have used this source.

8. Gutiérrez was born at Ramos Arizpe, Coahuila, in 1881, joined Madero in 1910 and fought Huerta in 1913. He survived the Revolution, dying in Mexico City in 1939. See Pablo C. Moreno, *Galería de coahuilenses distinguidos* (Torreón: Imprenta Mayagoitia, 1967); and Miguel A. Sánchez Lamego, *Historia militar de la revolución en la epoca de la revolución* (México, D.F.: Instituto Nacional de Estudios Históricos de la Revolución Mexicana, 1983).

9. See Robert E. Quirk, *The Mexican Revolution, 1914-1915: The Convention of Aguascalientes* (Bloomington: University of Indiana Press, 1960).

10. Both Villa and Zapata hoped to take control of Mexico, but only for vaguely similar reasons. See Richmond, *Venustiano Carranza*, 64-65.

11. For Zapata, see John Womack, Jr., *Zapata and the Mexican Revolution* (New York: Alfred A. Knopf, 1969). For a more recent treatment, see Samuel Brunk, *Emiliano Zapata: Revolution and Betrayal in Mexico* (Albuquerque: University of New Mexico Press, 1995). An insightful work based upon long study of the Carranza manuscripts at Condumex is Josefina Moguel Flores, *Venustiano Carranza: Primer Jefe y Presidente* (Saltillo: Talleres Gráficos, 1995). See also *Avances historiográficos en el estudio de Venustiano Carranza*, presentación de Alfonso Vázquez Sotelo (Saltillo: Instituto Estatal de Documentación, 1996).

12. Richmond, *Venustiano Carranza*, 66.

13. Smith, *The United States and Revolutionary Nationalism in Mexico*, 37.

14. Katz, *The Secret War in Mexico*, 271-72.

15. Richmond, *Venustiano Carranza*, 84.

16. Katz, *Secret War in Mexico*, 296.

17. For an interpretation of Carranza, see George Wolfskill and Douglas Richmond, eds., *Essays on the Mexican Revolution: Revisionist Views of the Leaders* (Austin: University of Texas Press, 1979). Particularly see Richmond's piece, "Carranza: The Authoritarian Populist as National President," 47-80.

18. For a good picture of Angeles, see R. González Garza, P. Ramos Romero, and J.R. Pérez Rul, *"Apuntes para la historia": la batalla de Torreón* (El Paso: El Paso Printing Company, 1914).

19. Adán Montecón Pérez, *Recuerdos de un villista: mi campaña en la revolución* (México, D.F: n.p., 1967). Luz Corral de Villa agreed with those who complimented Angeles, and she must have heard this from Villa. See interview with Luz Corral de Villa, Gonzálo Franceschi en la Ciudad de Chihuahua, 1973, Pho 1/23 INAH. Copies of all of the interviews at INAH are at the Instituto de Investigaciones Dr. José María Luis Mora in México, D.F.

20. See interview with Federico Cervantes, August 1960, México, D.F., PHO, 1/1, INAH. See also Bernardino Mena Brito, *Felipe Angeles, federal*, tomo 1 (México, D.F.: Ediciones Herrerías, 1936); and Odile Guilpan Peuliard, *Felipe Angeles y los destinos de la revolución mexicana* (México, D.F.: Fondo de Cultura Económica, 1991); and Federico Cervantes, *Felipe Angeles y la revolución de 1913* (México, D.F.: n.p., 1942). See also Matthew T. Slattery, *Felipe Angeles and the Mexican Revolution* (Dublin, Indiana: Prinit Press, 1982); and Felipe Angeles, *Documentos relativos al general Felipe Angeles* (México, D.F.: Domes, 1982).

21. Interview with Práxedes Giner Durán, María Isabel Souza, July 21, 1973, Ciudad Camargo, Chihuahua, PHO 1/75, INAH.

22. Langle Ramírez, *El ejército villista*, 30-32, 122-123. For general information that is somethat reliable, see Dr. Eugenio Toussant Aragón, *Quién y cómo fue Pancho Villa* (México, D.F.: Editorial Universo, S.A., 1979); Victor Ceja Reyes, *Yo decapité a Pancho Villa* (México, D.F.: Costa Amic, 1971); and Luis y Adrián Aguirre Benavides, *Las grandes batallas de la División del norte al mando de Pancho Villa* (México, D.F.: Editorial Diana, S.A., 1964).

23. An interesting discussion of Obregón and his military and personal leadership style can be found in Hector Aguilar Camín, *Obregón: estratego y político: Macbeth en Huatabampo* (México, D.F.: Secretaría de Educación Pública, 1980 [?]).

24. For his interpretation, see Alvaro Obregón, *Ocho mil kilómetros en campaña* (México, D.F.: Fondo de Cultura Económica, 1959). See also Miguel Alessio Robles, *Obregón como militar* (México, D.F.: Editorial Cultura, 1935). Other works on Obregón exist. See, for example, Manuel W. González, *Contra Villa: relato de la campaña, 1914-1915* (México, D.F.: Ediciones Botas, 1935).

25. Montecón Pérez, *Recuerdos de un villista* . For another participant's view, see Juan Bautista Vargas Arreola, *A sangre y fuego con Pancho Villa* (México, D.F.: Fondo de Cultura Económica, 1988).

26. Enríque C. Llorente, Confidential Agent of the Constitutional Government to Sec. of State Ad Interim, Washington, D.C., June 12, 1915, United States Department of State, *Papers Relating to the Foreign Relations of the United States, 1913-1921* (Washington, D.C., GPO, 1915) 812.00/15215, 704-707 (hereafter cited as RDS).

27. Sec. of State to Oliviera de Cardoso, Washington, D.C., June 2, 1915, 812.00/15123, 694-695, Ibid.

28. *NYT*, August 4, 1915.

29. Special Agent George Carothers to Sec. of State, Gómez Palacio, Durango, June 11, 1915, 812.00/15294, 701-703, RDS.

30. John R. Silliman to Sec. of State Ad Interim, Veracruz, México, June 22, 1915, 812.001/15288, 718, Ibid.

31. *NYT*, June 11, 1915.

32. *Periódico Oficial del Estado de Chihuahua*, Ciudad Chihuahua, October 17, 1915, 2 (hereafter cited as Per. Ofic. Chi.).

33. *NYT*, October 9, 1915.

34. Ibid., December 20, 1915.

35. Ibid., October 17, 1915.

2: FIND VILLA!

1. *Enciclopedia de México*, tomo 13 of 14 (México, D.F.: Secretaría de Educación Pública, 1987). Information about Treviño can also be found in General Jacinto B. Treviño, *Memorias*, Segunda Edición (México, D.F.: Editorial Orión, 1961). One has to be careful with this reminiscence. Treviño lived long after his frontier service and sought to defend his record. He omits much of what happened during 1916. See also General Jacinto B. Treviño, *Parte oficial rendido al C. Venustiano Carranza, primer jefe del ejército constitucional, con motivo de las operaciones llevadas a cabo por la Tercera División del Cuerpo de Ejército del Noreste, del 21 de marzo al 31 de mayo de 1915, en El Ebano, SLP* (Monterrey: El Constitucional, 1915).

2. Murguía was born in Zacatecas in 1873. As a young man, he worked as a miner and later in Coahuila as a photographer. When revolution broke out, he joined the Maderistas and, later, the Carrancistas, as they fought Huerta's regime. Both Generals Pablo González and Alvaro Obregón, like Carranza, had considerable confidence in Murguía. Murguía served in Durango and Chihuahua from 1916 to 1918, becoming chief of operations in both states in 1918 with the rank of general of division. He remained

faithful to Carranza and was with him when the president left Mexico City in May 1920. He fought at Aljibes and remained with Carranza at Tlaxcalantongo. After Carranza's death, he fled to the United States, returning in 1922 to participate in a rebellion against Obregón. He fell captive to the Obregonistas at Tepehuanes, Durango, and was executed that year. *Diccionario de Porrúa de historia, biografía y geografía de México* (México, D.F.: Editorial Porrúa, 1964), 1077.

3. Juan Gualberto Amaya, *Venustiano Carranza, caudillo constitucionalista: segúnda etapa, febrero de 1913 a mayo de 1920* (México, D.F.: n.p., 1947), 346. Many other sources exist for the Villista and Constitutionalist armies. I have used most of these in preparing my comments. See Rafael F. Muñoz, *¿Vamos con Pancho Villa?* Quinta edición (México, D.F.: Escasa-Calpe Mexicana, 1984). This work was originally published in 1934. Alvaro Matute, "Del ejército constitucionalista al ejército nacional," *Estudios de Historia Moderna y Contemporánea de México,* 6 (1977), 155-183; Alberto Calzadíaz Barrera, *Anatomía de un guerrero: el general Martín López; hijo militar de Pancho Villa* (México, D.F.: Editores Mexicanos Unidos, 1968).

4. Born in Villa Juárez, Coahuila, in 1886, González was a native of the frontier. He was educated in Saltillo and taught school there. He left teaching in 1913 to join the struggle against Huerta. Francisco R. Almada, ed., *Diccionario de Porrúa de historia, geografía y biografía chihuahuenses* (México, D.F.: Editorial Porrúa, 1968), 230-231.

5. *El Demócrata,* México, D.F., January 4, 1916.

6. Rubén Osorio, ed., *Pancho Villa ese desconocido: entrevistas en Chihuahua,* prólogo de Friedrich Katz (Chihuahua: Ediciones del Estado de Chihuahua, 1990). Interview with Domingo Domínguez Chacón and Francisca Martínez de Domínguez, Pilar de Conchos, Chihuahua, November 11-17, 1979 (hereafter cited as Osorio, *Pancho Villa*). Some documents pertaining to Villa's activities, especially after 1917 but also including materials from the earlier period, are in Rubén Osorio, *La correspondencia de Francisco Villa: cartas y telegramas de 1912 a 1923* (Ciudad Chihuahua: Ediciones del Gobierno del Estado de Chihuahua, 1986).

7. Juan Barragán Rodríguez, *Historia del ejército,* tomo 3, 67.

8. Ignacio Rodríguez to Venustiano Carranza, Ciudad Chihuahua, Chihuahua, January 13, 1916, Fondo XXI-4, telegram in Manuscritos de don Venustiano Carranza, Centro de Estudios de Historia de México, Fundación Cultural de Condumex, México, D.F. (hereafter cited as VCT when the document used was a telegram). General López was captured by Constitutionalist troops in 1917 and was executed.

9. Jacinto B. Treviño to Venustiano Carranza, Ciudad Chihuahua, Chihuahua, January 13, 1916, Núms. 911-912, Archivo de Jacinto B.

Treviño; Ramo: Ejército Constitucionalista; Subramo: Operaciones Militares, Centro de Estudios sobre la Universidad, Universidad Nacional Autónoma de México (hereafter cited as AJBT). General José Cavazos was born in Nuevo León and was a general of brigade in January 1916.

10. *Diccionario histórico y biográfico de la revolución méxicana*, tomo 2 (México, D.F.: Secretaría de Gobernación, 1991); 554-555. See also Jacinto B. Treviño to Venustiano Carranza, Ciudad Chihuahua, Chihuahua, January 13, 1916, XXI-4, VCT. Born in 1892 in Satevó, Chihuahua, Rodríguez joined the revolutionary movement in 1910 and was one of the first men to support Villa. He commanded the Brigada Villa in the Division of the North beginning in September 1913. He opposed Pascual Orozco, Jr., and Venustiano Carranza. He also fought in all Villa's principal battles against Huertista forces and later against Obregón at Celaya, León and Aguascalientes. He followed Villa to Sonora and on to Chihuahua in 1915 and 1916.

11. Venustiano Carranza to Jacinto B. Treviño, Ciudad Querétaro, Querétaro, January 14, 1916, VCT. See also Begoña Hernández y Lazo, *Las batallas de la plaza de Chihuahua, 1915-1916* (México, D.F.: Serie Cuadernos del Archivo Histórico de Universidad Nacional Autónoma de México, 1984). This work contains a few of the documents from the Treviño collection.

12. Jacinto B. Treviño to Venustiano Carranza, Ciudad Chihuahua, Chihuahua, January 17, 1916, XXI-4, VCT.

13. *El Demócrata*, México, D.F., January 18, 1916.

14. Charles A. Douglas to Venustiano Carranza, Washington, D.C., January 13, 1916, XXI-4, VCT.

15. Eliseo Arredondo to Venustiano Carranza, Washington, D.C., January 13, 1916, Ibid.

16. Michael M. Smith, "Carrancista Propaganda and the Print Media in the United States: An Overview of Institutions," *The Americas,* 52 (October 1995), 155-174; see also Smith, "The Mexican Immigrant Press Beyond the Borderlands: The case of *El Cosmospolita, 1914-1919, Great Plains Quarterly,* 10 (Spring 1990), 71-85; see also Richard Griswold del Castillo, "The Mexican Revolution and the Spanish-Language Press in the Borderlands," *Journalism History,* 4 (Summer, 1977), 42-47.

17. Arnulfo González to Venustiano Carranza, Ciudad Durango, Durango, January 15, 1916, VCT.

18. Arnulfo González to Venustiano Carranza, Ciudad Durango, Durango, January 1, 1916, Ibid.

19. Juan P. Marero to Venustiano Carranza, Loma, Durango, January 3, 1916, Ibid.

20. Arnulfo González to Venustiano Carranza, Yerbañez, Durango, January 6, 1916, Ibid.

21. Luis Gutiérrez to Venustiano Carranza, Torreón, Coahuila, January 10, 1916, Ibid.

22. Luis Herrera to Venustiano Carranza, Ciudad Chihuahua, Chihuahua, February 15, 1916, Ibid.

23. Alvaro Obregón to Venustiano Carranza, Monterrey, Nuevo León, January 6, 1916, Caja 4 (1), AGJB; *NYT*, January 4, 1916.

24. Mariano Arrieta to Venustiano Carranza, Ciudad Durango, Durango, January 28, 1916, AGJB.

25. Thomas M. Catache to Jacinto B. Treviño, Torreón, Coahuila, March 3, 1916, Núm. 1021, AJBT.

26. *Diccionario histórico y biográfico de la Revolución Mexicana*, tomo 2 of 8, 420-421 (México, D.F.: Instituto Nacional de Estudios Históricos de la revolución, 1991). Herrera, born in Hidalgo de Parral in 1877, was another of Chihuahua's native sons. He died in December 1916, trying to capture Torreón from the Villistas.

27. Jacinto B. Treviño to Venustiano Carranza, Torreón, Coahuila, January 22, 1916, no Núm., AJBT.

28. *El Demócrata*, México, D.F., January 25, 1916.

29. Ignacio C. Enríquez to Venustiano Carranza, Ciudad Chihuahua, Chihuahua, January 27, 1916, XXI-4, VCT.

30. *El Demócrata*, México, D.F., January 31, 1916.

31. Ignacio C. Enríquez to Venustiano Carranza, Ciudad Chihuahua, Chihuahua, January 31, 1916, XX1-4, VCT; see also *El Demócrata*, México, D.F., February 10, 1916.

32. Gerzayn Ugarte, Secretario Particular de Carranza, to Directores de Periódicos, México, D.F., February 6, 1916, XXI-4, VCT.

33. *Diccionario de Porrúa de historia, biografía, y geografía de México* (México, D.F.: Editorial Porrúa, 1964), 1185. Ramos was born in Zacatecas in 1891 and entered the rebellion against Díaz in 1911. He fought against Huerta and Villa. In a confrontation against Villa at Cusihuiriáchic in 1916, Ramos was wounded. He remained in the army after the Revolution, serving fifty-one years and rising to the rank of general de división and secretario de defensa nacional.

34. Gabriel Gavira, *Gabriel Gavira, general de brigada, su actuación político-militar revolucionaria*, segunda edición (México, D.F.: Talleres Tipográficos de S.A. del Bosque, 1933). Gavira, born in Mexico City in 1867, had long been a

supporter of the Revolution. Educated in the industrial arts, Gavira was one of the founders of the Club Anti-reeleccionista in Veracruz. For his opposition to the Porfirato, Díaz had him arrested and imprisoned at San Juan de Ulúa. Upon release, he ultimately joined Carranza and fought with Obregón against Villa in 1915 and later. See also *El Demócrata* (México, D.F.), February 13, 1916.

35. Jacinto B. Treviño to Venustiano Carranza, Piedras Negras, Coahuila, February 20, 1916, Núm. 1013, AJBT.

36. Venustiano Carranza to Luis Gutiérrez, Celaya, Guanajuato, February 29, 1916, in Isidrio Fabela, *Documentos de la revolución mexicana,* XII, *Expedición Punitiva,* I, Núms. 1, 13 (México, D.F.: Instituto Nacional de Estudios Históricos de la Revolución Mexicana, 1967; hereafter cited as FDRM).

37. Ignacio C. Enríquez to Juan Barragán, Ciudad Chihuahua, Chihuahua, February 21, 1916, XXI-4, VCT. See also Enríquez to Venustiano Carranza, Ciudad Chihuahua, Chihuahua, February 23, 1916, Ibid.

38. Francisco Murguía to Venustiano Carranza, Ciudad Durango, Durango, February 24, 1916, Ibid.

39. Francisco Murguía to Venustiano Carranza, Ciudad Durango, Durango, February 28, 1916, Ibid.

40. Francisco Murguía to Venustiano Carranza, Ciudad Durango, Durango, February 18, 1916, Ibid.

41. Barragán Rodríguez, *Historia del ejército,* tomo 3, 80.

3: THE RAID ON COLUMBUS

1. Several sources deal with Villa's attack on Columbus, New Mexico. They vary in length and in quality. Carranza was angry at U.S. violation of Mexican sovereignty, and he insisted from the first U.S. troop crossing of the border that the U.S. get its troops out of Mexico. See the following: Alberto Salinas Carranza, *La Expedición Punitiva,* segunda edición (México, D.F.: Ediciones Botas, 1937). Most of the works written in English are based rather heavily upon Colonel Frank Tompkins, *Chasing Villa: The Last Campaign of the U.S. Cavalry* (Harrisburg: Military Services Publishing Co., 1934), which was reprinted with an introduction by Louis R. Sadler by High-Lonesome Books, Silver City, New Mexico, in 1996. Charles H. Harris, III, and Louis R. Sadler have done considerable research on the Punitive Expedition. See also Harry Aubrey Toulmin, *With Pershing in Mexico* (Harrisburg: Military Services Publishing Co., 1935); Haldeen Braddy, *Pancho Villa at Columbus: The Raid of 1916* (El Paso: Texas

Western Press, 1965); Braddy, *The Cock of the Walk: The Legend of Pancho Villa* (Albuquerque: University of New Mexico Press, 1955); Braddy, *The Paradox of Pancho Villa* (El Paso: Texas Western Press, 1978); Clarence C. Clendenen, *Blood on the Border: The United States Army and the Mexican Irregulars* (New York: The Macmillan Co., 1969); Clendenen, *The United States and Pancho Villa: A Study in Unconventional Diplomacy* (Ithaca: Cornell University Press, 1961); Herbert Malloy Mason, Jr., *The Great Pursuit* (New York: Random House, 1970); John S.D. Eisenhower, *Intervention! The United States and the Mexican Revolution, 1913-1917* (New York: W.W. Norton and Co., 1993); Manuel A. Machado, Jr., *Centaur of the North: Francisco Villa, the Mexican Revolution, and Northern Mexico* (Austin: Eakin Press, 1988). See also Paul J. Vanderwood and Frank N. Samponaro, *Border Fury: A Picture Postcard Record of Mexico's Revolution and U. S. War Preparedness, 1910-1917* (Albuquerque: University of New Mexico Press, 1988), Samporano and Vanderwood, *War Scare on the Rio Grande: Robert Runyon's Photographs of the Border Conflict, 1913-1916* (Austin: Texas State Historical Association, 1992) and José Angel Aguilar, ed., *En el centenario del nacimiento de Francisco Villa* (México, D.F.: Instituto Nacional de Estudios Históricos de la Revolución Mexicana, 1978). For well-researched and insightful articles on this topic, see James A. Sandos, "Pancho Villa and American Security: Woodrow Wilson's Mexican Diplomacy Reconsidered," *Journal of Latin American Studies*, 13 (November 1981), 293-311; Sandos, "German Involvement in Northern Mexico, 1915-1916: A New Look at the Columbus Raid," *Hispanic American Historical Review*, 50 (February, 1970), 70-88; Friedrich Katz, "Pancho Villa and the Attack on Columbus, New Mexico," *American Historical Review*, 83 (February, 1978). See also Katz, *The Life and Times of Pancho Villa*. For United States attempts at intelligence gathering in Mexico, see W. Dirk Raat, "U.S. Intelligence Operations and Covert Actions in Mexico, 1900-1947," *Journal of Contemporary History*, 22 (1987), 615-638.

2. Slocum, born in Ohio in 1855, graduated from the United States Military Academy in 1876. He served in the conflicts against Native Americans, graduated from the Infantry and Cavalry School in 1883 and served in the Spanish-American War. The army assigned him in September 1914 as Colonel of the Thirteenth Cavalry. *Official Army Register*, no. 498, AGO, Washington, D.C., December 1, 1915, 194 (hereafter cited as *OAR*).

3. Lucas, born in 1890 in Virginia, was a graduate of the United States Military Academy class of 1911. Trained as an artillery officer, Lucas saw service in both world wars. *Marquis Who Was Who in American History— The Military* (Chicago: Marquis Who's Who, Inc., 1976), 340.

4. Castleman, born in Kentucky in 1877, enlisted in the army as a private in 1898 to fight in the Spanish-American War. He was commissioned second

lieutenant of infantry in February 1901. He later fought in the Philippines and was assigned to the Thirteenth Cavalry in March 1915. *OAR*, no. 498, 196.

5. *NYT*, March 10, 1916.

6. Tompkins, born in Washington, D.C., in 1868, received his commission from New York State in 1891. He graduated from the Infantry and Cavalry School in 1897, served in the Spanish-American War and in the Philippines, and was assigned as a major in the Thirteenth Cavalry in May 1915. *OAR*, Núm. 498, 194.

7. Smyser, born in Pennsylvania in 1882, enlisted as a private in a Pennsylvania regiment to fight in the Spanish-American War. In 1901 he received an appointment as second lieutenant in the Fourteenth Cavalry. In August 1915 he was assigned to the Thirteenth Cavalry as a captain. Ibid., 195.

8. Tompkins, *Chasing Villa*, 56.

9. For General Funston's attitude about the raid on Columbus, see Frederick Funston to Army Adjutant General, San Antonio, Texas, March 10, 1916, 812.00/17396, 482, RDS.

10. *NYT*, March 10, 1916.

11. Deputy Collector Cobb to Sec. of State, El Paso, Texas, March 9, 1916, 812.00/17377, 480, RDS.

12. *NYT*, March 11, 1916.

13. Ibid.

14. Ibid., March 10, 1916.

15. Ibid.

16. Plutarco Elías Calles to Venustiano Carranza, Agua Prieta, Sonora, March 9, 1916, FDRM.

17. Venustiano Carranza to Eliseo Arredondo, Ciudad Querétaro, Querétaro, March 11, 1916, 812.00/17501, 486, RDS.

18. See United States Senate Concurrent Resolution #17, 64th Cong., 1st Sess., relating to Wilson's decision and congressional expressions of support, 492, 1916, RDS.

19. *NYT*, March 11, 1916.

20. *La Opinión*, México, D.F., March 11, 1916, in Special Agent Belt to the Sec. of State, Ciudad Querétaro, Querétaro, March 12, 1916, 812.00/17458, 487, RDS.

21. *NYT*, March 11, 1916.

22. Hugh Lenox Scott, *Some Memories of a Soldier* (New York: Century, 1928), 516.

23. Ibid., 523.

24. Katz, *The Secret War in Mexico*, 331–338.

25. For Pershing's career, see Frank E. Vandiver, *Black Jack: The Life and Times of John J. Pershing*, 2 vols. (College Station: Texas A&M University Press, 1977).

26. *NYT*, March 16, 1916.

27. See the Katz–Sandos exchange in "Communications," *American Historical Review* (January, 1979), 304–307.

4: THE PUNITIVE EXPEDITION

1. On July 28, 1866, Congress had provided for the creation of two regiments of cavalry and two regiments of infantry to be comprised of African American soldiers with white officers in command. One was the Tenth, originally under command of Colonel Benjamin H. Grierson. See Major E. L. N. Glass, ed., *The History of the Tenth Cavalry, 1866-1921*, 2nd ed., introduction by John M. Carroll (Fort Collins, Colorado: The Old Army Press, 1972). See also William H. Leckie, *The Buffalo Soldiers* (Norman: University of Oklahoma Press, 1967).

2. Tompkins, *Chasing Villa*, 74.

3. *NYT*, March 21, 1916.

4. Ibid., March 23, 1916.

5. Ibid., March 23, 1916.

6. Tompkins, *Chasing Villa*, 78.

7. Ibid., 79. On seeing the condition of the train, Pershing became angry at the El Paso & Southwestern Railroad that had sent rolling stock in such poor condition.

8. Brown, born in Minnesota in 1854, graduated from the United States Military Academy in 1877. *Marquis Who Was Who*, 69.

9. Evans, born in Maryland in 1866, graduated from the United States Military Academy in 1887. *OAR*, Doc. 498, 180.

10. *NYT*, March 24, 1916.

11. Tompkins, *Chasing Villa*, 91.

12. Dodd, born in Pennsylvania in 1852, graduated from the United States Military Academy in 1876. Marquis, *Who Was Who*, 138.

13. Tompkins, *Chasing Villa*, 94.

14. Ibid., 97.

15. *NYT*, March 29, 1916.

16. Ibid., March 31, 1916.

17. Ibid., April 1, 1916.

18. Ibid., March 28, 1916.

19. Ibid., April 2, 1916.

20. Tompkins, *Chasing Villa*, 110.

21. Patton, well known for his expoits during World War II, was born in San Gabriel, California, in 1885. He graduated from the United States Military Academy in 1909. He served as a cavalry officer in several assignments before convincing Pershing that he should take him along on the Punitive Expedition. Patton's attitude and actions foreshadowed his later aggressiveness in battle. He served in World War I and witnessed some of the first tank battles in history. After the conflict he continued his interest in armored warfare. Much has been written about Patton. See, for example, Martin Blumenson, *The Patton Papers, 1885-1940* (Boston: Houghton-Mifflin, 1972) and *The National Cyclopaedia of American Biography*, vol. 38 (New York: James T. White & Co., 1951), 18-20.

22. Young, born in Kentucky in 1864, was appointed to the United States Military academy in 1884 and graduated in 1889. He was the third African American to graduate from West Point and was commissioned in the Tenth Cavalry. He also served with the Ohio Ninth Regiment in Cuba during the Spanish-American War. Assigned to the Tenth Cavalry for the Punitive Expedition, Young demonstrated his abilities in skirmishes with Villistas. Harry A. Ploski and Roscoe C. Brown, Jr., eds., *The Negro Almanac* (New York: Bellwelther Publishing Co., 1966).

23. Tompkins, *Chasing Villa*, 110, 145. See also RG-395, Entry 1201, April 1, 1916, Overseas Operations, National Archives and Record Services, Washington, D.C., for much of this detail.

24. Ibid., 148-149.

25. *NYT*, April 15, 1916.

26. Ibid., April 14, 1916.

27. Marion Letcher to Edwards, Office of the Sec. of State, El Paso, Texas, April 16, 812.00/17886, 520-521, RDS.

28. *NYT*, April 17, 1916.

29. Sec. of War to Sec. of State, Washington, D.C., April 21, 1916, 812.00/17952, 526-527, RDS. Several enclosures are in this file.

30. *NYT*, April 14, 1916.

31. Ibid., April 18, 1916.

32. Tompkins, *Chasing Villa*, 172, 192-195.

33. *NYT*, April, 22, 23, 24, 1916.

34. Adjutant General of the Army to General Hugh L. Scott and General Frederick Funston, Washington, D.C., April 28, 1916, 812.00/18003, 530-532, RDS.

35. *NYT*, April 24 and May 4, 1916.

5: THE CONSTITUTIONALIST ARMY

1. Sec. of State to Eliseo Arredondo, Mexican Ambassador, Washington, D.C., July 21, 1916, Expediente 7-9-14, IV, "Incidente Columbus," Archivo Histórico "Genaro Estrada," Secretaría de Relaciones Exteriores, México, D.F. (hereafter cited as AHSRE).

2. Venustiano Carranza to Luis Gutiérrez, Celaya, Guanajuato, March 10, 1916, Núm. 16, 45, FDRM.

3. *El Demócrata*, México, D.F., March 5, 16, 17, 1916.

4. Venustiano Carranza to Manuel M. Diéguez, Celaya, Guanajuato, March 11, 1916, Núms. 20, 60. FDRM.

5. Diéguez, born in 1874, was a native of Guadalajara. He was a miner who organized strikes against the Díaz government. He joined Madero's rebellion in 1911, unwisely opposed Obregón in 1923, and was captured and executed by the Obregonistas in 1924. *Enciclopedia de México*, tomo 3 of 14 (México, D.F., 1968), 487. Carranza's attitude toward war with the United States was clear. See "Revolución mexicana durante los años de 1910 a 1920. Informaciones diversas de la República y las oficinas de México en el exterior," L-E-798 (5), AHSRE.

6. Venustiano Carranza to Plutarco Elías Calles, Celaya, Guanajuato, March 11, 1916, "Revolución mexicana durante los años de 1910-1920," L-E-859 (1), AHSRE.

7. Venustiano Carranza to Agustín Millán, Celaya, Guanajuato, March 16, 1916, Ibid.

8. Millán was a woodworker by training. He opposed Victoriano Huerta and fought with Carranza. Carranza appointed him to the rank of general of brigade and military governor of his home state of Mexico. He defended Carranza at Aljibes on May 13, 1920, and died in the process. *Diccionario Porrúa de historia, geografía y biografía*, supplemento (México, D.F.: Editorial Porrúa, 1966), 232-233.

9. S. González to Jacinto B. Treviño, Gómez Palacio, Chihuahua, June 10, 1916, Núm. 1261, AJBT; see also Núm. 1009.

10. Fernández was a native of Durango and knew the region well. He continued to fight Constitutionalists long after Villa retired to Hacienda Canutillo in 1920. Barragán Rodríguez, *Historia del ejército*, Tomo 3, 190, 192, 482.

11. Francisco Murguía to Venustiano Carranza, Ciudad Durango, Durango, March 16, 1916, XXI-4, VCT.

12. Luis Cabrera to Charles A. Douglas, Querétaro, Querétaro, March 20, 1916, L-E-859(1), AHSRE.

13. Alvaro Obregón to General Cándido Aguilar, México, D.F., March 24, 1916, LE-792(8), "Revolución Francisco Villa," 542, AHSRE. Villa was a shrewd recruiter. While in El Valle on March 14, Villa called a town meeting to incite the locals to fight the invading gringos. To what extent this type of recruiting worked for Villa is difficult to determine.

14. Juan B. Fuentes to Venustiano Carranza, Ciudad Durango, Durango, March 23, 1916, XXI-4, VCT.

15. *El Demócrata*, México, D.F., March 20, 1916.

16. Andrés G. García, Mexican Consul in El Paso, to Cándido Aguilar, El Paso, Texas, March 26, 1916, L-E-859 (1), AHSRE.

17. Villa might have been shot by one of the recruits he had forced into his army. Later some soldiers claimed that they wanted to kill Villa and join the Constitutionalist forces. The blame for Villa's misfortune, however, could not be traced. Villa certainly would have retaliated had he known of a conspiracy. Cervantes, *Francisco Villa y la revolución*, 541-542.

18. Alvaro Obregón to Venustiano Carranza, México, D.F., May 3, 1916, "Expedición Punitiva," 7-9-14 (111), AHSRE. See also Andrés G. García to Venustiano Carranza, El Paso, Texas, March 29, 1916, XXI-4, VCT.

19. Several of these ideas are explained in Hall, *Alvaro Obregón: Power and Revolution in Mexico*.

20. Colonel Juan Barragán Rodríguez to General Pablo González, Querétaro, Querétaro, March 22, 1916, XXI-4, VCT.

21. Barragán Rodríguez, *Historia del ejército*, 187.

22. Alvaro Obregón to Cándido Aguilar, Querétaro, Querétaro, April 12, 1916, 7-9-14 (11), AHSRE. See also Cándido Aguilar to Eliseo Arredondo, Querétaro, Querétaro, April 12, 1916, Ibid.

23. James L. Rodgers, office of the Sec. of State, to Cándido Aguilar, Washington, D.C., April 18, 1916, Ibid.

24. General Luis Gutiérrez to Alvaro Obregón, Ciudad Chihuahua, May 4, 1916, Telegrams of General Alvaro Obregón, Núms. 83-88, in Fideicomiso Archivos Plutarco Elías Calles y Fernando Torreblanca, 11010501 (8), INV.75, México, D.F. (hereafter cited as FAPEC).

25. Jacinto B. Treviño to Alvaro Obregón, Torreón, Coahuila, April 15, 1916, Núms. 1108-1109, AJBT; see also Alvaro Obregón to General Pablo González, México, D.F., May 1, 1916, in Obregón Telegrams, 11010501-1-8, FAPEC. Mexican division strength was smaller than corresponding units in Europe and the United States.

26. General Arnulfo González to Venustiano Carranza, Ciudad Chihuahua, Chihuahua, March 1, 1916, XXI-4, VCT.

27. Francisco Murguía to Venustiano Carranza, Ciudad Durango, Durango, April 3, 1916, Ibid.

28. Francisco Murguía to Venustiano Carranza, Ciudad Durango, Durango, April 4, 1916, Ibid.

29. Alvaro Obregón to Venustiano Carranza, Ciudad Juárez, Chihuahua, April 28, 1916, 11010501, Exp. 2, Inv. 69, 18, FAPEC.

30. Jacinto B. Treviño to Venustiano Carranza, Ciudad Chihuahua, Chihuahua, May 20, 1916, Núms. 1160-1161, AJBT.

31. Jacinto B. Treviño to Venustiano Carranza, Ciudad Chihuahua, Chihuahua, May 16, 1916, Núm. 1156, Ibid.

32. Alvaro Obregón to Jacinto B. Treviño, México, D.F., May 20, 1916, Núm. 1160, Ibid.

33. Jacinto B. Treviño to Alvaro Obregón, Ciudad Chihuahua, Chihuahua, May 21, 1916, Núm. 1161, Ibid.

34. Timoteo Rodríguez to Jacinto B. Treviño, Esmeralda, Coahuila, May 22, 1916, Núms. 1184-1187, Ibid.

35. Ignacio Ramos to Jacinto B. Treviño, Ciudad Jiménez, Chihuahua, May 19, 1916, Núm. 1159, Ibid.

36. José A. Cavazos to Jacinto B. Treviño, Cusihuiriáchic, Chihuahua, May 21, 1916, Núm. 1183, Ibid.

37. Ignacio Ramos to Jacinto B. Treviño, Ciudad Jiménez, Chihuahua, May 19, 1916, Núm. 1163, Ibid.

38. Alvaro Obregón to Jacinto B. Treviño, México, D.F., May 20, 1916, Núm. 1164, Ibid.

39. Alvaro Obregón to Jacinto B. Treviño, México, D.F., May 21, 1916, Núm. 1166, Ibid.

40. P. Hernández to Jacinto B. Treviño, Parral, Chihuahua, May 20, 1916, Núms. 1168-1172, Ibid.

41. Alvaro Obregón to Jacinto B. Treviño, México, D.F., May 20, 1916, Núms. 1175-1177, Ibid.

42. Jacinto B. Treviño to Domingo Arrieta, Ciudad Chihuahua, Chihuahua, May 26, 1916, Núms. 1195-1196, Ibid. General Domingo Arrieta was a native of Durango, born in 1874 at Canelas. Originally engaged in mining, he organized forces to capture Durango from the Porfiristas. He fought against Huerta and became military commander of his native state during Carranza's presidency. Miguel A. Sánchez Lamego, *Generales de la revolución*, tomo 2 (México, D.F.: Instituto Nacional de Estudios Históricos de la Revolución Mexicana, 1981), 31-42.

43. Jacinto B. Treviño to Gabriel Gavira, Ciudad Chihuahua, Chihuahua, May 26, 1916, Núms. 1197-1198, AJBT.

44. John J. Pershing to Gabriel Gavira, Casas Grandes, Chihuahua, May 27, 1916, Núm. 1216, Ibid.

45. Gabriel Gavira to Jacinto B. Treviño, Ciudad Juárez, Chihuahua, May 27, 1916, Núms. 1216-1217, Ibid.

46. John J. Pershing to Gabriel Gavira, Colonia Dublán, Chihuahua, June 1, 1916, Núm. 1222, Ibid.

47. *El Demócrata*, México, D.F., May 30, 1916.

48. Enrique R. Nájera to Jacinto B. Treviño, Ciudad Camargo, Chihuahua, June 16, 1916, Núms. 1278-1279, AJBT. Nájera was a native of Durango, Durango. In 1914 he was director de los Establecimientos Fabriles Militares and later a senator to the national congress from his home region. *Diccionario histórico y biográfico de la revolución mexicana*, tomo 2 (México, D.F.: Instituto Nacional de Estudios Históricos de la Revolución Mexicana, 1991) 988-989.

49. Apolonio Treviño to Jacinto B. Treviño, Torreón, Coahuila, June 2, 1916, Núm. 1224, AJBT.

50. Jacinto B. Treviño to Venustiano Carranza, Ciudad Chihuahua, Chihuahua, June 13, 1916, Núm. 1267, Ibid. It is interesting that the men were in a bordello. General Pershing had established a system of prostitution for his men. The soldiers evidently complained about the looks of the

women, which might explain why they were seeking new opportunities. See James A. Sandos, "Prostitution and Drugs: The United States Army on the Mexican-American Border, 1916-1917," *Pacific Historical Review*, 49 (November 1980) 621-645. See also M. J. Exner, "Prostitution in its Relation to the Army on the Mexican Border," *Social Hygiene*, 3 (1917), 205-220.

51. Andrés G. García to Cándido Aguilar, El Paso, Texas, June 16, 1916, 7-9-14 (4), AHSRE.

52. Venustiano Carranza to Jacinto B. Treviño, México, D.F., June 15, 1916, Núm. 1271, AJBT.

53. Jacinto B. Treviño to all commanders, Ciudad Chihuahua, Chihuahua, June 16, 1916, Núm. 1273, 1274, Ibid. Zuazua was promoted to general on June 16, 1916.

54. Jacinto B. Treviño to John J. Pershing, Ciudad Chihuahua, Chihuahua, June 16, 1916, Núm. 1272, Ibid.

55. John J. Pershing to Jacinto B. Treviño, Casas Grandes, Chihuahua, June 16, 1916, Núm. 1274, Ibid.

6: CONFRONTATION AT CARRIZAL

1. *NYT*, April 25, 1916.

2. Howze, born in Texas in 1864, graduated from the United States Military Academy in 1888. He served in the wars against the Native Americans, in the Spanish-American War, and with the Punitive Expedition until being assigned to the general staff in September 1916. Marquis, *Who Was Who?* 272. The activities of Howze and his men can be found in greater detail in Mason, *The Great Pursuit*.

3. *NYT*, May 9, 1916.

4. *NYT*, May 7, 1916.

5. Vice Consul William P. Blocker to Sec. of State, Eagle Pass, Texas, May 7, 1916, 812.00/18073, 540, RDS. See also Frederick Funston to Sec. of War, El Paso, Texas, May 7, 1916, 812.00/18098, 542, Ibid.

6. *NYT*, May 8, 1916.

7. Frederick Funston to Sec. of War, El Paso, Texas, May 9, 1916, 546, 812.00/18106, RDS.

8. *NYT*, May 9, 1916.

9. Ibid., May 12, 1916.

10. Ibid., May 10, 1916.

11. U.S. Consul Bowman to Sec. of State, Fronteras, Sonora, May 16, 1916, 812.00/18171, 548, RDS; see also Sec. of Foreign Relations of the De Facto Govt. of Mexico to Sec. of State, Mexico City, May 22, 1916, 812.00/18450, 552-563, Ibid.

12. *NYT*, May 11, 1916.

13. Ibid., May 17, 1916.

14. Frederick Funston to Sec. of War, Fort Sam Houston, Texas, May 26, 1916, 812.00/18258, 564-565, RDS. See also Jerome W. Howe, *Campaigning in Mexico, 1916: Adventures of a Young Officer in General Pershing's Punitive Expedition* (Tucson: Arizona Pioneer's Historical Society, 1968).

15. *NYT*, May 27, 1916.

16. Ibid., June 1, 1916.

17. Ibid., May 30, 1916.

18. Frederick Funston to Sec. of War, Ft. Sam Houston, Texas, June 7, 1916, 812.00/18364, 568-569, RDS; see also Vice Consul Randolph Robertson to Sec. of State, Washington, D.C., June 9, 1916, 812.00/20165, 570-572, Ibid.; see also *NYT*, June 9, 1916.

19. The plan's origins may have been purely Mexican American, with no connections to the Mexican government. But Carranza might have influenced the movement to further his struggle with the United States. Some historians have suggested that Carranza used the cabal to win diplomatic recognition for his regime from the United States or to retaliate for the Veracruz occupation. It may have been part of his military strategy should the United States and Mexico wage war. There is no hard evidence implicating Carranza, but his government apparently did nothing until late 1915 to stop the organizers from taking sanctuary south of the international border. Carranza probably did not have complete control of his military commanders in the border region, and local officers might have acted independently, allowing the movement to continue.

The Plan of San Diego is not of critical importance to this volume, but it was one of the problems that shaped relations between the United States and Mexico in 1915 and 1916. For the most thorough study of the Plan of San Diego, see James Sandos, *Rebellion in the Borderlands: Anarchism and the Plan of San Diego, 1904-1923* (Norman: University of Oklahoma Press, 1992); Sandos, "The Plan of San Diego: War and Diplomacy on the Texas Border, 1915-1916," *Arizona and the West*, 14 (Spring 1972), 5-24. For an interpretation of Carranza's involvement, see Richmond, "La guerra de

Texas se renova," 1-32; see also Harris and Sadler, *The Border and the Revolution*, 71-98. See also Juan Gómez-Quiñones, "Plan de San Diego Reviewed," *Atzlán,* 1 (Spring 1970), 124-130.

20. *NYT,* June 18, 1916; for details of several of these episodes see also, James Linn Rodgers to Sec. of State, Washington, D.C., June 13, 1916, 812.00/18417, 774-579, RDS. See also Sec. of State to James Linn Rodgers, Washington, D.C., June 13, 1916, 812.00/18399, 575, Ibid.

21. *NYT,* June 15, 1916.

22. Frederick Funston to Sec. of War, Fort Sam Houston, Texas, June 17, 1916, 577, 812.00/18544, 577, RDS; see also *NYT,* June 17, 1916.

23. *Per. Ofic. Chi.,* Ciudad Chihuahua, Chihuahua, June 17, 1916.

24. Sec. of State to Sec. of Foreign Relations of the De Facto Government of Mexico, Washington, D.C., June 20, 1916, 812.00/18450, RDS.

25. *NYT,* June 20, 1916.

26. Much information can be found in John J. Pershing, "Report of the Punitive Expedition to June 30, 1916," and "Report of the Punitive Expedition July 16-February, 1917," AGO Records, RG-94, National Archives and Records Branch, Washington, D.C., micro copy in Oklahoma State University Library (hereafter cited as Pershing Report). Boyd, born in Iowa in 1870, graduated from the United States Military Academy in 1896. He served in the Spanish-American War, where he fought with the infantry. In 1903 he was assigned as a captain in the Tenth Cavalry. He was a distinguished graduate in 1912 of the Army School of the Line. See *OAR,* Doc. 498, 181.

27. Ibid., Doc. 1920, 202. Morey, born in New York in 1875, graduated from the United States Military Academy in 1900. He was a distinguished graduate of the Infantry and Cavalry School in 1907 and the Graduate Army Staff College in 1908.

28. For an early telegram about the battle at Carrizal, see James Linn Rodgers to Sec. of State, México, D.F., 812.00/18525, 592, RDS. See also *NYT,* June 22, 1916.

29. Frederick Funston to Sec. of War, Fort Sam Houston, Texas, June 22, 1916, 812.00/18686, 594, RDS. See also Funston to Sec. of War, Fort Sam Houston, Texas, June 23, 1916, 812.00/18686, 594, Ibid.

30. *NYT,* June 22, 1916; see also Eliseo Arredondo to Sec. of State, Washington, D.C. , June 24, 1916, 812.00/18574, 595, RDS.

31. Punitive Expedition, RG-395, Box 70, Entry 1204, Testimony of Corporal William Hogue, National Archives and Records Service, Washington, D. C.

32. Interview, Daniel González, "The Fight at Carrizal," The Clarence C. Clendenen Collection, Container Number 12, Stanford University.

33. C. General de División, Secretario de la Defensa Nacional, Estado Mayor (July 4, 1953), XIII, 9-139, 149-154, FDRM. These documents form the report of an investigation that the Defensa Nacional carried out to clarify some of the points of the Carrizal incident.

34. Frederick Funston to Sec. of War, Washington, D.C., June 25, 1916, 812.00/18916, 596, RDS.

35. *NYT*, June 23, 1916.

36. Ibid., June 25, 1916.

37. P. Edward Haley, *Revolution and Intervention: The Diplomacy of Taft and Wilson with Mexico, 1910-1917* (Cambridge: The MIT Press, 1970), 220-221.

38. Francisco González to Jacinto B. Treviño, Ciudad Juárez, Chihuahua, June 21, 1916, Núms. 1300-1302, AJBT. See also Jacinto B. Treviño to Alvaro Obregón, Ciudad Chihuahua, Chihuahua, June 21, 1916, L-E-1443 (2), AHSRE. Gómez, born in Gómez Farías, Coahuila, and reared in Zacatecas, was a miner by profession.

39. C. General de División, Secretario de la Defensa Nacional, Estado Mayor (July 4, 1953), XIII, 9-139, 149-154, FDRM.

40. Eliseo Arredondo to Sec. of State, México, D.F., June 28, 1916, 812.00/18609. 597, RDS.

41. Jacinto B. Treviño to E. P. Nafarrate, Tampico; García Vigil, Monterrey; Ignacio Ramos, Villa Aldama; Fortunato Maycotte, Torreón; Jesus S. Novoa, Torreón; José Isabel Robles, Torreón; Domingo Arrieta, Camargo; José E. Santos, Parras; Ernesto García, Parral; June 21, 1916, Núm. 1320, AJBT.

42. Cándido Aguilar to Eliseo Arredondo, México, D.F., July 3, 1916, Expediente 7-9-14, AHSRE.

43. Andrés G. García to Venustiano Carranza, El Paso, Texas, undated, unnumbered document filed immediately after document 9774 in VCT.

44. Ramón Arías to Jacinto B. Treviño, Ciudad Chihuahua, Chihuahua, June 21, 1916, Núms. 1321-1323, AJBT.

45. E. González to Jacinto B. Treviño, Gómez Palacio, Chihuahua, June 10, 1916, Núm. 1261, Ibid.

46. Ricardo Antonio Martínez to Venustiano Carranza, Guadalupe Hidalgo, Chihuahua, June 18, 1916, Núm. 9402, Manuscritos de don Venustiano Carranza, Centro de Estudios de Historia de México, Fundación Cultural

de Condumex. These documents are different from the telegrams previously cited (hereafter cited as VCD).

47. Governor of Zacatecas, illegible, to Jacinto B. Treviño, July 3, 1916, Ciudad Zacatecas, Zacatecas, Núm. 1374, AJBT.

48. *El Paso Morning Times*, June 29, 1916.

49. Arthur S. Link and William M. Leary, Jr., eds., *The Diplomacy of World Power: The United States, 1889-1920* (New York: St. Martin's Press, 1970), 89-92. For anyone who wishes to look closely at Wilson's diplomacy with Mexico, see Arthur S. Link, ed. *The Papers of Woodrow Wilson*, 64 vols. (Princeton, New Jersey: Princeton University Press, 1966-1991).

50. For German involvement in Mexico, see Katz, *The Secret War in Mexico*; see also Sandos, "German Involvement in Northern Mexico," 70-88; and Michael C. Meyer, "The Mexican-German Conspiracy of 1915," *The Americas,* 23 (July 1966), 76-89.

7: THE JOINT COMMISSION

1. Cándido Aguilar to Eliseo Arredondo, México, D.F., July 3, 1916, 17-11-185 (1), AHSRE; see also Luis Gutiérrez to Alvaro Obregón, Ciudad Chihuahua, Chihuahua, April 12, 1916, 7-9-14 (1), Ibid., 175-176, and Cándido Aguilar to Eliseo Arredondo, México, D.F., April 12, 1916, 7-9-14 (1), Ibid.

2. Carranza's motives are discussed in Richmond, *Venustiano Carranza's Nationalist Struggle*. See also Josefina Moguel Flores, *Venustiano Carranza: antología* (México, D.F.: Instituto Nacional de Estudios Históricos de la Revolución Mexicana, 1986). Many sources treating diplomacy between the two countries are available. See, for example, James A. Sandos, "Pancho Villa and American Security: Woodrow Wilson's Mexican Diplomacy Reconsidered," *Journal of Latin American Studies*, 13 (November, 1981), 293-311. For the most complete treatment of the United States side of the joint commission, see, Haley, *Revolution and Intervention*; for clarification of the United States' perspective of the diplomatic problems with Mexico, see Gilderhus, *Diplomacy and Revolution*; see also Katz, *The Secret War in Mexico*. Perhaps the best work in Spanish is Luis G. Zorrilla, *Historia de las relaciones entre México y Los Estados Unidos de América, 1800-1858*, 2 tomos (México, D.F.: Editorial Porrúa, 1977). Information relating to the United States and Mexico can also be found in Investigative Case Files of the Bureau of Investigation, 1908-1922; Investigative Records Relating to Mexican Neutrality Violations ("Mexican Files"), 1909-1921 Microfilm Publication M1085, The

National Archives and Records Service, Washington, D.C.: 1982, Roll 863 (hereafter cited as Bureau of Investigation Case Files).

3. Cándido Aguilar to Secretary of State, México, D.F., July 11, 1916, 7-9-14 (5), AHSRE.

4. Secretary of State to Eliseo Arredondo, Washington, D.C., July 7, 1916, in Salinas Carranza, *La expedición punitiva*, 327-328.

5. For general information, see Ricardo L. Vázquez, *Hombres de la revolución: Eliseo Arredondo* (México, D.F.: Ediciones Botas, 1945); Luis Gabriella de Beer, *Luis Cabrera: un intelectual en la revolución mexicana* (México, D.F.: Fondo Cultura Económica, 1984); Fernando Zertuche, *Luis Cabrera: una visión de México* (México, D.F.: Secretaría de Educación Pública, 1988).

6. Cándido Aguilar to Luis Cabrera, México, D.F., August 3, 1916, in Salinas Carranza, *La expedición punitiva*, 333-334.

7. Juan B. Rojo to Cándido Aguilar, New London, Connecticut, September 6, 1916, 7-9-14 (7), AHSRE.

8. Juan B. Rojo to Cándido Aguilar, New London, Connecticut, September 9, 1916, in Salinas Carranza, *La expedición punitiva*, 338-339.

9. Mexican Consul to Venustiano Carranza, New York, June 1, 1916, Núm. 8956, VCD.

10. Juan B. Rojo to Cándido Aguilar, New London, Connecticut, September 18, 1916, 7-9-14 (7), AHSRE.

11. Mexican understanding and interpretation of these events can be found in a special "Informe" that Alberto Pani delivered personally to Carranza at Querétaro, 7-9-14 (13, 14), AHSRE. This document is thirty-six pages long and summarizes all the proceedings that had taken place between the U.S. and Mexican commissioners.

12. Juan B. Rojo to Cándido Aguilar, New London, Connecticut, September 28, 1916, in Salinas Carranza, *La expedición punitiva*, 348-349.

13. "Informe" to Carranza, 7-9-14 (13), AHSRE.

14. Luis Cabrera to Cándido Aguilar, New London, Connecticut, September 12, 1916, 7-9-14 (7), Ibid.

15. Luis Cabrera to Cándido Aguilar, Atlantic City, New Jersey, October 2, 1916, in Salinas Carranza, *La expedición punitiva*, 356-357.

16. "Informe" to Carranza, 7-9-14 (13), AHSRE.

17. Ibid.

18. Luis Cabrera to Cándido Aguilar, Atlantic City, New Jersey, October 7, 1916, 7-9-14 (8), AHSRE.

19. The text of this proposal is in the "Informe" to Carranza, Ibid.

20. Ibid.

21. See the response to the United States in "Informe" to Carranza. See also the proposal of October 27, 1916, also in the "Informe." It is important to note that a number of prominent and influential Americans had valuable investments in Mexico that they wished to protect. William Randolph Hearst, the powerful publisher of newspapers, owned a large ranch near Babícora, Chihuahua, and Albert B. Fall, U.S. senator from New Mexico who also profited from Mexican assets and resources, pressured Wilson to take strong action to protect these properties, as did the American Smelter and Refining Company executives who had investments in Mexico. For information about Hearst, see Lindsay Chaney, *The Hearsts: Family and Empire, The Later Years* (New York: Simon and Schuster, 1981) and Ferdinand Lundberg, *Imperial Hearst: A Social Biography* (Westport, Connecticut: Greenwood Press, 1970).

22. "Informe" to Carranza, (13), Ibid.

23. Alberto J. Pani, *Apuntes autobiográficas* (México, D.F.: Talleres de la Editorial Stylo, 1945), 208-219.

24. Juan B. Rojo to Cándido Aguilar, Atlantic City, New Jersey, October 17, 1916, 7-9-14 (8), AHSRE.

25. Juan B. Rojo to Cándido Aguilar, Atlantic City, New Jersey, in "Tratados y Convenciones," 7-9-14 (8), AHSRE.

26. Salinas Carranza, *La expedición punitiva*, 372-373.

27. Pani, *Apuntes autobiográficas*, 208-219.

28. "Informe" to Carranza, 7-9-14 (13), AHSRE.

29. From the time Wilson first took office, business leaders attempted to convince him that order and stability in Mexico were in the best interests of the United States and that Wilson should secure a promise from Mexican revolutionary leaders that they would protect United States citizens and their property. Wilson had agreed basically with business interests, but his ideology of government operation was more important in shaping his actions. To some extent this explains the motives of the American team during the joint negotiations. These concepts are explained clearly in Smith, *The United States and Revolutionary Nationalism in Mexico*.

8: CARRANCISTAS VERSUS VILLISTAS

1. Jacinto B. Treviño to Alvaro Obregón, Torreón, Coahuila, May 16, 1916, Núm. 1155, AJBT.

2. Francisco Murgía to Alvaro Obregón, Jiménez, Chihuahua, November 23, 1916, Núm. 383, 11010502, FAPEC.

3. Juan A. Mateos to Andrés G. García, Galveston, Texas, July 26, 1916, LE-806-2, AHSRE.

4. Jacinto B. Treviño to Alvaro Obregón, Ciudad Chihuahua, Chihuahua, July 7, 1916, Núm. 1379-1381, AJBT.

5. Matías Ramos to Jacinto B. Treviño, Parral, Chihuahua, July 31, 1916, Núms. 1446, 1447, 1448, 1449, Ibid.

6. Carlos A. Zenteño to Andrés G. García, no place given, July 11, 1916, L-E-806 (2), AHSRE.

7. Luis Herrera to Venustiano Carranza, Parral, Chihuahua, July 11, 1916, XXI-4, VCT; see also *El Pueblo: Diário de la Mañana* (México, D.F.: ano III, No. 627), 1.

8. "Informe to Venustiano Carranza," July 11, 1916, XXI-4, Núm. 9802, VCD.

9. Juan A. Mateos to Andrés G. García, Galveston, Texas, July 26, 1916, L-E-806 (2), AHSRE.

10. Dario F. Cortes to Jacinto B. Treviño, Jiménez, Chihuahua, September 6, 1916, Núm. 1547, 1548, AJBT.

11. Ysidrio Cardona to J. Váldez Leal (of Treviño's staff), Jiménez, Chihuahua, September 7, 1916, Núms. 1549, 1550, Ibid.

12. Jacinto B. Treviño to Alvaro Obregón, Ciudad Chihuahua, Chihuahua, September 15, 1916, 7-9-14, AHSRE. The statement was both untrue and an exaggeration. American troops paid for supplies and generally did not abuse local citizens.

13. Jacinto B. Treviño to Alvaro Obregón, Ciudad Chihuahua, Chihuahua, September 15, 1916, Núms. 6-8, 11010502, FAPEC.

14. Juan Gualberto Amaya, *Venustiano Carranza, caudillo constitucionalista: febrero de 1913 a mayo de 1920* (Segunda Etapa, México, D.F.: n.p., 1947), 348. Villa had decided to attack Ciudad Chihuahua not only to discredit the Carrancistas and demonstrate his support in the state, but also to release Villista prisoners held there.

15. Jacinto B. Treviño to Alvaro Obregón, Ciudad Chihuahua, Chihuahua, September 20, 1916, Núm. 1556, AJBT.

16. Barragán Rodríguez, *Historia del ejército*, tomo 3, 308; Jacinto B. Treviño to Alvaro Obregón, Ciudad Chihuahua, Chihuahua, no date, 11010502, FAPEC.

17. Alvaro Obregón to Jacinto B. Treviño, México, D.F., September 16, 1916, 11010502, FAPEC.

18. Jacinto B. Treviño to Alvaro Obregón, September 26, 1916, Ciudad Chihuahua, Chihuahua, Núm. 39, Ibid.

19. Jacinto B. Treviño to Alvaro Obregón, Ciudad Chihuahua, Chihuahua, September 23, 1916, Núm. 29, FAPEC.

20. See, for example, reports for June 16, 1916, Núms. 9350, 9352, 9353, 9377, 9388, 9393 and 9394, VCD.

21. For information about ammunition, see Núms. 8955, 9112, 8981 of May 18, June 1, June 6, 1916, Ibid.

22. Jacinto B. Treviño to Alvaro Obregón, September 25, 1916, Ciudad Chihuahua, Chihuahua, Núms. 39-41, 11010502, FAPEC.

23. Jacinto B. Treviño to Alvaro Obregón, Ciudad Chihuahua, Chihuahua, September 30, 1916, Núms. 66-68, 11010502, Ibid.

24. Alvaro Obregón to Jacinto B. Treviño, México, D.F., October 4, 1916, Núm. 69, Ibid.

25. Osuna, born at Mier, Tamaulipas, joined Madero in 1911. He served under Murguía and was interim governor of Durango during some months of 1916 and 1917. *Diccionario Porrúa*, Quinta Edición, 2159. See also Jacinto B. Treviño to Alvaro Obregón, Ciudad Chihuahua, Chihuahua, October 6, 1916, Núm. 70, 11010502, FAPEC.

26. Alvaro Obregón to Jacinto B. Treviño, México, D.F., October 14, 1916, Núm. 77, Ibid.

27. Alvaro Obregón to Fortunato Maycotte, México, D.F., October 19, 1916, Núm. 88; see also, Jacinto B. Treviño to Alvaro Obregón, Ciudad Chihuahua, Chihuahua, October 20, 1916, Núm. 93, both in Ibid.

28. Various works exist detailing the part women played in the revolution. One recent example is Ana Lau-Carmen Ramos, *Mujeres y revolución* (México, D.F.: Instituto Nacional de Estudios Históricos de la Revolución Mexicana, 1993).

29. Andrés G. García to Venustiano Carranza, El Paso, Texas, October 3, 1916, XXI-4, VCT.

30. Eliseo Arredondo to Venustiano Carranza, Washington, D.C., October 20, 1916, Ibid.

31. *El Universal*, México, D.F., October 17, October 20, 1916.

32. Jacinto B. Treviño to Alvaro Obregón, Ciudad Chihuahua, Chihuahua, October 26, 1916, Núm. 102, 11010502, FAPEC.

33. Jacinto B. Treviño to Alvaro Obregón, Ciudad Chihuahua, Chihuahua, October 22, 1916, Núm. 99, Ibid.

34. Alvaro Obregón to Jacinto B. Treviño, México, D.F., October 22, 1916, Núm. 100, Ibid.

35. Jacinto B. Treviño to Alvaro Obregón, Ciudad Chihuahua, Chihuahua, October 23, 1916, Núm. 108, Ibid. See also *El Universal,* México, D.F., October 26, 1916.

36. Alvaro Obregón to Jacinto B. Treviño, Cuidad Chihuahua, Chihuahua, October 26, 1916, Núm. 101, Ibid.

37. Jacinto B. Treviño to Alvaro Obregón, Ciudad Chihuahua, Chihuahua, October 27, 1916, Núm. 102, Ibid.

38. General Domingo Arrieta to Alvaro Obregón, Jiménez, Chihuahua, October 27, 1916, Núm. 139, Ibid. See also Boletín Informativo, Núm. 165, November 2, 1916, L-E-806 (2), AHSRE.

39. General Domingo Arrieta to Alvaro Obregón, Jiménez, Chihuahua, October 28, 1916, Núm. 141, 11010502, FAPEC.

40. Maycotte, a native of Músquiz, Coahuila, joined the Madero movement in 1910 and Carranza in 1913. *Diccionario Porrúa*, 1964, 902.

41. Alvaro Obregón to Jacinto B. Treviño, México, D.F., October 28, 1916, Núm. 133, 11010502, FAPEC.

42. Jacinto B. Treviño to Alvaro Obregón, Ciudad Chihuahua, Chihuahua, October 30, 1916, Núms. 147-148, Ibid.

43. Alvaro Obregón to Francisco Maycotte, México, D.F., October 28, 1916, Núm. 133, Ibid.

44. Francisco Maycotte to Alvaro Obregón, Bermejillo, Chihuahua, November 2, 1916, Núms. 217-219, Ibid.

45. Francisco Murguía to Alvaro Obregón, Jiménez, Chihuahua, November 23, 1916, Núms. 377-379, Ibid.

46. Alvaro Obregón to Francisco Murguía, México, D.F., November 24, 1916, Núm. 380, Ibid.

47. Herrera, *Francisco Villa*, 181.

48. Domingo Arrieta to Alvaro Obregón, Bermejillo, Chihuahua, November 2, 1916, Núm. 204, 11010502, FAPEC.

49. Gustavo Espinosa Mereles to Venustiano Carranza, Saltillo, Coahuila, November 2, 1916, XXI-4, VCT.

50. Alvaro Obregón to Jacinto B. Treviño, México, D.F., November 3, 1916, Núm. 222, FAPEC.

51. Alvaro Obregón to Jacinto B. Treviño, México, D.F., November 3, 1916, Núms. 224-225, FAPEC.

52. Jacinto B. Treviño to Alvaro Obregón, Ciudad Chihuahua, Chihuahua, November 10, 1916, Núm. 147, Ibid.

53. Jacinto B. Treviño to Alvaro Obregón, Ciudad Chihuahua, Chihuahua, November 4, 1916, Núms. 226-227, Ibid. No doubt the presence of U.S. troops continued to help Villa recruit, at least to a point. Many people in Chihuahua were willing to fight the Americans but not the Constitutionalists. To a great extent Villa's resurgence in the fall of 1916 was temporary and due in large part to his intimidation of the villagers. Katz in *The Life and Times of Pancho Villa* also explains Villa's recruiting tactics in Chihuahua. Katz suggests that Villa did recruit more effectively while the Pershing Expedition was in Mexico.

54. Alvaro Obregón to Francisco Murguía, México, D.F., November 15, 1916, Núm. 315, Ibid.

55. Jacinto B. Treviño to Alvaro Obregón, Ciudad Chihuahua, Chihuahua, November 10, 1916, Núm. 283, Ibid.

56. *El Universal*, México, D.F., October 2, 1916.

57. Ibid., October 15, 1916.

58. Ibid., October 17, 1916.

59. Ibid., November 6, 1916.

60. Barragán Rodríguez, *Historia del ejército*, tomo 3, 311.

9: THE PUNITIVE EXPEDITION AND THE CONSTITUTIONALIST ARMY: SUCCESSES AND FAILURES

1. *NYT*, July 4, 1916.

2. The following articles are useful in explaining vice during the period. Sandos, "Prostitution and Drugs: The United States Army," 621-645; Exner, "Prostitution in Its Relation to the Army," 205-220.

3. *Periódico Official*, México, D.F., August 5, 1916, Núm. 31, 1-2.

4. John J. Pershing to Frederick Funston, Colonia Dublán, November 21, 1916, 812.00/19867, 613, RDS.

5. Consul Alonso Garrett to Sec. of State, Laredo, Texas, December 28, 1916, 812.00/20172, 625, Ibid.

6. Vice Consul William P. Blocker to Sec. of State, Eagle Pass, Texas, November 13, 1916, 812.00/19848, 615, Ibid.

7. *NYT*, January 3, November 13, 1917. By this time the U.S. had tried everything to eliminate or neutralize Villa, except occupying the entire state of Chihuahua. The research of Charles H. Harris, III, and Louis R. Sadler into U.S. intelligence archives has shown that Americans, with the help of Japanese citizens in Chihuahua, even tried to poison Villa. The attempt failed. See Harris and Sadler, "Termination with Extreme Prejudice: The United States Versus Pancho Villa," *The Border and the Revolution*, 7-23.

8. *NYT*, January 20, January 31, 1917.

9. Jacinto B. Treviño to Alvaro Obregón, Ciudad Chihuahua, Chihuahua, November 4, 1916, Núms. 212, 11010502, FAPEC.

10. Oficina de Información, El Paso, Texas, November 4, 1916, L–E–806 (2), AHSRE.

11. Alvaro Obregón to Jacinto B. Treviño, México, D.F., November 18, 1916, Núm. 339, 11010502, FAPEC; Alvaro Obregón to Francisco Murguía, México, D.F., November 15, 1916, Núm. 315, Ibid.

12. Francisco Murguía to Alvaro Obregón, Rellano, Chihuahua, November 20, 1916, Núm. 344, 11010502, Ibid.

13. Francisco Murguía to Alvaro Obregón, Dolores, Chihuahua, November 21, 1916, Núm. 371, 11010502, Ibid.

14. Francisco Murguía to Alvaro Obregón, Rellano, Chihuahua, November 20, 1916, Núm. 346, Ibid.

15. Jacinto B. Treviño to Alvaro Obregón, Ciudad Chihuahua, Chihuahua, November 18, 1916, Núm. 340, Ibid.

16. Boletín de Información, Núm. 188, November 8, 1916, L–E–806 (2), AHSRE.

17. Alvaro Obregón to Jacinto B. Treviño, México, D.F., November 24, 1916, Núm. 396; see also Jacinto B. Treviño to Alvaro Obregón, Ciudad Chihuahua, Chihuahua, November 24, 1916, 11010502, FAPEC.

18. Alvaro Obregón to Francisco Murguía, México, D.F., November 21, 1916, Núm. 347, Ibid.

19. Venustiano Carranza to Alvaro Obregón, Ciudad Querétaro, Querétaro, November 22, 1916, Núm. 349, Ibid.

20. Jacinto B. Treviño to Alvaro Obregón, Hacienda Horcasitas, Chihuahua, November 30, 1916, Núm. 508, Ibid. See also Jacinto B. Treviño to Venustiano Carranza, Ciudad Chihuahua, Chihuahua, November 23, November 24, 1916, VCT.

21. Alvaro Obregón to Venustiano Carranza, México, D.F., December 2, 1916, Caja 4 (1), AGJB.

22. Andrés G. García to Venustiano Carranza, El Paso, Texas, November 27, 1916, Ibid.

23. Alvaro Obregón to Venustiano Carranza, México, D.F., November 29, 1916, Caja 4 (5), AGJB.

24. Francisco Murguía to Alvaro Obregón, Ortíz, Chihuahua, November 29, 1916, Núm. 489, 11010502, FAPEC.

25. Barragán Rodríguez, *Historia del ejército*, tomo 3, 333.

26. Alvaro Obregón to Jacinto B. Treviño, México, D.F., November 26, 1916, Núms. 409, 11010502, FAPEC.

27. Francisco Murguía to Alvaro Obregón, El Rellano, Chihuahua, November 19, 1916, no number, Ibid.

28. Alvaro Obregón to Venustiano Carranza, México, D.F., December 8, 1916, Caja 4 (7), AGJB.

29. Treviño, *Memorias*, 137. By the time that Treviño wrote his memoirs, both Murguía and Obregón were dead.

30. Jacinto B. Treviño to Francisco Murguía, Monterrery, Nuevo León, March 24, 1917, 812.00\20945, Bureau of Investigation Case File. The materials in this file are translations of letters the U.S. State Department somehow obtained. There may be copies in Defensa, but this author has been unable to get access to them.

31. Francisco Murgía to Jacinto B. Treviño, Ciudad Chihuahua, Chihuahua, May 10, 1917, Ibid.

32. Alvaro Obregón to Francisco Murguía, México, D.F., November 29, 1916, Núm. 483, 11010502, FAPEC. See also Venustiano Carranza to Alvaro Obregón, Querétaro, Querétaro, November 25, 1916, Caja 4, (5), AGJB.

33. Alvaro Obregón to Francisco González, México, D.F., November 30, 1916, Núms. 502, 11010502, FAPEC.

34. Venustiano Carranza to Alvaro Obregón, México, D.F., November 30, 1916, Núm. 503, Ibid.

35. Alvaro Obregón to Manuel M. Diéguez, México, D.F., November 30, 1916, Núm. 512., Ibid.

36. Alvaro Obregón to Venustiano Carranza, México, D.F., November 30, 1916, Núm. 513, Ibid.

37. Alvaro Obregón to Venustiano Carranza, México, D.F., November 30, 1916, Núm. 503, Ibid. See also Alvaro Obregón to Venustiano Carranza,

México, D.F., December 30, 1916, Caja 4 Expediente 5, AGJB. (These are essentially the same documents and they illustrate how duplicates are often in more than one archive.)

38. Francisco Murguía to Alvaro Obregón, Estación Ortíz, Chihuahua, November 30, 1916, Núm. 520, 11010502, FAPEC.

39. Alvaro Obregón to Francisco Murguía, México, D.F., November 30, 1916, Núm. 521, Ibid.

40. Francisco Murguía to Alvaro Obregón, December 4, 1916, Núm. 7, Cuartel General, México, D.F. in, *El Pueblo: Diario de la Mañana* (México, D.F.), December 31, 1916.

41. Barragán Rodríguez, *Historia del ejército*, tomo 3, 337.

42. Francisco Murguía to Alvaro Obregón, Ciudad Chihuahua, Chihuahua, December 7, 1916, Núms. 611-617, 11010502, FAPEC.

43. Alvaro Obregón to Venustiano Carranza, México, D.F., December 3, 1916, Núm. 584, Ibid.

44. Barragán Rodríguez, *Historia del ejército*, tomo 3, 340.

45. Alvaro Obregón to Francisco Murguía, México, D.F., December 8, 1916, Núm. 603, 11010502, FAPEC.

46. Francisco Murguía to Alvaro Obregón, Ciudad Chihuahua, Chihuahua, December 7, 1916, Núms. 611-617, Ibid.

47. Alvaro Obregón to Venustiano Carranza, México, D.F., December 8, 1916, Núm. 608, Ibid.

48. Arnulfo González to Venustiano Carranza [place unknown], Chihuahua, December 15, 1916, XXI-4, VCT.

49. Juan G. Amaya, *Venustiano Carranza: caudillo constitutiónalista*, 358-359.

50. Alvaro Obregón to Venustiano Carranza, México, D.F., December 12, 1916, Caja 4, Expediente 8, AGJB. There is no record that the committee ever supplied a report, but it is possible it remains a part of Obregón's file in the defense archive.

51. Francisco Murguía to Alvaro Obregón, Ciudad Chihuahua, Chihuahua, December 26, 1916, Núms. 626-627, 11010502, FAPEC.

52. Barragán Rodríguez, *Historia del ejército*, tomo 3, 481. Talamantes' inability to command had been evident before the fall of Torreón. The presidente municipal de Torreón had sent a message earlier via the governor of Coahuila to Carranza, complaining that Talamantes could not control his troops. The soldiers had abused local citizens in Torreón, taking horses and supplies, and otherwise violating the civilian population. The municipal

leader asked that Carranza place a more judicious commander over the region. Carranza agreed and ordered Obregón to place the Laguna area under a more competent officer. See Venustiano Carranza to Alvaro Obregón, Ciudad Querétaro, Querétaro, December 21, 1916, Caja 4 (10), AGJB.

53. Juan G. Amaya, *Venustiano Carranza: caudillo constitutiónalista*, 364.

10: END OF AN ERA

1. Richmond, *Venustiano Carranza's Nationalist Struggle*, 226.

BIBLIOGRAPHY

▼▼▼▼▼▼

PRIMARY DOCUMENTS: MÉXICO

Archivo del General Jacinto B. Treviño, Ramo, Ejército Constitucionalista; Subramo, Operaciones Militares. Centro de Estudios sobre la Universidad. Universidad Nacional Autónoma de México.

Archivo de General Juan Barragán, Ramo Ejército Constitucionalista; Subramo, Operaciones Militares. Centro de Estudios sobre la Universidad, Universidad Nacional Autónoma De México, México, D.F.

Archivo Histórico "Genaro Estrada" de la Secretaría de Relaciones Exteriores. México, D.F.

Chihuahua, México, *Periódico Oficial del Estado de Chihuahua.*

Coahuila, México, *Periódico Oficial del Estado de Coahuila.*

Interview with Doña Luz Corral de Villa. n.d. [1973?]. Gonzalo Franceschi, Chihuahua, Chihuahua. Pho 1/23. Interviews from the oral history collection at the Instituto Nacional de Antropología y Historia, México, D.F. (INAH).

Interview with Práxedes Giner Durán, Chihuahua, 21 de Julio 1973, Ciudad Camargo, Chihuahua, Pho 1/23 (INAH).

Interview with Federico Cervantes, México, D.F. August, 1960. Pho 1/1 (INAH).

Fabela, Isidrio. *Documentos de la revolución mexicana: Expedición Punitiva*, vol. 3. México, D.F.: Editorial Jus, S. A., 1967.

Fideicomiso Archivos Plutarco Elías Calles y Fernando Torreblanca. México, D.F.

Labor internacional de la revolución consticionalista de México, Ediciones de la Comisión Nacional para la Celebración del Sesquicentenario de la Proclamación de la Independencia Nacional y Del Cincuentenario de la Revolución Mexicana. México, D.F., 1960.

Manuscritos de don Venustiano Carranza; Centro de Estudios de Historia de México, Fundación Cultural de Condumex. México, D.F.

PRIMARY DOCUMENTS: UNITED STATES

Interview with Daniel González, "The Fight at Carrizal," The Clarence C. Clendenen Collection, Hoover Institute, Stanford University.

Investigative Case Files of the Bureau of Investigation 1908-1922, Investigative Records relating to Mexican Neutrality Violations, 1909-1921, Roll 863, National Archives and Records Service, Microfilm Publications MJ 1085, 1982.

John J. Pershing. "Report of the Punitive Expedition to June 30, 1916," and "Report of the Punitive Expedition July 16-February 1917 in Adjutant General's Office Records, RG-94, National Archives and Records Service, GPO, Washington, D.C. Microfilm copy in Oklahoma State Univerity library.

Official Army Register. Washington, D.C.: Adjutant General's Office, 1915.

United States Department of State. *Papers Relating to the United States Department of State,* 1916.

United States Department of State. *Records Relating To Internal Affairs of Mexico, 1910-1920,* Record Group 59, Microfilm Publications, Microcopy 274, National Archives, Washington, D.C.

"Punitive Expedition." RG-395, Box 70, Entry 1204. Testimony of Corporal William Hogue, National Archives and Records Service. Washington, D.C. GPO.

NEWSPAPERS: MEXICO

El Demócrata, México, D.F.

El Nacional, México, D.F.

El Pueblo: Diario de la Manaña, México, D.F.

El Universal, México, D.F.

NEWSPAPERS: UNITED STATES

El Paso Morning Times

New York Times

BOOKS AND ARTICLES:

Aguilar Camín, Hector. *Obregón: estratego y político: Macbeth in Huatabampo.* México, D.F.: Secretaría de Educatión Pública, 1980.

Aguirre Benavides, Luis Y Adrián. *Las grandes batallas de la división del norte al mando de Pancho Villa.* México, D.F.: Editorial Diana, 1964.

Alessio Robles, Miguel. *Obregón como militar.* México, D.F.: Editorial Cultura, 1935.

Almada, Francisco R., ed. *Diccionario de Porrúa de historia, geografía, y biografía chihuahuenses.* México, D.F.: Editorial Porrúa, 1968.

_____. *La revolución en el Estado de Chihuahua.* Vol. 2, 1913-1921. México, D.F.: Biblioteca del Instituto Nacional de Estudios Históricos de la Revolución Mexicana, 1971.

Amaya, Juan Gualberto. *Venustiano Carranza, caudillo constitucionalista segunda etapa, febrero de 1913 a mayo de 1920.* México, D.F.: n.p., 1947.

Angel Aguilar, José, ed. *En el centenario del nacimiento de Franciso Villa.* México, D.F.: Instituto Nacional de Estudios Históricos de la Revolución Mexicana, 1978.

Angeles, Felipe. *Documentos relativos al general Felipe Angeles.* México, D.F.: Domés, 1982.

Barragán Rodríguez, Juan. *Historia del ejército y de la revolución constitucionalista.* 3 vols. México, D.F.: Instituto Nacional de Estudios Históricos de la Revolución Mexicana, 1985-86. Volumes 1 and 2 are reprints of the original edition published in 1946.

Beezley, William H. *Insurgent Governor: Abraham González and the Mexican Revolution in Chihuahua.* Lincoln: University of Nebraska Press, 1973.

Blumenson, Martin. *The Patton Papers, 1885-1940.* Boston: Houghton Mifflin, 1972.

Braddy, Haldeen. *Pancho Villa at Columbus: The Raid of 1916.* El Paso: Texas Western Press, 1965.

_____. *The Cock of the Walk: The Legend of Pancho Villa.* Albuquerque: University of New Mexico Press, 1955.

_____. *The Paradox of Pancho Villa.* El Paso: Texas Western Press, 1978.

Brunk, Samuel. *Emiliano Zapata: Revolution and Betrayal in Mexico.* Albuquerque: The University of New Mexico Press, 1995.

Calzadíaz Barrera, Alberto. *Anatomía de un guerrero: el general Martín López; hijo militar de Pancho Villa.* México, D.F.: Editores Mexicanos Unidos, 1968.

Cervantes, Federico. *Francisco Villa y la revolución.* México, D.F.: Instituto Nacional de Estudios Históricos de la Revolución Mexicana, 1985.

_____. *Felipe Ángeles en la revolución Biografía (1869-1919).* 3rd ed. México, D.F.: n.p., 1964.

_____. *Felipe Angeles y la revolucion de 1913.* México, D.F.: n.p., 1942.

Chaney, Lindsay. *The Hearsts: Family and Empire, the Later Years.* New York: Simon and Schuster, 1981.

Clendenen, Clarence C. *Blood on the Border: The United States Army and the Mexican Irregulars.* New York: Macmillan, 1969.

————. *The United States and Pancho Villa: A Study in Unconventional Diplomacy.* Ithaca: Cornell University Press, 1961.

Coerver, Don M. and Linda B. Hall. *Texas and the Mexican Revolution: A Study in State and National Border Policy, 1910-1920.* San Antonio: Trinity University Press, 1984.

Cosío Villegas, Daniel, ed. *Historia moderna de México*, 10 vols. México, D.F.: Editorial Hermes, 1953.

Cumberland, Charles C. *The Mexican Revolution: The Constitutionalist Years.* Austin: University of Texas Press, 1972.

Dávila, José María. *El ejército de la revolución: Contribución histórica del ejército mexicano.* n.p., n.d. [1938?].

De León Toral, Jesús. *El ejército mexicano.* México, D.F.: Secretaría de la Defensa Nacional, 1979.

Diccionario histórico y biográfico de la revolución mexicana. Vol. 2 of 8. México, D.F.: Instituto Nacional de Estudios Históricos de la Revolución Mexicana, 1991.

Diccionario de Porrúa de historia, biografía, y geografía de México. México, D.F.: Editorial Porrúa, 1964.

Enciclopedia de México. 14 vols. México, D.F.: Secretaría de Educación Pública, 1987. See also 1968 edition.

Eisenhower, John S. D. *Intervention: The United States and the Mexican Revolution, 1913-1917.* New York: W. W. Norton and Co., 1993.

Exner, M. J. "Prostitution in Its Relation to the Army on the Border," *Social Hygiene*, 3 (1917), 205-220.

Gabriella de Beer, Luis. *Luis Cabrera: un intelectual en la revolución méxicana.* México, D.F.: Fondo de Cultura Económica, 1984.

Garfias M., Luis. *Breve historia militar de la revolución mexicana.* México, D.F.: Secretaría de la Defensa Nacional, 1981.

Gavira, Gabriel. *Gabriel Gavira, General de brigada, su actuación político-militar revolucionaria.* Segunda edición. México, D.F.: Talleres Tipográficos de S.A. del Bosque, 1933.

Gilderhus, Mark T. *Diplomacy and Revolution: U.S.-Mexican Relations Under Wilson and Carranza.* Tucson: University of Arizona Press, 1977.

————. *Pan American Visions: Woodrow Wilson in the Western Hemisphere, 1913-1921.* Tucson: University of Arizona Press, 1986.

Glass, Major E.L.N., ed. *The History of the Tenth Cavalry, 1866-1921.* 2nd ed. Introduction by John M. Carroll. Fort Collins, Colorado: The Old Army Press, 1972.

Gómez-Quiñones, Juan. "Plan of San Diego Reviewed," *Atzlán,* 1 (Spring 1970), 124-130.

González Garza, R., P. Ramos Romero and Rul Pérez. *La batalla de Torreón,* México, D.F.: Secretaría de Educación Pública, 1960 [?]. (Originally published by El Paso Printing Co, El Paso, Texas, 1914.)

González, Manuel W. *Contra Villa: relato de la campaña, 1914-1915.* México, D.F.: Ediciones Botas, 1935.

Griswold del Castillo, Richard. "The Mexican Revolution and the Spanish-Language Press in the Borderlands," *Journalism History,* 4 (Summer 1977), 42-47.

Guzmán, Martín Luis. *Memoirs of Pancho Villa.* Translated by Virginia H. Taylor. Austin: University of Texas Press, 1965.

Haley, P. Edward. *Revolution and Intervention: The Diplomacy of Taft and Wilson with México, 1910-1917.* Cambridge: Massachusetts Institute of Technology Press, 1970.

Hall, Linda B. *Alvaro Obregón: Power and Revolution in Mexico, 1911-1920.* College Station: Texas A&M University Press, 1981.

Hall, Linda B. and Don M. Coerver. *Revolution on the Border: The United States and Mexico, 1910-1920.* Albuquerque: University of New Mexico Press, 1988.

_____. "Woodrow Wilson, Public Opinion, and the Punitive Expedition: A Re-Assessment," *New Mexico Historical Review,* 72 (April 1997), 171-194.

Harris, Charles H., III, and Louis R. Sadler. *The Border and the Revolution: Clandestine Activities of the Mexican Revolution, 1910-1920.* Silver City, New Mexico: High-Lonesome Books, 1988.

_____. "The Plan of San Diego and the Mexican-United States War Crisis of 1916: A Re-examination," *The Hispanic American Historical Review,* 58 (August 1978), 381-408.

_____. "Termination with Extreme Prejudice: The United States Versus Pancho Villa," *The Border and the Revolution: Clandestine Activities of the Mexican Revolution, 1910-1920.* Silver City, New Mexico: High-Lonesome Books, 1988.

Hart, John M. *Revolutionary Mexico: The Coming and Process of the Mexican Revolution.* Berkeley: University of California Press, 1987.

Henderson, Peter V. N. *Félix Díaz, The Porfirians, and the Mexican Revolution.* Lincoln: University of Nebraska Press, 1981.

Hernández y Lazo, Begoña. *Las batallas de la plaza de Chihuahua, 1915-1916.* México, D.F.: Serie Cuadernos del Archivo Histórico de UNAM, 1984.

Herrera, Celia. *Francisco Villa ante la historia.* Quinta edición, México, D.F.: Costa Amic Editores, S.A., 1989. (Originally published in 1939.)

Hill, Larry D. *Emissaries to a Revolution: Woodrow Wilson's Agents in Mexico.* Baton Rouge: Lousiana State University Press, 1973.

Howe, Jerome W. *Campaigning in Mexico, 1916: Adventures of a Young Officer in General Pershing's Punitive Expedition.* Tucson: Arizona Pioneer's Historical Society, 1968.

Katz, Friedrich. *The Secret War in Mexico: Europe the United States, and the Mexican Revolution.* Chicago: University of Chicago Press, 1981.

_____. *The Life and Times of Pancho Villa.* Stanford: Stanford University Press, 1998.

_____. "Pancho Villa and the Attack on Columbus, New Mexico," *American Historical Review*, 83 (February 1978), 101-130.

Katz, Friedrich and James A. Sandos. "Communications," *American Historical Review*, 84 (January 1979), 304-307.

Knight, Alan. *The Mexican Revolution*, 2 vols. London: Cambridge University Press, 1986.

_____. *U.S.-Mexican Relations: 1910-1940: An Interpretation.* San Diego: University of California at San Diego, Center for U.S.-Mexican Studies, 1987.

LaFrance, David G. and Errol D. Jones, eds. *Latin American Military History: An Annotated Bibliography.* New York: Garland Publishing Co., 1992.

Langle Ramírez, Arturo. *El ejército Villista.* México, D.F.: Instituto Nacional de Antropología e Historia, 1961.

Lau-Carmen Ramos, Ana. *Mujeres y revolución.* México D.F.: Instituto Nacional de Estudios Históricos de la Revolución Mexicana, 1993.

Leckie, William H. *The Buffalo Soldiers.* Norman: University of Oklahoma Press, 1967.

Lieuwen, Edwin. *Mexican Militarism: The Political Rise and Fall of the Revolutionary Army, 1910-1940.* Albuquerque: University of New Mexico Press, 1968.

Link, Arthur S., ed. *The Papers of Woodrow Wilson.* 64 vols. Princeton, New Jersey: Princeton University Press, 1966-1991.

Link, Arthur S. and William M. Leary, Jr., eds. *The Diplomacy of World Power: The United States, 1889-1920.* New York: St. Martin's Press, 1970.

_____. *Wilson the Diplomatist: A Look At His Major Foreign Policies.* Baltimore: Johns Hopkins University Press, 1957.

Lozoya, Jorge Alberto. "El ejército mexicano, 1911-1965." Unpublished MA thesis, El Colegio De México, 1970.

Lundberg, Ferdinand. *Imperial Hearst: A Social Biography.* Westport, Connecticut: Greenwood Press, 1970.

Machado, Manuel A., Jr. *Centaur of the North: Francisco Villa, the Mexican Revolution, and Northern Mexico.* Austin: Eakin Press, 1988.

Magaña, Gilardo. *Así nació la División del Norte.* México, D.F.: SEP-Conasupo, 1981.

Marquis Who Was Who in American History: The Military. Chicago: Marquis Who's Who, Inc., 1976.

Martínez, Oscar J. *Border Boom Town: Ciudad Juárez Since 1848.* Austin: University of Texas Press, 1975.

_____, ed. *U.S-Mexico Borderlands: Historical and Contemporary Perspectives.* Wilmington, Delaware: Scholarly Resources Inc. 1996.

_____, ed. *Fragments of the Mexican Revolution: Personal Accounts from the Border.* Albuquerque: University of New Mexico Press, 1983.

Mason, Herbert Malloy, Jr. *The Great Pursuit.* New York: Random House, 1970.

Matute, Alvaro. "Del ejército constitucionalista al ejército nacional," *Estudios de Historia Moderna y Contemporánea de México,* 6 (1977), 153-183.

Mena Brito, Bernardino. *Felipe Angles, Federal.* México, D.F.: Herrerías, 1936.

Meyer, Michael C. *Mexican Rebel: Pascual Orozco and the Mexican Revolution, 1910-1915.* Lincoln: University of Nebraska Press, 1967.

_____. "The Mexican-German Conspiracy of 1915," *The Americas,* 23 (July 1966), 76-89.

Moguel Flores, Josefina. *Venustiano Carranza: Antología.* México, D.F.: Instituto Nacional de Estudios Históricos de la Revolución Mexicana, 1986.

_____. *Venustiano Carranza: Primer Jefe y Presidente.* Saltillo: Talleres Gráficos del Estado de Coahuila, 1995.

Montecón Pérez, Adán. *Recuerdos de un Villista: mi campaña en la revolución.* México, D.F.: n.p., 1967.

Moreno, Pablo C. *Galería de coahuilenses distinguidos,* 2a. Serie. Torreón, Coahuila: Imprenta Mayagoitia, 1967.

Muñoz, Rafael F. *¿Vamos con Pancho Villa?* Quinta edción. México, D.F.: Escasa-Calpe Mexicana, 1984. (Originally published in 1934.)

Muro, Luis y Berta Ulloa. *Guía del Ramo Revolución Mexicana, 1910-1920, del Archivo Histórico de la Defensa Nacional y de Otros Repositorios del Gabinete de*

Manuscritos de la Biblioteca Nacional de México. México, D.F.: El Colegio de México, 1997.

National Cyclopaedia of American Biography. vol. 38. New York: James T. White and Co., 1951.

Obregón, Alvaro. *Ocho mil kilómetros en campaña.* Segunda edición. México, D.F.: Fondo de Cultura Económica, 1959.

Osorio, Rubén, ed. *Pancho Villa ese desconocido: Entrevistas en Chihuahua,* prólogo por Friedrich Katz. Ciudad Chihuahua: Ediciones del Estado de Chihuahua, 1991.

_____, ed. *La correspondencia de Francisco Villa: cartas y telegramas de 1912-1920.* Ciudad Chihuahua: Ediciones del Gobierno del Estado de Chihuahua, 1986.

Pani, Alberto J. *Apuntes autobiográficas.* México, D.F.: Talleres de la Editorial Stylo, 1945.

Peuliard, Odile Guilpan. *Felipe Angeles y los destinos de la revolución mexicana.* México, D.F.: Fondo de Cultura Económica, 1991.

Ploski, Harry A. and Roscoe C. Brown, Jr., eds. *The Negro Almanac.* New York: Bellwelther Publishing Co., 1966.

Quirk, Robert E. *An Affair of Honor: Woodrow Wilson and the Occupation of Veracruz.* New York: W.W. Norton, 1967.

_____. *The Mexican Revolution, 1914-1915: The Convention of Aguascalientes.* Bloomington: University of Indiana Press, 1960.

Raat, W. Dirk. *Revoltosos: Mexico's Rebels in the United States, 1903-1923.* College Station: Texas A&M University Press, 1981.

_____. "U.S. Intelligence Operations and Covert Actions in Mexico, 1900-1947," *Journal of Contemporary History,* 22 (1987), 615-638.

Reyes, Victor Ceja. *Yo decapité a Pancho Villa.* México, D.F.: B. Costa Amic, 1971.

Richmond, Douglas, ed. *La frontera Mexico-Estados Unidos durante la epoca revolucionaria, 1910-1920: Antología documental.* Saltillo: Consejo Editorial del Estado, 1996.

_____. "La guerra de Texas se renova: Mexican Insurrection and Carrancista Ambitions, 1900-1920, *Atzlán,* 11 (Spring 1980), 1-32.

_____. *Venustiano Carranza's Nationalist Struggle, 1893-1920.* Lincoln: University of Nebraska Press, 1983.

Salas, Elizabeth. "Soldaderas in the Mexican Military: Myth and Mythology," Ph.D. dissertation, University of California Los Angeles, 1987.

Salas, Elizabeth, *Soldaderas in the Mexican Military: Myth and History.* Austin: University of Texas Press, 1990.

Salinas Carranza, Alberto. *La Expedición Punitiva.* Segunda edición. México, D.F.: Ediciones Botas, 1937.

Sampanaro, Frank. "The Political Role of the Army in Mexico." Unpublished Ph.D. dissertation, The State University of New York at Stonybrook, 1974.

Samparano, Frank N. and Paul J. Vanderwood. *War Scare on the Rio Grande: Robert Runyon's Photographs of the Border Conflict, 1913-1916.* Austin: Texas State Historical Association, 1992.

Sánchez Lamego, Miguel A. *Generales de la revolución.* 2 vols. México, D.F.: Instituto Nacional de Estudios Históricos de la Revolución Mexicana, 1981.

_____. *Historia militar de la revolución en la epoca de la convención.* México, D.F.: Instituto Nacional de Estudios Históricos de la Revolución Mexicana, 1983.

Sandos, James A. *Rebellion in the Borderlands: Anarchism and the Plan of San Diego, 1904-1923.* Norman: University of Oklahoma Press, 1992.

_____. "German Involvement in Northern Mexico, 1915-1916: A New Look at the Columbus Raid," *Hispanic American Historical Review,* 50 (February 1970), 70-88.

_____. "The Plan of San Diego: War and Diplomacy on the Texas Border, 1915-1916," *Arizona and the West,* 14 (Spring 1972), 5-24.

_____. "Pancho Villa and American Security: Woodrow Wilson's Mexican Diplomacy Reconsidered," *Journal of Latin American Studies,* 13 (November, 1981), 293-311.

_____. "Prostitution And Drugs: The United States Army On The Mexican-American Border, 1916-1917," *Pacific Historical Review,* 49 (November 1980), 621-645.

Scott, Hugh Lenox. *Some Memoirs of a Soldier.* New York: Century Co., 1928.

Slattery, Matthew T. *Felipe Angeles and the Mexican Revolution.* Dublin, Indiana: Prinit Press, 1982.

Smith, Michael M. "Carrancista Propaganda and the Print Media in the United States: An Overview of Institutions," *The Americas,* 52 (October 1995), 155-174.

_____. "The Mexican Immigrant Press Beyond the Borderlands: The Case of *El Cosmopólita,* 1914-1919, *Great Plains Quarterly,* 10 (Spring 1990), 71-85.

Smith, Robert Freeman. *The United States and Revolutionary Nationalism in Mexico, 1916-1932.* Chicago: University of Chicago Press, 1972.

Tompkins, Frank. *Chasing Villa: The Last Campaign of the U.S. Cavalry.* Harrisburg, Pennsylvania: Military Services Publishing Co., 1934.

Toulmin, Harry Aubrey. *With Pershing In Mexico.* Harrisburg, Pennsylvania: Military Services Publishing Co., 1935.

Toussant Aragón, Dr. Eugenio. *Quién y cómo fué Pancho Villa*. México, D.F.: Talles de Editorial Universo, 1979.

Treviño, Jacinto B. *Memorias*. Segunda edición. México, D.F.: Editorial Orion, 1961.

_____. *Parte oficial rendido al C. Venustiano Carranza, primer jefe del ejército Constitucional, con motivo de Las operaciones llevadas a cabo por la Tercera División del Cuerpo de Ejército del Noreste, del 21 de marzo al 31 de mayo de 1915, en El Ebano, SLP*. Monterrey: El Constitucional, 1915.

Urquizo, Francisco L. *Organización del ejército constitucionalista: apuntes para la ley orgánica*. México, D.F.: Secretaría de Guerra Y Marina, 1916.

Vanderwood, Paul J. and Frank N. Samponaro. *Border Fury: A Picture Postcard Record of Mexico's Revolution and U.S. War Preparedness, 1910-1917*. Albuquerque: University of New Mexico Press, 1988.

Vandiver, Frank E. *Black Jack: The Life and Times of John J. Pershing*. 2 vols. College Station: Texas A&M University Press, 1977.

Vargas Arreola, Juan Bautista. *A sangre y fuego con Pancho Villa*. Compilación de Berta Vargas de Corona. México, D.F.: Fondo de Cultura Económica, 1992.

Vázquez, Ricardo L. *Hombres de la revolución: Eliseo Arredondo*. México, D.F.: Ediciones Botas, 1945.

Vázquez Sotelo, Alfonso, ed. *Avances historiográficos en el estudio de Venustiano Carranza*. Saltillo: Instituto Estatal de Documentación, 1996.

Wager, Stephan J. "The Mexican Army, 1940-1992." Unpublished Ph.D. dissertation, Stanford University, 1992.

Wolfskill, George and Douglas Richmond. *Essays on the Mexican Revolution: Revisionist Views of the Leaders*. Austin: University of Texas Press, 1979.

Womack, John, Jr. *Zapata and the Mexican Revolution*. New York: Alfred A. Knopf, 1969.

Zertuche, Fernando. *Luis Cabrera: una visión de México*. México, D.F.: Secretaría de Educación Pública, 1988.

Zorrilla, Luis G. *Historia de las relaciones entre México y los Estados Unidos de América, 1800-1958*. 2 vols. México, D.F.: Editorial Porrúa, 1965.

INDEX